THE MORAL LIFE
OF SCHOOLS

THE MORAL LIFE
OF SCHOOLS

Philip W. Jackson
Robert E. Boostrom
David T. Hansen

JOSSEY-BASS
A Wiley Imprint
www.josseybass.com

Copyright © 1993 by John Wiley & Sons, Inc. All rights reserved.

Published by Jossey-Bass
A Wiley Imprint
989 Market Street, San Francisco, CA 94103-1741   www.josseybass.com

FIRST PAPERBACK EDITION PUBLISHED IN 1998.

Jossey-Bass books and products are available through most bookstores. To contact Jossey-Bass directly
call our Customer Care Department within the U.S. at (800) 956-7739, outside the U.S. at (317) 572-
3986 or fax (317) 572-4002.

Jossey-Bass also publishes its books in a variety of electronic formats. Some content that appears in
print may not be available in electronic books.

Library of Congress Cataloging-in-Publication Data

Jackson, Philip W. (Philip Wesley), date.
    The moral life of schools / Philip W. Jackson, Robert E. Boostrom,
David T. Hansen. — 1st ed.
      p. cm. — (The Jossey-Bass education series)
   Includes bibliographical references (p.) and index.
   ISBN 1-55542-577-1
   ISBN 0-7879-4066-6 (paperback)
    1. Moral education—United States. 2. Classroom management—
United States. 3. School management and organization—United
States. 4. Education—United States—Aims and objectives.
I. Boostrom, Robert E., date. II. Hansen, David T., date.
III. Title. IV. Series.
LC268.J33 1993
370.11'4—dc20   93-22370

Printed in the United States of America
FIRST EDITION
HB Printing   10 9 8 7 6 5 4 3 2 1
PB Printing   10 9 8 7 6 5 4

THE JOSSEY-BASS
EDUCATION SERIES

Contents

*To the eighteen teachers
who participated in the Moral Life Project:*

*By welcoming us into your classrooms and by speaking with candor about
your own teaching experience, you enabled us to learn far more about the
moral life of schools than we had ever anticipated.*

⤚ Introduction ⤙

Audience and Purpose

This book principally addresses three groups of readers: practicing teachers and school administrators, persons who aspire to become teachers or administrators, and those who teach or advise either today's or tomorrow's practitioners. We further hope that a significant number of educational researchers, particularly those who are either presently engaged in naturalistic studies of classrooms or planning to become so, will find here ample food for thought. Parents and citizens-at-large may do the same, for in the final analysis the question of what goes on within schools and classrooms is truly everyone's business. Consequently, though we suspect that what we have to say will chiefly be of interest to the subgroups of professionals we have named, we invite the readership of all who care about our schools.

As its title implies, our book is about moral matters as they impinge upon the work of the school, a topic of great interest these days. However, our treatment of that topic differs markedly from most other works; we do not concentrate on *specific* ways to remedy the current situation. We have relatively little to say about moral *instruction,* for example, other than to note that a lot of it seemed to be going on within the schools we visited. Nor do we deal with the question of how to structure regular classroom activities in a way that might enhance the likelihood of their having positive moral *outcomes*. In fact, we largely ignore outcomes per se, just as we do the specific methods by which they might be reached.

What we offer instead is *a generalized way of looking at and thinking about what goes on in classrooms,* one that highlights the moral significance of much that occurs there. This perspective is important because the world of classrooms — and by extension the world in general — becomes a far more interesting and more vibrant place in which to live and work when its moral complexity, which is to say its full potential for communicating the moral meaning of all that surrounds us, begins to come into focus. Only then do we realize how shortsighted it is to think of schools as institutions whose sole function is to equip students with the knowledge and skills they will need to get by in the world. The latter function certainly is the foremost reason for our having schools, but the formative potency of these institutions extends far beyond the goals of the official curriculum.

To anyone who takes a close look at what goes on in classrooms it becomes quickly evident that our schools do much more than pass along requisite knowledge to the students attending them (or fail to do so, as the case may be). They also influence the way those students look upon themselves and others. They affect the way learning is valued and sought after and lay the foundations of lifelong habits of thought and action. They shape opinion and develop taste, helping to form likings and aversions. They contribute to the growth of character and, in some instances, they may even be a factor in its corruption. Schools in the aggregate do all this and more to and for the students they serve. Moreover, and here is the important point, they do much of it without the full awareness and thoughtful engagement of those in charge.

The perspective we shall develop in this book can help to improve that state of affairs by heightening the sensitivity of practitioners, and indirectly all others, to the myriad events and features of moral consequence that they may presently be overlooking within their own schools and classrooms. Our perspective may also help to make practitioners more aware of the moral implications of their own habitual ways of responding to students and to the overall demands of their work. For some readers this may constitute a new way of looking and thinking and for others it will not. To the former we need say nothing further about why adopting this point of view is worth the effort. To those who already look at schools and classrooms in these ways we would point to the value and satisfaction of having their customary views confirmed or reaffirmed. Those benefits turned out to be one of the most important things we discovered — or rediscovered — in the course of our own work.

A word about the form and style of what is to come. Because we chiefly address an audience whose members are in a position to put this book's underlying ideas into practice, either within schools and classrooms directly or within training programs that prepare teachers, we have sought to present our ideas in a way that will facilitate their adoption and application. One of our chief means of doing that has been to enact in our own writing the same kinds of reflective processes that the book as a whole seeks to encourage in its readers. Thus, Parts Two and Three, which offer examples of our way of looking and thinking, contain not only a lot of observational material but also our ruminations on those observations. We hope our readers will come to think in a similar way about what is going on in their own classrooms and in the descriptions of classroom life that others have prepared.

Another way in which we have tried to be mindful of our readers is by offering suggestions for further reading. These come at the end of the book in the form of a Postscript. In compiling these suggestions we started with the chief topics explored within the book itself. We then added one or two others of tangential relevance to cover the likelihood that some readers' interests will move in those directions. For each of these topics we have listed several texts to which readers might turn in pursuit of further knowledge. We have also annotated each text or set of entries by the same author in order to provide a bit more information about them than is given by their titles alone. We obviously do not intend those listings and our commentary to be at all definitive. We offer them in response to the imagined question: Where might I go from here? Each subset of references serves only to suggest further help.

Background of the Study

The ideas expressed in this book and the scenes and events used to give life to those ideas derive from a study called the Moral Life of Schools Project, from which comes the title of the book.

Because the study served as the source of all the classroom observations and statements from teachers that follow, a brief overview of its purpose and design seems in order at this point. Additional details will emerge throughout the book.

The Moral Life Project, as its participants came to call it, sought to investigate the ways in which moral considerations permeate the everyday life of schools and classrooms. The study lasted for two and a half years, from January 1988 to June 1990; during this time the three of us constituted its research staff. The project involved extensive observations in eighteen classrooms, located in two public, two independent, and two parochial schools (an elementary and a high school of each type) situated in the Midwest. It also included conversations and periodic discussions with the teachers in charge of those rooms. The nine elementary school teachers were drawn from various grade levels of the participating schools; each grade had at least one representative. The nine high school teachers included teachers of English, science, mathematics, social studies, physical education, religion, and special education. Ten of the teachers were women; eight were men. Four were African Americans; the remainder were white. All but two had taught for at least a decade. Six had taught for twenty years or more.

The classroom observations began almost as soon as the project was under way and continued throughout its duration. Each classroom was visited dozens of times over the two and a half years. The typical visit covered the better part of a morning or an afternoon, though some were only an hour or so in length and others lasted all day. In addition to visiting classrooms, we periodically attended special events in each of the schools. These included assemblies, field trips, pep rallies, class parties, parent meetings, and athletic contests. We further spent a considerable amount of time simply wandering the halls and grounds of each institution. Our visits did not occur on any schedule and were usually unannounced.

The conversations we had with the teachers occurred under both formal and informal conditions. We often chatted informally with them before or immediately following our visits to their classrooms. We also talked off-the-cuff with groups of them at parties and other social events. Under somewhat more formal conditions, each of us conducted one separate interview of each teacher. We also held biweekly meetings consisting of dinner followed by a seminar with the group as a whole throughout the school year. These formal and informal exchanges greatly enriched our understanding of what we had observed.

We decided upon the title of the project, The Moral Life of Schools, long before we had a firm idea of what we would actually be looking for when our work began or even of what terms like *moral* and *moral life* could possibly mean when they were applied to what goes on in schools. We made a point of confessing our ignorance on this score as we went about recruiting teacher-volunteers, telling everyone who expressed an interest in joining us that we had no formal definition of morality to start with beyond the commonsense understanding that *moral* usually refers to desirable human conduct and to personal qualities, such as virtue or strength of character, believed to ensure its occurrence. (Many of the teachers to whom we spoke asked for definitions of such key terms almost before we had a chance to interject our disclaimer.) We usually went on, however, to declare a strong belief about the school's role in moral education. We said then, and on the strength of what our work has revealed, we now reiterate with even stronger conviction, that we believe that most of our schools and most of the teachers within them contribute to the moral well-being of students in many important ways. However, we further believe — and this too we thought from the start — that teachers and school administrators are not always fully aware of the moral potency of their actions.

Our hunch that teachers and school administrators are only partially aware of how they contribute to the moral upbringing of their students led us to believe that there is much to be learned about the moral influence schools and teachers have on their students. That prior belief helps to explain why we undertook the Moral Life Project in the first place. It also accounts for a related hunch of ours, which was that if educators knew more about what they were already doing in this regard they might be capable of doing it more effectively or at least more self-consciously. Either way would be an improvement over present practice.

Where did we get the idea that schools and teachers are already more influential in moral terms than they typically understand themselves to be? It arose from the most ordinary of sources, a combination of common sense and personal experience. We knew, to start, that our schools tacitly subscribe to a broad policy of acting in the best interests of the students they serve. That unspoken policy automatically entails a concern for the moral well-being of those students. This concern is evident in the school's efforts to sanitize or purify the institution in moral terms by barring unsavory intruders such as drug peddlers or vagrants and by trying to weed out teacher applicants who have criminal records or who otherwise look as though they might have a "bad influence" on the young. To the extent that such efforts are successful, the adults within our schools are basically good people who are out to serve students as best they can. This being so, we might expect some of their goodness to rub off or at least to become evident without their explicitly intending that to happen and therefore without their being aware that it had. We extended this line of reasoning to include the school as a whole. We thought that the structure of a school might have moral premises built into it without conscious intent, the way a house or factory might reflect an attitude of consideration (or lack of it) for the building's inhabitants, even though its builder or architect may never have consciously planned it that way. The same holds true for a school's operation. The forms of daily governance that characterize it may unintentionally reflect moral assumptions in the same way that the routines of a business or a public agency might.

At this point, we sense the likelihood of a demur from some of our readers. So far we have spoken solely about a school's potential for doing good, for having a positive moral influence on those it serves. But it is apparent to most of us that schools and teachers also have the potential for doing moral harm to those in their care. Doubtless there are some schools and classrooms in which that harm is realized. Why have we not yet spoken of that possibility? And were those harmful effects among the things we were looking for?

The quick answer to those questions is that we have so far ignored mention of possible ill effects principally because they did not lie at the heart of our investigation. We were, and are, chiefly interested in understanding the school's potential as a positive moral force. We recognized that some teachers and perhaps even some entire schools may actually do more harm than good to their students, but we tried to avoid encountering such unfortunate (and we would hope rare) situations by choosing to work only in schools and with teachers that were reputedly doing a good job. We were prepared, of course, to witness even in those schools and with those teachers incidents that revealed moral shortcomings of one kind or another. In Parts Two and Three of this book we will examine some of the shortcomings we observed. But we did not specifically go looking for such phenomena.

Partly because of the exploratory nature of the Moral Life Project and additionally because of the congenial relationships we hoped to establish with participating teachers, we eschewed many if not most of the qualities that typify textbook examples of empirical research. We did not begin with formal hypotheses, nor was our work guided by a theoretical framework. And we did not end with findings, at least not in the usual sense of a set of propositions whose truth is buttressed by tests of statistical significance. We also avoided making use of many of the terms that researchers typically employ. Thus, we do not refer to the teacher-participants as "subjects," nor do we speak of our observational notes as "data" or even as "protocols." Instead, throughout the life of the project and in this final rendering of our work, we have tried to keep our language as informal and as close to ordinary speech as possible.

This informality extended to the way we went about observing in classrooms as well as to the format and conduct of our biweekly discussions. We did not make use of observation schedules or try to systematize and regularize our observations in other ways. Not only did we usually arrive in the classrooms unannounced, we also commonly arrived without intending to observe anything in particular. Instead, we would typically focus on whatever happened to attract our attention that day. In our biweekly discussions with teachers and in our interviews, a similar kind of informality reigned. The biweekly meetings had no set agenda and the interviews were not guided by a list of questions that we wanted to have answered. Instead, the topic of each discussion was established by the group as a whole and varied from week to week, as did its chairperson. The interviews were allowed to move anywhere the participants jointly wished to take them. Our gradual appreciation of the advantages of this way of working, particularly as it relates to observing the subtlety of what goes on in classrooms, constitutes one of the major outcomes of our work.

The Moral Life of Classrooms and Schools

Returning to our decision to use the name of our project as the title of this book, we must offer an additional word or two of explanation. From the standpoint of its detailed contents, this work might properly be called *The Moral Life of Classrooms* rather than *The Moral Life of Schools,* for almost all of the observations we make use of were gathered in classrooms and all of the practitioners whose experiences and remarks we report on were themselves classroom teachers. Without doubt, this is much more a book about classrooms than it is about schools. Why, then, retain the word *schools* in the book's title?

We do so in part as a salute to the Moral Life of Schools Project and to all who helped to make it possible. Without it and without them, there would be no book. But there is a more cogent reason than that for our keeping the word *schools* in the book's title. We do so chiefly because all we have to say applies as much to schools in toto as it does to classrooms, even though the latter turned out to be the actual sites of most of our observations. Every detail of school life, from the interior of the principal's office to the way the school's cafeteria operates, from the schoolwide policy that governs the giving of grades to the rules that deal with the way students move through the halls, can be examined with an eye to moral significance. Thus, the word *schools* advertises the broad applicability of the perspective our book seeks to develop.

Classrooms do, of course, form the heart of every school. They are where the action is, as the saying goes, which is why we have concentrated almost all of our observations on what goes on within them. But the larger institutional settings in which they are lodged — schools in general — are not to be ignored as sources of moral influence. They too are capable of having a powerful impact upon their inhabitants. This, again, is why we invite school administrators and other educational personnel, from building principals to state superintendents, to join their teaching colleagues in cultivating a heightened sensitivity to the moral significance of their total surroundings. Classrooms, we discovered, are the perfect place to start. They are so jam-packed with people, objects, and events that it takes only a short time there to witness something — a scrap of dialogue, an action on the part of the teacher, a feature of the physical environment — that is glaringly obtrusive in a moral sense.

The transition from that first crude witnessing of what is going on to the discernment of some of the more subtle ways in which moral matters become manifest in the life of both schools and classrooms is chiefly a matter of practice and patience. Naturally, we must also continually reflect on what we have witnessed. And it helps to have someone to talk with along the way, especially someone who shares the same goal and has his or her own observations to add to our own. This book offers that kind of companionship, at least vicariously, to anyone who picks it up and begins to read. It is obviously no substitute for joining with colleagues or fellow students in pursuit of a refined understanding, but it does provide a starting place for both individuals and groups who seek greater insight into the complexities of school life. Once that journey of discovery has begun, there is no telling where it will end. In a grand sense, it never does.

Chicago, Illinois   Philip W. Jackson
July 1993   Robert E. Boostrom
                          David T. Hansen

THE MORAL LIFE
OF SCHOOLS

◈ PART ONE ◈

Looking for the Moral:
AN OBSERVER'S GUIDE

*I*magine a trio of researchers setting out to visit a school or a set of classrooms scattered over a number of different schools with the express purpose of studying the moral significance of what is going on there. Where would they begin? What would they look for? That was the situation we faced at the beginning of our work. Prior to starting our observations we had explicitly declared ourselves to be interested in anything at all that might have the remotest chance of leaving a moral mark of some kind on those present — students, principally, of course, but possibly teachers and school administrators and perhaps even the casual observer as well. That sounded like a reasonably clear statement of purpose to us. It also temporarily assuaged the fears of the teachers we were planning to visit, some of whom were a bit uneasy over the prospect of having us as regular visitors and all of whom wanted to know what we would be looking for in their classrooms. Yet despite the straightforwardness and all-inclusiveness of our objective, it left us unprepared for what we might find when we got there. More importantly, it did not provide a clue as to how we should go about looking for what we were interested in seeing. In the absence of such guidelines, all each of us could do when he settled down in the rear of the room on the first day of his visits to one of the eighteen participating classrooms was to keep his notebook handy, his pencil poised, and his eyes and ears open, and to hope for the best.

1

What emerged at the start was pretty much what we would have expected under the circumstances. We first noted the presence or absence of activities that were explicitly moral in content and purpose. These included moral "lessons" of one kind or another, sometimes presented as a separate part of the curriculum but more commonly embedded within some larger context; they might be an integral and recurring part of one of the regular school subjects or a nonrecurring event that arose contingently and interrupted the normal flow of classroom events. Gradually, however, our awareness of the moral significance of what was going on around us expanded to include events, actions, and even aspects of the physical environment that were much less obviously moral in nature than were the explicit instructional efforts that had initially caught our attention. Some of these less obvious aspects of the schools' engagement in moral matters took us days to uncover; others required weeks or even months.

The fact that it took a long time for us to become aware of all the categories of moral influence that we will discuss in this part indicates the difficulties we faced as observers. It also raises a host of questions about how the process of moral development actually works. Must it occur consciously, for example? Can students be influenced morally without knowing that such a thing is happening to them? If they can, which it seems reasonable to suppose, does that mean that their testimony about such matters, the fact that they may not be able to recall what happened or when, counts for nothing? And what about teachers? Do *they* need to be aware of the possible moral consequences of what they are doing in order for those consequences to take place? Again, it seems reasonable to suppose that they do not, any more than parents or friends or anyone else must always be aware of the full extent of the influence they exert on those with whom they associate daily. But having said that, we are left to wonder about the desirability of that state of ignorance, especially as it pertains to teachers. Might it not be advantageous for all educators, no matter what their job or where they work, to become increasingly aware of the moral potency of their actions?

Such questions are of obvious relevance to anyone interested in the moral consequences of schooling. We will address each of them, plus a number of related matters, in due course.

For the time being, however, we will sidestep these and other issues in order to get on with what the title of this part promises, which is an observer's guide — a taxonomy, one might call it — of the categories of moral influence within classrooms as we came to understand and appreciate them. We will return in subsequent sections to various questions noted here in passing.

For the present, then, we need only reiterate that some of what we took to be morally significant in the eighteen participating classrooms was evident on the very first day of our visits or shortly thereafter, whereas other aspects emerged much more slowly. Our presentation of the categories will reflect that difference. We will begin with what came to our attention most readily and proceed to items and ideas that took longer for us to recognize. This plan also allows us to follow the common practice of starting with what is easiest to talk about and moving by degrees to matters that are rather more difficult to describe and explain.

All such distinctions are relative, of course, as we ourselves discovered again and again during our months of observing. Some of the things that we first thought were quite easy to see and talk about became more and more opaque and progressively more complicated the longer we looked at them and discussed their significance. Other phenomena that took a longer time for us to notice gradually became so apparent that we wondered how we could have overlooked them in the first place. All told, however, our understanding of nearly all of the categories we shall describe became richer and deeper as our observations multiplied.

Moral Instruction

For a long time we thought in terms of a single set of categories arrayed along a continuum from more readily visible to less visible categories. But then we began to see that we had in fact two sets of categories, which might be distinguished in several ways. The five categories of the first set consist of activities that are avowedly moral. They are deliberate attempts to promote moral instruction and to encourage moral behavior. The three categories of the second set consist of activities that *embody* the moral. To recognize the moral in these activities requires us to probe beneath the surface of events. Although the influences of the second type are not immediately obvious, we have found them to be pervasive throughout all aspects of classroom life, including attempts at direct moral instruction. We will therefore spend considerably more time discussing the second set of categories than the first. However, we will begin with the first category.

Category I. Moral Instruction as a Formal Part of the Curriculum

Although it was the most obvious thing to look for, formal moral instruction as a recurrent and identifiable piece of the curriculum was close to absent in the classrooms we visited. The clear exceptions were in the two Roman Catholic schools. In the Catholic elementary school, twenty minutes a day was set aside for religious instruction at each grade level. In the Catholic high school, religion was a required course for all students. We encountered nothing remotely similar in any of the other schools. There were no courses in civics or ethics, "values clarification" sessions, Kohlbergian discussion groups, or any other form of moral instruction as a separate curricular entity in either of the other two high schools.

The religious instruction in both of the Catholic schools was manifestly moral in content although it often treated liturgical, geographical, and historical matters as well. Frequently the lesson consisted of the reading of a Bible story from the New Testament, followed by a discussion of its moral significance interspersed with information about its historical place within the Catholic tradition. During the discussion students were encouraged to draw upon their own experience and relate it to the moral message of the text. At other times, the teachers would lead students in discussions of contemporary situations requiring a moral choice guided by Catholic doctrine. For example, a religion lesson in a fifth-grade class focused on the story of Sally, a girl who had been sent by her parents to get some groceries. She had more money than she needed and was tempted to keep the extra money for herself. "What rules," the teacher asked his fifth graders (apparently expecting them to cite the "Honor thy father and thy mother" and "Thou shalt not steal" commandments), "would help her make a decision?" In some of the classes workbook exercises and written assignments accompanied the lessons.

As far as we could tell as observers, there was nothing unusual about these religion classes from a pedagogical point of view. They were conducted in about the same way as were classes in the other school subjects. Students seemed to approach them with neither more nor less enthusiasm or piety than they did any of their other subjects. Likewise, the teachers in charge taught them with about the same degree of involvement that typified other classes.

Category II. Moral Instruction Within the Regular Curriculum

In almost all of the classrooms, we encountered lessons that were decidedly moral in tone, though part of the regular curriculum. Often these dealt with the character of real or legendary figures (e.g., the *Challenger* astronauts, Dr. Martin Luther King, Jr., Anna Karenina, Charlotte of *Charlotte's Web*) or with issues of social injustice (e.g., slavery among the Greeks, the displacement of Native Americans by European settlers, the plight of the homeless in our society today). Such sessions were especially frequent in English and social studies classes in the three high schools and in equivalent curricular locations in the elementary schools.

In these sessions students were often called upon to relate their own experiences and to venture their own opinions. They often were also asked to place themselves in the position of the character or type of character being discussed and to imagine how they might feel or react under similar circumstances. Very often such discussions generated differences of opinion and sometimes sharp disagreements. Not infrequently the sessions became so animated that the teacher in charge had some difficulty keeping order.

Although moral judgments of many different kinds were prominent in these lessons, it was seldom evident that the teacher was trying to teach a moral lesson per se. Usually the focus was on trying to understand a social phenomenon or fictional character rather than on trying to instill a particular moral habit or attitude within the students themselves. Of course, it was often clear when people or actions under discussion were to be admired or deplored, and so in that sense they were held before the class as moral models or their opposites. But "the moral" of their actions for the students present in the room was more often implied than explicitly drawn. In short, though these lessons were clearly designed to bring moral matters, such as acts of heroism and issues of social injustice, to students' attention, they usually lacked the hard-edged prescriptive tone that typified the religion lessons in the two Catholic schools.

For example, to commemorate Martin Luther King's birthday, Mr. Jordan, a teacher at an independent school, showed his second graders a television drama about Booker T. Washington's boyhood as a slave. His reason for choosing Washington over King was that he didn't think King was a figure children could readily appreciate. "King was just another adult," he explained, "and he didn't really do anything of interest to seven-year-olds. He gave speeches, he was a minister, and both of those things are kind of boring as far as seven-year-olds are concerned." At least with the Booker T. Washington tape, the teacher reasoned, the children would be exposed to the issues that Martin Luther King fought for and spoke about, and because the tape focused on Washington when he was about the same age as the children in Mr. Jordan's class, they would be exposed to a figure with whom they could readily identify.

Category III. Rituals and Ceremonies

In all of the schools and classrooms we visited, we encountered rituals and ceremonies of a moral nature. Some of them were schoolwide affairs, such as pep rallies, graduations, and assemblies that featured, for example, lectures by guest speakers against drug abuse. Others occurred within the confines of the individual classroom. The latter included opening ceremonies, such as the Lord's Prayer or the Pledge of Allegiance, birthday parties for individual students, a commemorative service in honor of a recently deceased mayor, and the like. These were not usually part of the regular instructional activities, which makes them extracurricular in a formal sense, even though they took place during the regular school day.

What made us think of these activities as being essentially moral in nature was the mood or attitude they sought to engender. This included feelings of pride, loyalty, inspiration, reverence, piety, sorrow, prudence, thankfulness, and dedication. These activities also called upon students to identify themselves with causes, social missions, and social and political entities whose goals and purposes lay outside the framework of the students' individual interests and daily concerns. The ceremonial staging of many of these activities (e.g., gathering as a student body in the school auditorium or standing, rather than sitting, in the classroom), the presence of musical accompaniment (along with musical directors, vocalists, cheerleaders, etc.), and the attendance of special visitors (e.g., the school principal, groups of parents, invited speakers, or police officers) gave to these occasions a special character and added to their mood-inducing effectiveness.

The monthly schoolwide assemblies held at the public elementary school we visited were an example of these kinds of activities. Each month a different grade was responsible for providing the assembly program. The program for February was entitled "Peace — Brotherhood — Greatness" and was put on jointly by the fifth-grade classes and the special education classes in the school. As was customary, they were charged with presenting stories, skits, and the like related to the theme of the month. One class presented "Great People": children portrayed (and recited from the works of) George Washington, Sojourner Truth, Frederick Douglass, Harriet Tubman, Abraham Lincoln, Susan B. Anthony, Ralph Bunche, and Mary Bethune. Another class presented a silent drama called "Love Our Earth." In front of a large paper globe in the center of the stage, two boys engaged in an escalating battle. First they punched one another with boxing gloves, then they pretended to shoot one another, then they began throwing large paper rocks. Finally, they moved toward one another with rockets in their hands, meeting in the middle of the stage at the globe, which suddenly fell to the floor as the stage went ominously dark. It was left to the children in the audience to discern for themselves the message of this pantomime, and of the assembly as a whole. The symbolic richness of ceremonies of this kind (and we witnessed them in all of the schools) hardly stands in need of further comment.

Category IV. Visual Displays with Moral Content

In each and every classroom and on the walls of every school we saw signs, pictures, and posters of all kinds. Many of them exhorted viewers to behave in a morally approved manner with respect to a specific issue, such as abstinence from drugs or premarital sex, or encouraged them to maintain or adopt a positive attitude toward an imminent challenge, such as getting good grades or staying in school. A classroom bulletin board in one of the high schools read: "Hey Graduates! We look forward to May 1988. But will there be a different FATE for a few less fortunate?" In some instances the message urged a particular orientation toward the self, such as "In This Classroom Be Yourself—Please" or "Take Pride in What You Do"; in others it advocated the adoption of a more global viewpoint, such as "Peace on Earth" or "Join the Family of Man."

Typically the messages displayed in such materials were brief and to the point. But it was not uncommon to find posted an entire poem or even an essay whose contents were manifestly intended to be inspiring or morally uplifting. Much of this work contained quotations from famous people, but sometimes the display was completely designed and written by students. For example, one classroom featured a bulletin board in the center of which were the words "Values for 1989" in bold letters. These were surrounded by student essays on topics such as friendship, love, honesty, and effort. In another room a bulletin board with the heading "Beauty is Everywhere" contained a spread of color photographs of nature, more than a dozen in all, each about the size of a magazine cover.

Some of these displays were changed regularly; others remained in place throughout the school year and sometimes for much more than a year. As a general rule, posters and signs in the elementary school classrooms were changed more frequently than those in the high school. Also, the former were far more colorful and decorative environments throughout than were the latter, a difference that will hardly come as a surprise to anyone who has visited both types of school. We will have more to say about this later in this part. Some of the signs and decorations were handmade by either teachers or students or both, and others were commercially manufactured. Posters containing well-known cartoon characters who offered moral advice to a school-age audience were common (e.g., Snoopy says, "Don't be a fool, stay in school!"), as were pictures of sports heroes with similar advice (e.g., Walter Payton, of football fame, is shown reading a book and saying, "Reading is an important part of my life").

Among ourselves we began to speak of these many signs and slogans as constituting a kind of "bumper-sticker morality," whose pithy phrases and eye-catching designs seemed patterned for quick consumption by passersby rather than being intended as subject matter for reflection and discussion. Not all of the displays were of that character, of course, as we have already acknowledged, but there were enough to make the phrase seem appropriate. The impression the displays gave of being designed more for show and instantaneous recognition than for sustained inspection was confirmed by the fact that we seldom saw them being discussed by the teacher and the class as a whole. It is possible, of course, that many such discussions took place and we just happened to miss them. However, the frequency of our visits makes that possibility seem unlikely.

Category V. Spontaneous Interjection of Moral Commentary into Ongoing Activity

From time to time, in each of the classrooms, the teachers introduced moral subject matter that had almost nothing to do with the lesson at hand or the activity in progress. What sometimes triggered its introduction was a breach of moral conduct so egregious that it could not be ignored—for example, the theft of someone's belongings, or an act of cruelty or poor sportsmanship

on the playground. In these often dramatic and emotionally up-
setting situations, the teacher would commonly bring a halt to
whatever was going on at the time and then proceed to discuss
the matter with the class as a whole, while at the same time giving vent to his or her own feelings of consternation, dismay,
disappointment, and regret. To single out one of the numerous examples, a seventh-grade teacher once began a class by
describing how one of the students' classmates, since suspended
from school, poured acid on another student's belongings. The
teacher spent a considerable part of the period asking the students why such behavior was wrong and dangerous and how
they could work together to prevent it from happening again.
She was obviously troubled by the incident and her students
appeared equally unsettled.

    Not all of the events that triggered such talk were nearly
as dramatic as this; in fact, the vast majority were not. More
commonly, some quite ordinary event, yet one with moral overtones, would cause the teacher to digress momentarily in order
to offer commentary of a moral kind. For example, in a social
studies discussion a teacher responded to a student's "cute" answer to a question with "Robert, are you contributing to our
discussion, or are you just trying to show off?" Minute interruptions and digressions such as these occurred untold numbers
of times during our visits. Hardly a class was free of them.

    The examples we have used so far to illustrate this category
may create the impression that teachers broke from the constraints of their lesson plans and launched into moral commentary only in response to misbehavior of some kind. That was
not the case. Often the teachers' asides were occasioned by exemplary conduct and were laudatory rather than condemnatory
in their intent—for example: "Class, can I have your attention
for a minute? Has everyone noticed how carefully Marsha and
Sarah are preparing the exhibit for tonight's visitors? Good work,
girls." Things like that happened on countless occasions. Indeed,
some of the teachers so habitually interjected praise and encouragement into their running commentary during a lesson
that the flow of instruction was undisturbed and the remarks
seemed like part of the lesson itself—for example, "Good ques-

tion, Samantha! That's really paying attention! Now let's see, if the area bounded by X is three times the circumference. . . ."

These positive examples give rise to a question of their own. Their brevity and ubiquity might lead us to ask whether all of a teacher's praise or blame, no matter how fleetingly communicated or how seemingly trivial, ought to be considered a form of moral commentary that falls within the bounds of the present category. We think it should on the grounds that all judgments of a person's conduct are ultimately moral in the sense of being based on a conception of what ought to be. They imply a standard of goodness or its opposite against which a comparison has been made. Teachers communicate those comparative judgments by words and deeds in terms that leave no doubt of the worthiness or unworthiness of what the student has done. And they often do so publicly, which usually increases the sting of discomfort or the feeling of pride and delight for the person being judged. Moreover, teachers usually add to the judgment itself a clear indication of how they personally feel about the matter; for instance, a teacher facing the class as a whole might say, "I'm really disappointed in you, Virgil. I thought you told me you were going to try harder to. . . ." In our view, all such talk is a form of moral commentary.

Moral Practice

Our second set of categories of moral influence constitutes a change of perspective. The focus shifts from direct moral instruction to classroom practices and personal qualities of teachers that — sometimes unintentionally — embody a moral outlook or stance. Whereas the first set dealt with phenomena that can be relatively quickly discerned by those on the lookout for moral matters in the school and classroom, these next three categories are far less obvious than the first five and may require considerable effort on the part of the observer to bring them into view. At least that was so for us. They are also the more important of the two sets, in our judgment, with respect to their possible moral impact on students. They help us to see how morals might be "caught, not taught," as the old adage says. They also reveal how the agency of such contagion may include not just the teacher but the classroom environment itself.

Category VI. Classroom Rules and Regulations

Every classroom constitutes a small society embedded within a complex web of social entities whose overlapping systems of laws, customs, and traditions it partially shares and sometimes adds to or contradicts. In many classrooms, especially in the lower grades, the rules and regulations deemed to be essential for the conduct and well-being of the room's inhabitants are made explicit to those present at the beginning of the school year or shortly thereafter and may even be posted for all to see. These small regulatory systems, which function somewhat like miniature constitutions or codes of law, usually consist of an assortment of do's and don'ts whose contents can range from the pious and the vacuous ("Be kind to one another") to the mundane and the specific ("No talking during fire drills"). In some classrooms these rules remain unchanged from year to year and are simply announced by the teacher to each incoming body of students, with or without explanation or justification. In other rooms they are developed anew each fall with much discussion and participation by the students themselves. Some rules are fairly constant from class to class and from grade to grade ("Raise your hand to be recognized during discussions"); others are more idiosyncratic and apply only to one grade or classroom ("Do not feed the gerbil without permission").

From the standpoint of someone looking for sources of moral influence within classrooms, the rules and regulations that are found there constitute, at first glance, an obvious subject of observation and reflection, because they come the closest of anything we have mentioned so far to constituting an explicit moral code that all of the students in the room are expected to obey. Although there are other ways of getting in trouble in classrooms, none is more surefire than transgressing the locally defined boundaries of their duties and responsibilities. As most students soon discover, those who follow the rules become known as good students; those who disobey them suffer the wrath of their teachers and additionally run the risk of being thought of as troublemakers or worse by teachers and classmates alike.

Even though many such rules may at times seem arbitrary and even peculiar to the outsider (the way the English custom of driving on the left-hand side of the road looks to an American), attending to them can be serious business to local residents, as our observations revealed again and again. In one of the elementary classrooms we visited, for example, the students were assigned the task of writing a letter of advice to an imagined member of next year's class. Almost without exception their letters contained a list of rules the newcomer must follow, that being the best and most urgent advice they could think of offering.

Yet as simple and as direct as rules sound when they are put into words ("Pay attention at all times," "No fighting," "Raise your hand when you want to speak"), they turn out to be quite complicated when we try to understand their enactment. This is partly because most such rules seem, at first, to be inconsistently enforced. Sometimes the teacher overlooks inattention and sometimes not. Sometimes fighting brings swift and severe punishment and at other times it elicits only a command to stop and a frown of disapproval. Students who call out answers rather than raising their hands are not always rebuked for doing so. Sometimes they even receive praise. What gradually becomes evident, however, is that many of these apparent inconsistencies are not actually instances of rules being ignored. Instead, they reflect refinements of the rules that are clearly understood by almost everyone present except the observer. In other words, the rule as stated turns out to be a general maxim to which there are many exceptions.

Another puzzling aspect of these small but locally significant regulatory systems is the way the same rule, such as "Pay attention" or "Raise your hand before talking," works itself out differently in different classrooms, not only in the details of its application and enforcement but also in what it contributes to the moral climate of the room. In one of the classrooms we observed, "Pay attention" meant, in effect, "Always obey what your teacher tells you to do." In another classroom we observed, it gradually dawned on us that it meant "Be respectful to your fellow students so that you can be a successful member of the community." In short, we discovered that rules are often the surface manifestations of broader moral principles that reflect the individual teacher's vision of his or her role in the classroom. But these and other nuances became apparent to us, as outsiders, only after much observation and reflection.

Category VII. The Morality of the Curricular Substructure

To most people, and perhaps even to many seasoned educators, the curriculum is simply the subject matter of instruction. It consists of what is to be taught or, turned the other way around, of what students are expected to learn. However, the *content* of the curriculum, the actual material that is contained in textbooks or included on tests, is not all there is to it. For in addition to containing content, every curriculum is also structured in a variety of ways.

At the most rudimentary level, the structure determines how the curricular content is organized and presented to students. The principles of organization are numerous and vary markedly from one subject or grade level to another. In one school subject the material is arranged chronologically; in another, narratively; in a third, topically; and so on. The visibility of this structure to those engaged in teaching and learning also varies from subject to subject and from grade to grade. Sometimes students are not only led to see that there *is* a structure but are required to incorporate it as knowledge. The structure, in other words, becomes part of the lesson. This is often the case in history, for example, where chronology is usually the organizing principle. There students not only must learn a set of facts but must be able to place them within a time frame that roughly approximates the order in which they were presented in class. In mathematics and other skill-oriented subjects, the ordering of material according to its level of difficulty is the most salient characteristic. No formal announcements are required to let everyone know how instruction proceeds in those subjects. First come the easy problems, then the hard ones. Nothing could be more obvious.

At other times, however, the structural elements of the curriculum that determine the order in which the material is taught receive scant attention during the lesson itself and thus remain barely noticeable to those present, including, it would seem, the teachers themselves in many classrooms. This is especially likely in rooms where the teacher relies heavily on textbooks and workbooks and in school subjects where the material is topically arranged, as it often is in social studies, for example. Why does Topic A come before Topic B in such a subject? "Because that's the way it appears in the text," is the answer one is liable to receive straight from the teacher. Subjects like social studies, along with others that are topically arranged, are not at all lacking in structure, of course; it is only that the principle of sequencing what is to be learned does not derive in any obvious way from the nature of the material itself as it does elsewhere. Instead, the sequential arrangement is the brainchild of a textbook writer or a designer of instructional materials who may or may not go to the trouble of explaining it to those who use the book or materials.

We slowly began to realize during our visits to classrooms that the situation was much more complicated than has just been described. Beyond a set of organizing principles, such as those we have named, we detected other shaping forces that also remained out of sight much of the time yet continued to function behind the scenes and that appeared to be crucial to a full understanding of what was going on. Many of these forces also deserved to be thought of as structural, it seemed to us, even though they had nothing to do with either the form or the content of the curriculum per se. What prompted us to think of them as structural was the way they seemed to lend a kind of helping hand to the ongoing activity, buoying it up like a cushion of air or a buried foundation of some kind, a layer of bedrock, perhaps. In fact, they often seemed to reside so far beneath the surface of what was being done and talked about within the lesson itself that we ultimately abandoned the term *structural* in favor of *substructural*.

Either term will do for the present, however, as long as it manages to convey the basic notion that there are conditions that operate to sustain and facilitate every teaching session in every subject within the curriculum. A curious feature of these conditions, we reiterate, is their near invisibility much of the time. They are seldom explicitly acknowledged by either teachers or students except when they are absent to start with or when things go wrong. Indeed, we would venture to say that many teachers and students never realize their existence in the first place, so deeply embedded are they in the everyday functioning of many classrooms. Another feature, and the one that made them stand out for us, is their moral coloration. Each condition that we report on here is part of a complex web of obligations and responsibilities whose strands interlock to form a kind of moral substratum of understanding — one whose absence makes instruction impossible.

The most helpful approach we have found thus far in trying to understand these enabling conditions is to envision them as composing an elaborate amalgam of shared understandings, beliefs, assumptions, and presuppositions, all of which enable the participants in a teaching situation to interact amicably with each other and work together, thus freeing them to concentrate on the task at hand. Some of the amalgam's elements are school-specific and even subject- and classroom-specific. Others have a much broader range of applicability. Indeed, it would seem that many are close to universal and can be seen to operate in many social circumstances. However, even these broadly shared understandings and beliefs work differently in classrooms than they do elsewhere. They do so because all forms of social understanding are inevitably conditioned or qualified, usually in important ways, by the settings in which they operate, which is why it pays to study each of them in context.

To illustrate both the substance and the operation of these substructural elements, we have chosen to begin with the widely shared expectation of truth telling as it operates in classrooms. Our choice was made almost at random. Other examples could have served as well and we will turn to a few of them as soon as we have finished with the one we have chosen to open the discussion.

Teachers the world over are expected to speak the truth

when addressing their students, and students are expected to do the same when speaking up in class. Moreover, this expectation of truthfulness is not just a moral obligation to be honored for its own sake, although that may be the way it is typically introduced to young people by teachers and parents. The expectation that both teachers and students speak the truth is absolutely essential to the conduct of instruction. To appreciate how conclusively this is so, imagine the educational consequences of having a teacher who lies about the facts of history as he or she understands them or who knowingly gives the wrong answer to students' questions about science or math or any other school subject. Surely such practices would be grounds for the prompt dismissal of the offender. In addition, a teacher who behaves so bizarrely would doubtless be looked upon as morally perverse if not downright evil by almost everyone.

And what of students who knowingly falsify answers to their teachers' questions? They are likely to be treated as if they are either sick or criminal. A teacher cannot allow such behavior to pass because falsehoods from students inevitably subvert the educational process. If a teacher cannot tell what the students know and do not know, he or she cannot plan how to proceed with them or assess the effects of past lessons. Instruction can only proceed smoothly and properly when everyone involved is telling the truth or something close to it.

Most of the time, however, teachers and students alike can only *presume* that the condition of truthfulness is being upheld. For how can either party possibly know that the other is always being truthful? Obviously, they can never know for sure. Moreover, the process of trying to find out whether one or the other is lying at any particular moment can be very costly in a variety of ways. First, it takes a lot of time. Second, it disrupts the course of instruction. Third, and probably most importantly, if it is not handled skillfully it can irreparably damage the quality of the interpersonal relationship between the two parties. For all of these reasons, teachers and students, like the participants in most other social situations, usually strive to create and maintain a framework of mutual trust within which the work of the day can be carried on, thus keeping to a minimum the instances in which that trust is called into question. This *assumption of truthfulness* is one of the substructural elements within the total amalgam of tacit understandings that combine to facilitate instruction and enable it to proceed smoothly.

As we have already acknowledged, the assumption of truthfulness operates to some degree in most social situations. In a few of these, as when a doctor interviews a patient to obtain a medical history, the assumption governs all communication. In other situations — when people are bargaining with each other, for example, or when they are playing certain games — the assumption governs only portions of what is said. A diplomat representing a nation does not assume the truthfulness of all that is claimed by the diplomat representing an opposing nation. Neither does the buyer of a used car assume the truthfulness of everything the dealer claims about the car. But the diplomats do assume that their opponents are truthful in claiming to represent the other side, and the buyer does believe that the dealer is truthful in claiming to represent the dealership. Likewise, a poker player who assumed the truthfulness of all that was said by opposing players about their hands would be misunderstanding the game, but the player must assume that everyone is following the rules if the game is to be played at all.

When instruction is under way, the assumption of truthfulness takes on a special character that distinguishes it not only from other social situations but also from other situations occurring within the confines of schools and classrooms. In teaching situations the assumption of truthfulness revolves chiefly and most recognizably around issues of knowledge and ignorance. The belief that instruction is possible incorporates the assumption that there are truths that can be told, that knowledge is different from ignorance. Everyone present is expected to be scrupulously truthful in these encounters about what they know or don't know or, more broadly, what they understand or do not understand. We might refer to this obligation as a demand for intellectual honesty as opposed to honesty in general. However, the former term is usually reserved for the expectations we hold about advanced scholars and intellectuals, whereas the kind of intellectual truthfulness assumed to exist in classrooms when instruction is under way is of a far humbler variety. What it usually boils down to in practice, at least from the standpoint of the teacher, is the assumption that the students are being truthful in their answers to questions about the state of their knowledge, that they are being honest about their grasp of the subject matter, and that they believe what they are saying. From the students' point of view, the equivalent assumption is that their teachers know what they are talking about and are not trying to pretend to knowledge that they do not possess.

There are countless times in every classroom, of course, in which the assumption of truthfulness turns out to be untenable, either because events have proved it to be false or because there is strong reason to suspect that it is. In some instances it is the teachers themselves who undermine the mutuality of trust in the truthfulness of what is being said. However, at least in the classrooms we visited, it was much more often the students who were responsible.

The most common way in which students undermine the assumption of truthfulness is by pretending that they possess knowledge. The episodes of this type that stand out most dramatically involve cheating, or the suspicion of it, when students are taking paper-and-pencil tests. In fact, within the classroom itself the term *cheating* is almost exclusively reserved for that special form of dishonesty. The stress that testing places on the normal assumption of truthfulness in many classrooms is a topic worthy of extended treatment in its own right. Here we will only pause to mention a few of its more familiar forms and variations.

Among the many aspects of cheating on tests that the attentive classroom observer runs across sooner or later, none is more noticeable than the way the practice varies from one school subject to another. This happens chiefly because the practice of testing also varies markedly from subject to subject, as does the dominant instructional format. These differences provide ample illustrations of the way curricular and moral matters interact. In both math and spelling, for example, where quizzes and tests are more the norm than elsewhere and where the answers to test questions are usually short enough to be read quickly and from a distance or to be easily communicated across a room, the temptation to cheat and therefore both the frequency of cheating and the suspicion that it is happening are noticeably greater than in subjects such as English or social studies where longer answers prevail. As a consequence, teachers of math and spelling tend to be more vigilant when they are giving tests (thus communicating a mild sense of distrust) than teachers of other subjects or the same teachers when monitoring tests in other subjects. One math teacher we observed always moves students around the classroom in order to eliminate the temptation to cheat. He executes this rearrangement by speaking in a particularly formal manner, calling out his students' last names — "Mr. Patterson, Mr. Robinson . . ." — while pointing out where the students should move. His formality lends an aura of seriousness to the test situation, which may further encourage his students to refrain from cheating.

Beyond these subject matter differences, it also becomes evident to the observer who spends a sufficient amount of time in several different classrooms that some teachers are simply more suspicion-prone than others and thus are more vigilant when tests are being taken. In some rooms the frequency of commands like "Do your own work" and "Keep your eyes on your own paper" are noticeably greater than elsewhere. One teacher we visited, who taught in the lower grades, had the habit of trying to cloak her suspicions in humor, though this did little to reduce their salience. When she monitored quizzes in spelling or math she would roll her eyes and say things like "I think someone in this room has a case of wandering eyeballs" or "My goodness, what sharp eyes some people have this morning." Beyond what such practices reveal about a teacher's concern for the possibility of cheating, they also speak volumes about the person's overall orientation to his or her job. We will have more to say about such general characteristics shortly.

As we have already pointed out and as these examples help to substantiate, the term *cheating*, as used in classrooms, tends to be reserved for instances of dishonesty during the taking of a test of some kind. There are, in addition, many other forms of dishonesty that take place when teaching is under way. For example, when the teacher asks the class as a whole, "How many did their homework?" or, as we heard in a math class,

"How many got the same answer as Richard?" it is by no means certain that every student whose hand is or is not in the air is telling the truth, as subsequent events sometimes make clear. Yet the assumption that every student is telling the truth is signaled by the teacher gazing upon the students whose hands are and are not raised and saying something noncommittal like "Good" or "Only that many?" before moving on with the lesson.

But matters can be more complicated than this — as we so often found in the course of our observations. For example, a high school English teacher with whom we worked often gave quizzes in class in order to ensure that his students were doing the assigned reading. Yet he disliked giving them, so he said. He worried, in particular, about the signals he was giving students by requiring them, before each test, to move their seats farther apart. Addressing the need for the new seating arrangement, he would say things like "It's not that *I* don't trust you, but *society* doesn't, so you just have to get used to it." What he did not seem to understand was that the practice of giving quizzes was emblematic of distrust in its own right, quite apart from his worries about cheating. He worried about his students copying from each other, while disavowing any such concern, and at the same time he did not trust any assurances they might have given about having read the assignment (hence the need for a quiz to check up on them). Thus the assumption of truthfulness was twice brought into question by his practice.

A corollary of the assumption that students are telling the truth about what they know or don't know is that they are also telling the truth about what they think and feel. This companion assumption is particularly important in subjects like English and social studies, where the focus is often as much on the formation of belief and opinion as it is on the acquisition of knowledge per se. Thus, when teachers ask questions that emphasize personal belief or opinion, such as "How many believe that Achilles acted like a hero?" or "How did you like the poem?" or "How do you think you would feel if you were in Holden Caulfield's predicament?" their trust in the truthfulness of what is told to them is no different than when they ask a "Who knows *X*?" type of question.

Before moving on to another substructural element of the

curriculum, we cannot resist commenting briefly on a special form of dissembling that teachers are reputed to engage in rather frequently, even though we ourselves did not see a lot of it during our visits to classrooms. We refer to the practice of feigning interest and enthusiasm during the teaching of a lesson in order, presumably, to arouse a similar reaction from students. Teachers who behave this way clearly violate the conditions that underlie the assumption of truthfulness and therefore would seem to be courting danger insofar as that assumption is essential to the smooth progress of the lesson itself. However, whether such violations or any other forms of dishonesty create a disturbance depends entirely on whether they are perceived as such by the other party. The crucial question, in other words, is whether the students perceive the teacher to be dissembling when he or she gushes with enthusiasm or otherwise expresses feelings that are not really his or her own.

One of the things we noticed when *we* felt the teacher was less surprised or excited than he or she was acting was that the students often seemed not to notice the deception. Instead, they seemed to be completely taken in by the teacher's "ooohs" and "aaahs," whereas we saw them as exaggerated. This was particularly so in the lower grades, where such reactions on the teachers' part tend to be more prevalent than in the upper grades or high school.

One question these observations raise is whether this form of dissembling isn't natural and almost unavoidable when adults interact with young children. Is it possible, in other words, for an adult to converse with seven- or eight-year-olds, let's say, without falsifying his or her normal reactions in the least? If not, should we continue to read such behavior as a form of falsehood? Might it not be more like the air of cheerfulness a person automatically adopts when he or she is greeted with the usual "Good morning. How are you?" We have no answer to the question of how many adults respond to children in this way, but we do note that some of the teachers we observed seemed to be much more effusive and childlike in their reactions to students than others were. The former almost invariably struck us as being more phony than the latter. We might also note that such a way of responding was not confined to teachers of the very young. High school teachers, too, gush with enthusiasm from time to time or react in other ways that might reasonably make the adult who is watching them begin to doubt their sincerity. Perhaps it is the prevalence of such actions that has led some people to claim that there is a bit of the ham actor in every teacher.

Even if this is true, however, we would still be left with our observation that some teachers are clearly more inclined to behave that way than others. We are not sure what to make of that fact, but one possibility, which ties the phenomenon to issues of curriculum, is that certain school subjects provide more opportunities for the teacher to ham it up than others. It may be, for example, that mathematics requires a teacher to appear more serious than does, say, English or social studies. Also, in some subjects, it may seem inappropriate for a teacher to be a ham. For example, one teacher at a Catholic school often made hyperbolic threats, such as warning noisy students: "Would you like to live to go on to the fourth grade?" or "I'm about ready to get the tape for your lips." But we never heard her speak in that way during prayer time. Another possible explanation of gushing enthusiasm and exaggerated reactions, one that ties these phenomena to issues of instruction, is that certain teaching formats, such as the lecture, lend themselves to histrionics by the teacher more than others. When leading small discussion groups, for example, teachers may be less inclined to behave theatrically than when they are standing in front of the whole class. It may also be that some teachers enjoy behaving theatrically simply because they have a talent for it. Subject matter, instructional format, and dramatic talent can all be contributing factors in accounting for classroom histrionics.

As we ponder the effects of such behavior on the assumption of truthfulness, we cannot help but wonder whether it is correct to assume that low-key presentations are more sincere than those that are more flamboyant. Why should gushing sentiment be thought of as more artificial or less truthful than steely-eyed sobriety? The idea that all instances of teaching, no matter how bland, involve an element of performance is one we will return to when we consider the expressiveness of teaching. For now, we will conclude that the assumption of truthfulness need not be undone by behavior that strikes some observers as phony.

We turn now to a second substructural element, one that we will treat much more briefly than the first. This is the mutually shared assumption that the material being taught is important and the activity being engaged in is worthwhile. We shall refer to this dual expectation as the *assumption of worthwhileness.* Like the assumption of truthfulness, it too is one of the enabling conditions that allow instruction to take place. Conversely, its absence practically ensures instructional breakdowns and difficulties of one kind or another; it is hard to imagine how either teaching or learning could occur, or at least do so effectively, if either teacher or students totally lacked the conviction that what they were doing was worthwhile. Indeed, it is difficult to imagine either party wanting to remain in the classroom under those conditions.

Why should it be necessary to *assume* the worthwhileness of what goes on in classrooms when instruction is under way? Why shouldn't that condition be abundantly evident to all concerned without having to assume anything at all? In some subjects — the so-called basic skills, for example — the usefulness and importance of what is being taught does indeed seem evident to everyone. It sounds odd to talk about assuming the worthwhileness of reading or arithmetic as subject matter. Few people will doubt that it is worthwhile for elementary school children to learn to read or to understand the basic principles of arithmetic. Even children themselves, we might presume, could not harbor such doubts. There are many subjects, however, whose worthwhileness is far from obvious. History and geometry might be examples for many students. Teachers may explain the benefits of such subjects and many obviously do. But if no explanation is proffered, the subject's worthwhileness has to be assumed.

The justification of certain subjects within the curriculum is, however, only a small part of the role played by the assumption of worthwhileness. For even if it is granted that a subject is worthwhile, it does not follow that the activities offered in the name of that subject are equally worthwhile. Students may recognize the value of English without seeing the value of reading *Hamlet* or of writing a term paper.

Consider, for example, the second grader who asked his harried teacher why he needed to complete a math worksheet. The boy was questioning the worthwhileness not of mathematics, but only of this particular activity. In reply to the question, the teacher said, "Just do it." This reply may sound unhelpful, but it probably reflects a pragmatic response to the demands of classroom life as well as a realization of the importance of the assumption of worthwhileness. If each activity had to be fully justified to each student, there would not be time for any activities. The teacher requested the boy to take it on faith that the assignment was worthwhile. Whether the teacher's request succeeded depended not on the boy's completing the worksheet (which he could do even while believing it was a waste of time), but rather on his resuming the assumption of worthwhileness that the other children seemed (by their working) to accept. This second grader's question illustrates the fragility of the assumption of worthwhileness. To recognize that worthwhileness is often taken on faith is to raise the question of whether or not a given activity is truly worthwhile. And once the question has been asked, it is always possible that no satisfactory answer can be produced.

What does this assumption have to do with moral affairs? Why speak of it in a book like this? We do so because of the tacit understanding that undergirds it. What makes the assumption of worthwhileness moral is the even more deeply embedded assumption on which it rests, which is that schools and classrooms are places where one goes to receive help, to be made more knowledgeable and more skillful. Schools and classrooms are designed to be beneficial settings. This implies that the people in charge care about the welfare of those they serve and only ask them to do things that are expected to do them good. Without that underlying assumption, schools start to resemble prisons, which is how they must begin to feel to those who lack faith in the institution's good intentions. Thus, the assumption of worthwhileness is a tacit acknowledgment of the moral character of the institution.

How do we observe the assumption of worthwhileness in action? What do we look for? One of the best indicators we have found, though a very crude one, we must add, is the quality of attention both students and teachers give to their work, particularly when the task at hand is arduous or dull. What makes this indicator crude is the fact that there are many reasons for students to pay attention in class above and beyond the assumption that what they are being called upon to do is fundamentally worthwhile. They pay attention because the work is intrinsically interesting or because their teacher has an eye on them or because they are trying to impress the observer in the back of the room. It is seldom easy to differentiate those kinds of attentiveness from ones motivated by the assumption of worthwhileness. Indeed, it is often impossible to do so. Yet if we look carefully and regularly enough, those discriminations can sometimes be made. Enforced attention, with the teacher standing guard, is often accompanied by furtive glances and numerous signs of self-consciousness — squinted eyes, studied frowns, and the occasional head scratching that is supposed to signal intense concentration. The attention of the intrinsically interested yields an entirely different form of bodily expression, a total absorption that is usually hard to mistake. Its postures are unselfconscious and often uncomfortable looking or even grotesque. Hair is twisted, nails are bitten, pencils are chewed. Dutiful attention, which is the kind we are speaking of here, is more in between. It lacks the intensity of the intrinsically absorbed but also the playacting phoniness of the head-scratching student who is trying to impress the teacher or the observer. It is the posture of the person with a job to do, someone who may not fully understand the rationale behind his or her task but who takes for granted the wisdom of those who set it.

Student questions to the teacher about why something has to be done provide the most direct evidence that the assumption of worthwhileness is on the shelf, at least for the moment. Signs of boredom and inattention form the next best clump of indicators. Again, however, there is no foolproof way of knowing what makes a student's mind wander from the task at hand or why the youngster in the back row sits staring out the window most of the time. Directly questioning such a student about the source of his or her inattentiveness may prove informative under certain circumstances, but even where that is possible or advisable, which it almost never was for us, we could hardly expect the student to confirm in so many words his or her inability to accept the assumption of worthwhileness. What we would more likely get instead would be an answer describing the work or the activity as simply boring or uninteresting.

This last possibility raises an interesting question about the psychological reality (or the ontic status, as a philosopher might say) of the two assumptions we have been discussing. In essence, the question is this: Can we say that most of the time teachers and students *actively assume* that each is being truthful during the course of instruction and that the work they are engaged in is fundamentally worthwhile, or should we say merely that their behavior is consistent with these assumptions? Thus far we have been speaking as though these assumptions or something very much like them were consciously entertained by participants when a lesson was under way. However, the fact that students, if queried, would probably not use those terms to describe themselves suggests either that such assumptions operate on something like an unconscious level or that they simply fit the observable facts without necessarily referring to anything beyond that. As we suggested earlier, our hunch is that many teachers and students do not begin to realize how importantly these assumptions undergird their everyday classroom life.

What makes these assumptions important from a moral perspective is the possibility that living and acting under such conditions for an extended period of time — for some years and even decades — will begin to have an enduring effect on the moral makeup of the participants. This would imply that the assumptions we have been talking about do actually *register* somehow, either consciously or unconsciously, on the psyches of those present and are not simply a convenient way of describing how things look. Can a question like this even be answered and is it an empirical question? Might someone gather some evidence that would settle it once and for all?

Our own view is that both the central question and the

subsidiary ones we have raised lie at the heart of current worries about the school's role in the moral upbringing of students. We will return to these questions in Part Four. For the present we need only note that the forms of influence we are now considering lie far beyond those that are usually talked about in discussions of moral education.

Before turning to our eighth and final category of the moral dimensions of schooling, we need to mention yet another cluster of assumptions that belong to the category of curricular substructures. These center on issues of social justice. They include the assumption that teachers will ask fair questions and give reasonable exams, that turns will be taken when it comes time to speak, that speakers will be given sufficient time to compose their thoughts, that others will listen to what they say, and that everyone will face similar standards of judgment when it comes to grading and evaluation. Many of these assumptions might be grouped under the general rubric of fair play, which might make them seem commonplace, but, as with the other substructural elements we have discussed, they are special in the sense of being uniquely adapted to what goes on in instructional settings.

How can we tell that just practices are being taken for granted in the classroom? To cite only a few clues: by the patience with which students' hands are held in the air to be recognized; by their readiness to share ideas, feelings, and opinions; and by their willingness to accept that their grades on papers, tests, and report cards truly reflect their achievement. Once again, however, it is when *un*just practices occur that the assumption of justice is most readily noticeable to the observer. Open complaints about the teacher's unfairness, the students' readiness to tattle on classmates who misbehave behind the teacher's back, student indignation over an instance of supposed favoritism — all of these responses help to make apparent to the observer the underlying assumption that just practices will ordinarily prevail.

There are doubtless other assumptions and expectations beyond those discussed here that the classroom observer who is on the lookout for such things might possibly uncover. All we have tried to do is to introduce the category and back it up with a few fairly obvious examples. The key point to keep in mind is the idea of there being a set of underlying, typically invisible enabling conditions that are moral in nature and that allow instruction to proceed smoothly and amicably.

Category VIII. Expressive Morality Within the Classroom

The easiest way we could think of to introduce this final category of things to look for when searching for the moral in classrooms was by considering the facial expressions of teachers and the moral messages they convey. At the same time, we also envisioned some difficulty with that approach. We feared that by starting with something as familiar and as easily understood as the notion of facial expressions, we might inadvertently reinforce an overly narrow usage of terms like *express* and *expressive*, thus making it difficult later on to extend the range of their applicability as we shall insist on doing. When it came time for a decision, however, the attractiveness of starting with something familiar outweighed the risk involved. We thus decided to travel the easy road and to worry about how to stretch the boundaries of common usage when it becomes necessary to do so.

To begin with the blandest of assertions, it is certainly incontrovertible that the face, particularly the region around the eyes, is the most expressive part of the human body and the area on which people invariably focus their gaze when they want to find out how to respond to others. "The face is the mirror of the mind," Saint Jerome once wrote, "and eyes without speaking confess the secrets of the heart."[1] True enough, we all must surely agree. And if looks could kill, as another old saying has it, homicide rates would zoom out of sight.

Teachers, of course, are no different from anyone else when it comes to their faces revealing what is on their minds. As every classroom observer quickly learns, the look on the teacher's face is frequently the key to understanding what's going on. Students know that too, which is why they spend a lot of time looking at the teacher, even when he or she is not looking at them. They look to find out how their teacher "takes" things, to see whether it's safe to laugh at another student's smart-alecky remark or whether their own cleverness has evoked an appreciative response. They also quickly figure out how to "take" their teacher. They learn to discriminate between looks that mean the teacher is to be taken seriously and those that indicate that he or she is only kidding. In one of our elementary classrooms, for example, when the children were engaged in what educators normally call "seatwork," the teacher suddenly put on an angry mien and shouted from her desk in the corner of the room, "Shut up, all of you, or I'll cut out your tongues!" Heads lifted momentarily as all eyes focused on the teacher. Then, as the pupils detected her suppressed grin, giggles and smiles broke out around the room.

The range of expressions that cross a teacher's face in the course of a single lesson is often much greater than one might imagine, given the workaday nature of the activity itself. Moreover, the rapidity with which changes of countenance come and go on the faces of both teachers and students, but especially the former, make them nearly impossible to catalog. Teachers are hardly unique in this regard, of course. One thinks of the stand-up comic, for example, whose act often depends on quick changes of expression. But what makes the teacher's facial expressions of special interest from a moral perspective is what they communicate about the value — the goodness or the badness — of what is going on. Looks of kindness, impatience, good humor, sternness, incredulity, indignation, pity, discouragement, disapproval, delight, admiration, suspicion, disbelief — the list could easily go on — are all part of a teacher's normal repertoire of expressions that routinely come into play in the course of teaching a lesson or managing a class activity. All convey a moral outlook of one kind or another whose focus is on what the class as a whole and its individual members say and do.

Often those looks are combined with gestures and bodily postures that serve to make their meaning even more explicit. The teacher who folds her arms across her chest and taps her toe impatiently as she waits for the class to become quiet speaks expressively, with greater firmness and clarity, than does the one who merely stands there scowling. Most students quickly learn to read their teacher's body language as fluently as they do the look on his or her face.

In the crudest of terms, all that has been said so far about what we are calling expressive morality reduces to the observation that teachers smile and frown a lot when they teach and that this can often be read as a kind of moral commentary on the activity in which they are engaged. That summary is accurate enough as far as it goes but it doesn't go very far. It doesn't begin to capture the complexity of what can be seen to go on expressively in most classrooms even if observation is limited to the looks on the teacher's face and the gestures that accompany them. We would like to trace a few of the sources of that complexity. Our goal, as we have already suggested, is to move the discussion from its initial focus on an overly narrow conception of expression to one that is broader and more inclusive.

To begin, the looks on teachers' faces are not always as easily interpreted as our prior listing of a few of them might make them seem. When the teacher abruptly stops what he is saying, walks to the side of the classroom, rests against a bookcase, and looks sternly at the children, what are we to make of his stern look? Is he angry with the children or is he teasing them? When a teacher turns her head from a student who has just answered a question, is she curtly dismissing the answer or reflecting on it? How should we understand the science teacher's blank look as he waits for a puzzled student to formulate his question? Is he exhibiting patience or does his blankness mask a feeling of exasperation? Sometimes it is easy to tell such things, but not always. Moreover, as a couple of those examples imply, coming to a decision about what the teacher means when he or she looks a certain way is not simply a matter of deciphering the look itself. There is often the additional question of whether the look is to be trusted.

Does the teacher mean what his or her facial expression or gestures imply? The question is a familiar one. It reminds us that looks can sometimes be deceiving. And that fact, if pondered closely, leads us to recognize that the expressiveness of an object like a human face does not work like a window to another world, a transparency that allows us to see *into* something, even though that's the way we commonly think of it as operating. It is both more direct and more superficial than that. Its meaning as expression resides on the surface of the object. It *is* what we see, though not what we might describe if we were called upon to report on the object's physical properties. We see anger in the teacher's face, not in the innermost regions of his or her being, and that is where we also see patience or surprise or any of the other psychological qualities we have been describing. It is the *look* of patience and the *look* of attentiveness that we learn to discern in the facial expressions of others.

The full significance of this conception of how expressiveness is perceived and how it applies to physical objects as well as to humans will become increasingly apparent as we go along. For now all we need to take from it is the realization that what is expressed — the meaning we perceive — does not have to correspond to conditions that lie beyond or outside of the medium of expression. To rephrase Marshall McLuhan's famous slogan of a few decades back, the medium, we might say, *contains* the message. The latter, returning again to facial expressions, need not be a faithful report of how someone feels about something or of the outcome of that person's intentions. This means, of course, that people can and do tell lies with their faces and their bodily movements just as surely as they do with words (teachers being no exception, naturally enough). It also means that people's faces and gestures can reveal more than their owners want them to, and sometimes more than they realize. "You should have seen the look on your face," we say to a companion who was unaware of how candidly revealing his or her expression was. Teachers too commonly reveal a great deal about themselves without intending to.

We have been making two points here. One is that classroom observers can glean a great deal about what teachers intend from their facial expressions. The other is that looks can't always be trusted, not even by the person expressing them. That fact alone makes reading the expressive qualities of what goes on in classrooms a tricky business. Another source of complexity — indeed the major one — is the fact that facial expressions are only the most obvious loci of expressivity. We have already noted that gestures and bodily postures can augment or contradict what the face expresses. But the boundaries of the expressive do not stop there either. The truth is that they have no limits. Everything that teachers and students say and do together, every activity in which they engage, every physical object within the room, and even the environment as a whole can be scrutinized expressively if the observer chooses to do so. The challenge is to know when and how to adopt such a perspective.

As an instance of how broadly the net of observation might be cast in search of expressive meaning, consider the well-known sense of trust (or distrust) in the teacher that students and outside observers gradually develop. Here, surely, is a morally relevant quality if there ever was one. And for no one more than a teacher. After all, what greater virtue than trustworthiness could we ask of a person who is in a position to so potently influence the young?

Where does that sense of trust come from? What makes a teacher, or anyone else for that matter, appear trustworthy or untrustworthy? How do we explain, for example, the trust evinced by one of the second graders we observed who checked his spelling first with a classroom observer, then with a dictionary, and finally (just to be sure) with his teacher? Or, to take another instance from that same classroom, what do we make of the group of students who decided to consult their teacher to find out whether *hell* was a "bad word" (a matter they agreed they would not want to ask their parents about)? Did this teacher seem a trustworthy person to go to with these questions because he had demonstrated good spelling and sensitive word choice? Or was it that the children felt they could go to him with these questions because he seemed trustworthy?

It could be, of course, that it only takes a few acts to establish such a reputation. We know, certainly, that one dramatic instance of dishonesty can undo a lifetime of exemplary living and brand someone as a thief or a liar from then on. Yet it seems to us that that's not the way such things usually work. More commonly we come to trust or distrust people not because of any particular thing they have done but because that's the way they strike us, because that's how we come to look upon them. We see them as trustworthy or untrustworthy even when we have practically no grounds for doing so or at least none that can be rationally defended. We say things like: "I don't know, there's just something about him I don't trust" or "She has a sneaky look in her eyes" or "He has such an open and engaging manner" or "I just feel comfortable and relaxed when I'm around her."

Such judgments are not without error, as we know, and sometimes these errors are serious. Moreover, they may on occasion help to bring into being or at least intensify the very quality judged to be present. When that happens they become, in effect, self-fulfilling prophecies. Erving Goffman is alleged to have said somewhere, "A paranoid person is someone about whom others feel suspicious." He was right, of course, but what his quip left out was the recognition that the suspicions of others help to make the paranoid person paranoid.

Yet laying aside all exceptions to the rule, there is typically a lot of truth in the judgments we make of others. And this is so even when we cannot quite put our finger on the source of our opinion. That truth, we would suggest, *emerges expressively*. It is given off by what a person says and does, the way a smile gives off an aura of friendliness or tears a spirit of sadness. Emerson framed the idea memorably when he said, "We pass for what we are. Character teaches above our wills. Men imagine that they communicate their virtue or vice only by overt actions, and do not see that virtue or vice emit a breath every moment."[2] These vaporlike emanations of character that even our smallest acts give off mean that our judgment of a quality like trustworthiness does not usually depend on any single event or noteworthy instance, which is why we sometimes have a hard time putting our finger on its source. Rather than a discovery that hits us like a bolt from the blue — although the latter can occasionally happen, of course — it is something we arrive at or come to after an extended period of time. This implies that almost everything a teacher says and does, including the way she stands about when doing nothing, can potentially reveal something that will heighten or diminish an observer's impression of her trustworthiness. This is provided, of course, that the observer, whether a student or an outsider, is looking for such things.

Earlier we said that the expressiveness of an object like a human face resides on its surface. Now it is time to refine and somewhat revise that observation. In the interest of accuracy we might better have said at the start that the expressive meaning of what we can see and experience resides *in* the surface of a thing, rather than *on* it. By this we mean that what an object or person or even a total situation might express cannot be separated from the thing itself though it can be talked about separately as one of the object's or the person's or the situation's properties. It is not like a label that can be removed intact from the surface of what we see, the way we might peel a stamp from an envelope or a skin from a banana. More like the design in a rug, it is integral to the thing being witnessed. It belongs to the object or situation the way a grin belongs to the face expressing it. The disappearing Cheshire Cat in *Alice's Adventures in Wonderland,* the one that left its grin behind, humorously reminds us that in reality such a separation is impossible.

What this quality of embeddedness implies for the classroom observer is that the expressive significance of what we are looking at can never be fully appreciated or understood apart from the thing itself; a portion of its meaning always has to be left behind whenever we try to describe it to others. Thus, we who observe classroom teachers in action can say all we want about their giving off an aura of trustfulness or distrustfulness as they go about their work. But to appreciate fully the basis of that judgment one would have to have been there, seated beside us in the back of the room. And even that may not be enough. For someone could have been seated beside us all that time and still not have seen precisely what we saw. Why not? Because expressive meaning is usually quite subtle and because people differ in their receptivity to it, the way they differ in their receptivity to art, for example, or to the subtleties of what children say and do. In addition, even the most astute observer must leave some meaning behind when he or she begins to describe what was seen and heard. Any teacher who has tried to describe a student or a classroom setting to someone else knows this full well.

Does this mean that expressive meanings are purely subjective and therefore fundamentally unsharable? We will say more about this question at the beginning of Part Two, but our short answer here is no. On the contrary, a heightened sensitivity to the expressive quality of things is eminently teachable, as demonstrated by the popularity of courses on appreciation of the arts. For in large measure that's what learning to appreciate any of the arts is all about: becoming increasingly sensitive to the expressive potential of that particular artistic medium, be it literature, drama, painting, or dance.

It should now be clear that an effort to determine what a teacher expressively communicates to students in moral terms goes far beyond trying to figure out what his or her posture and facial expressions convey at any given moment. It takes in patterns of actions whose shape and contour can only be discerned through repeated visits and possibly over a long period of time. For example, consider what it means for a principal to be seen day after day in front of the school building, supervising the morning arrival and afternoon departure of the students. What do such actions communicate? By themselves, possibly nothing. Seen only once, they might mean little at all. It may just be that no one else is free at that time and someone has to be on duty at that spot. But as part of a larger pattern of actions, one that can only be understood by close and prolonged observation, the principal's habit of being on hand to greet students in the morning and attend their departure at the end of the day starts to take on a different character entirely. We begin to read it symbolically, which is to say, expressively. Seen in that light, it now reflects. the principal's commitment to her work.

Or picture the high school teacher who stands by his classroom door at the beginning of each period, ushers in the near latecomers, closes the door promptly at the sound of the bell, and then immediately strides to the center of the room, calling for attention as he launches into the day's lesson. The teacher's actions themselves are fairly routine and their meaning reasonably clear. They signal the fact that the period has begun and the class is about to get under way. But the manner of their execution, especially if it is repeated daily, communicates something more. The abruptness of the teacher's movements conveys a sense of the importance of what is about to take place in that room. They are *expressive* of that importance and of more besides. They say that here is a teacher who cares about what he is doing. Here is someone who doesn't have a moment to lose. The teacher may not have intended his actions to speak in that way, but they do all the same.

This last example reminds us that within the classroom a teacher's actions over time take on a certain consistency that allows fairly accurate prediction of how he or she will respond to recurrent situations such as outbreaks of misbehavior or students' failure to make themselves clearly understood. This consistency of manner, reaction, poise, and so forth we tend to call style. Style refers to the teacher's typical ways of handling the demands of the job. What makes a teacher's style noteworthy from a moral perspective is the way it embodies attributes that we normally think of as moral — many of the same attributes, in fact, that we find encapsulated in facial expressions. A teacher's style can be reserved and aloof or warm and intimate. It can express kindness or cruelty. It can be scatterbrained or methodical. A teacher's style is not the same as his or her personality, although the two notions are closely intertwined. Style, in contrast to personality, is more task-specific. It is not something that teachers necessarily take home with them at the end of the day, although some surely do. Others seem to shed their style and leave it behind them, the way they might hang a smock in the teacher's closet. They become different people as they step out the door and enter their out-of-school life.

In subsequent sections of this book we will offer detailed portrayals of some of these stylistic attributes and will discuss their moral relevance. For now it will suffice to point out that style, like all of the other items described in this section, is an expressive quality. The adjectives we attach to the term, words like reserved and effusive, convey only the scantiest notion of the complexity that, through repeated observation, we come to recognize as a teacher's characteristic way of leading a discussion or giving a lecture or supervising seatwork or even routinely navigating the short space between the classroom door and the front of the room, as we have just seen.

Thus far we have concentrated our search for the expressive dimensions of schooling on the teacher alone. And there is certainly good reason for doing so, since teachers are clearly the foci of attention in most classrooms. However, we earlier claimed that everything in classrooms, including the physical objects that crowd their interiors, has the potential of conveying expressive meaning if it is viewed from a certain angle. Now it is time to elaborate on that claim.

Certainly one of the most obvious differences among classrooms lies in the fullness or sparseness of their furnishings. Some classrooms are relatively devoid of objects, save for the usual scattering of chairs and desks; others are relatively cluttered. Some of the cluttered ones have so many things displayed on walls and tables that there is scarcely a bare space remaining, except perhaps for the tops of the students' desks. Such rooms might also contain their share of living things—some plants perhaps, a terrarium or two, a couple of small animals such as gerbils or rabbits, and sometimes a jar of captive insects or a cocoon waiting to be hatched. One classroom in which we observed usually had an array of objects hanging from the ceiling as well—student-made mobiles, papier-mâché masks, decorative glass ornaments, and so forth. In the sparest of classrooms, by way of contrast, the walls were nearly empty, except for the ubiquitous blackboard and perhaps a small bulletin board for notices. The furniture in such rooms is usually limited to desks for students and a larger desk for the teacher, the latter set apart from the others. There might also be a podium at the front of the room where the teacher holds forth when conducting a lesson.

These variations in furnishings differ according to the age and grade level of the students being served. Elementary school classrooms, by and large, tend to have more things in them and thus appear more cluttered than do high school or college classrooms. There are notable exceptions to this rule, of course—science labs, for example, tend to house a lot of objects no matter where they are—but the generalization still holds. Elementary classrooms are simply "busier" places visually than are those serving older students.

For the observer interested in the moral influences present within classrooms, the question becomes this: What do these differences in furnishings express and, whatever that might be, what is its significance in moral terms? The answer to that double-barreled question will certainly vary from room to room and may also vary somewhat from observer to observer, for not everyone is equally sensitive to such things, nor does everyone interpret them the same way. Sometimes the clutter has an uncared-for look about it, like a closet that needs cleaning. At other times it resembles a curio shop whose objects have been positioned with loving care and whose owner goes around dusting them all the time. At least superficially, the difference in moral terms is fairly straightforward: one room looks neglected, the other cared for.

In sparely furnished rooms differences in caretaking do not stand out as starkly as they do in more cluttered enclosures. Almost all rooms of the former type look more or less neglected from a housekeeping point of view, at least when compared with the latter. Yet even among these more Spartan settings we can discern variations in the expressive "feel" of the place. The bare look of some is cold and off-putting, like a hospital corridor or a deserted warehouse. Others exude a kind of barracks warmth — austere, to be sure, but not uninviting. It is not always easy to put our finger on the source of such differences. In one room it may have to do with the balls of dust under the teacher's desk or the torn window shade; in another, a faded poster or a piece of crushed chalk that never gets swept up contributes to the overall impression of neglect. One of the classrooms we visited in a Catholic high school was almost totally bare except for desks and chairs. But there was a visually compelling poster on the wall in a corner of the room that depicted an image of God reaching out with exaggeratedly large hands, below which were the words "For God So Loved the World." We leave readers to imagine the impact of such a poster on its audience and, hence, its expressive power.

What can we make of such differences in the expressive tone of classrooms? Does a room that looks neglected mean that the teacher in charge is generally neglectful? By no means. Nor, unfortunately, can we count on the opposite being true. Signs of a cared-for *environment* do not necessarily indicate a teacher who cares about *teaching*, although the two forms of caring often seem to go hand in hand. There are classrooms, however, in which the evident attention given to displays and decorations actually arouses our suspicions. The showcase quality of such rooms reminds us of the interiors pictured in housekeeping magazines, nice to look at but not to live in. The closer we look at such rooms the more we begin to wonder whether the teacher cares as much for the substance of what is going on there as for its appearance. What this says is that any simple formula that translates classroom clutter into an expression of pedagogical attentiveness is clearly off the mark.

However, if there is no one-to-one correspondence between how the room's appearance strikes those who gaze upon it and the attitude the teacher takes toward his or her work in general, what difference does it make what the room looks like or what impression it makes upon those who visit? The first answer is that there is always some correspondence between the appearance of the room and the person responsible for its care, even though the relationship may not be apparent and may even turn out to be the opposite of what we might think. Thus when we happen upon an excessively tidy or uncommonly sloppy classroom, it is always at least reasonable to wonder what the room's condition may be expressing about the character of the teacher in charge. On sight, such rooms pose a question that is waiting to be answered.

Beyond what the room's appearance may say about the teacher in charge, it also says something about the room itself, and what it says is often tinged with moral significance. Some classrooms are bright and cheerful; others are gloomy and depressing. And it doesn't matter, in a sense, who made them that way. That's just the way they are. The teachers and students who are obliged to spend large amounts of time there have no choice but to accommodate themselves to those conditions. There are many ways of doing so, of course. One of the most common, when the environment is dull and uninviting, is to "turn it off," to shift one's attention elsewhere. That is certainly what happens in many classrooms. Moreover, we could plausibly argue that this is what *should* happen. After all, classrooms are places where people should concentrate on work and not on the environment in general. However, if we closely observe students who are supposedly concentrating on their work, it quickly becomes evident that this concentration does not entail being completely inattentive to their surroundings. Even among the most hard-at-work students in a classroom, heads are constantly being raised and lowered. Eyes sweep the room from floor to ceiling between moments of concentrated focus on a text or workbook. Those eyes may not take in all of the features they fall upon during their momentary breaks from the task at hand, but it's hard to imagine them registering nothing at all.

What does it mean to spend several hours a day for months or even years in a dull and uninviting environment or a pleasant and inviting one? Does it make sense to think of the moral costs and benefits that may derive from such experiences? That question is one we shall return to in Part Four. For now we need only take from what has just been said the central point of the discussion, which is that every classroom, like every person or every situation, is unique and, most importantly, that part of its uniqueness is communicated expressively, registering on those present as a mood or feeling occasioned by their being there. The source of that feeling is not usually localized, at least not at the start. It somehow belongs to the place as a whole, pervading it the way a uniform climate or atmosphere might pervade a region of the earth. To epitomize the feeling aroused in a particular classroom, the visitor may seize upon a prominent feature, such as the peeling paint or the colorful bulletin board, and use that to stand for the whole. But the isolation of one or more such features cannot serve as a causal explanation for a room's aura.

What we have said about the classroom environment as a whole can be applied to even the smallest of its parts, such as the dusty eraser leaning against the blackboard or the faded Stuart portrait of George Washington hanging in the far corner of the room or the thank-you card from a former student tacked to the bulletin board. These objects too can be read expressively if the observer is open to doing so. To some, the worn eraser may speak of the temporality of the written word; to others, it may serve as an emblem of just how much work has gone on in the room year after year. The portrait of Washington may trigger a feeling of nostalgia. It may serve as a faded reminder of an educational past that is now gone, of days when school-children could recite the names of past presidents and even feel a sense of pride in being able to do so. The thank-you card could stand for many things, not the least of which might be the reciprocity of giving and receiving that constitutes the main order of business in classrooms.

When is it appropriate to undertake a detailed reading, in expressive terms, of the objects classrooms contain? That question invites us to take a backward look at all eight of the observational categories that have been discussed, for we need to know not only when to look for the expressive significance of classroom objects but also when and how to make use of the whole set of categories that have now been explicated. As a prelude to doing so, let us list the categories in the order in which we have presented them. The first group included

1. Moral instruction as a formal part of the curriculum
2. Moral instruction within the regular curriculum
3. Rituals and ceremonies
4. Visual displays with moral content
5. Spontaneous interjections of moral commentary into on-going activity

The second were

6. Classroom rules and regulations
7. The morality of curricular substructure
8. Expressive morality within the classroom

Using the Observer's Guide

To speak of *using* those eight categories may not be the best way of introducing what we want to say. The idea of use generally implies putting something to work for some ulterior purpose, as one might use a tool to repair a broken object. But the use of an observer's guide, which is what we have called our two sets of categories, is rather different from that of an ordinary tool. Its chief function is to help others *see* things, to alter their customary view of the world. It has often been said that teaching is a moral affair. But what we hope most for this taxonomy is that it will prove useful in calling our readers' attention to the myriad ways in which the moral significance of all that can be seen and heard within classrooms might become manifest. We hope it will impress upon them the pervasiveness of such matters and will alert them as observers to what might otherwise have gone unnoticed.

The categories should perform a second service as well. If the main function of this outline is to call attention to the pervasiveness of moral considerations as they impinge upon educational affairs, a secondary function and one of hardly less importance than the first is to reveal the subtlety of this effect. That subtlety is reflected in our two sets of categories, the first set focusing on the moral influences that are most readily observable and the second set on those that are least easily observed. But ease of observation is only one of the principles at work within that structure. Additionally, the categories, in the first set differ from those in the second set by their planfulness and their separateness as discrete items of observation. A word or two about each of these differences may help to make them clear.

Some of the things teachers and school administrators do to affect the moral well-being of their students are done intentionally. For example, when teachers put up signs that encourage students to be charitable or to adopt a positive attitude toward their personal goals and ambitions, they are almost certainly hopeful that these actions will lead their students to become better persons. The same is doubtless true when they organize ceremonies that are intended to be uplifting and when they spend time in class discussing the moral significance of some passing episode or event. The intent of all such actions is to leave a moral mark of some kind. Of course, not everything that teachers and administrators hope might leave such a mark actually does. And the mark it leaves is not always the one that was intended.

Of far greater significance for this discussion, however, is the opposite fact: many of the things that turn out to be of great influence from a moral standpoint are not purposefully undertaken as a moral act. We would go further than that in declaring our own convictions. We believe that the unintentional outcomes of schooling, the ones teachers and administrators seldom plan in advance, are of greater moral significance — that is, more likely to have enduring effects — than those that are intended and consciously sought. In terms of our taxonomy, this means that we place greater stock in the long-term moral potency of the items in our second set of categories than of those in the first set. One of our chief reasons for doing so, which should be fairly clear by now, is that many of the unintended influences are in operation *all or most of the time,* whereas the intended ones are more episodic and self-contained. The rules that structure the classroom, assumptions that undergird the curriculum, and the teacher's style or character are almost always present. They may seldom be the focus of attention but they remain in operation all the same.

We have devoted the bulk of this chapter to our last three categories not only because we believe that rules, substructure, and the expressive have long-term moral potency but also because we have found that their pervasiveness changes our perception of all of the preceding categories. When we finally arrive at the eighth category, we are taking the most expansive view of moral life — a view that reconceives the items examined in the other categories. It is for this reason that the expressive will be our main concern throughout this book.

What our observer's guide offers, then, is not a list of identifiable moral influences to be searched for in every classroom — a checklist to be used in a mechanical fashion. Instead, it provides some suggestions about where to look for those influences while at the same time offering a perspective, a *way* of looking, that extends beyond the focus on explicit programs of moral education that is the center of so much of the recent discussion about the place of morals and morality in today's schools. We have no wish to disparage such programs nor should classroom observers overlook them. On the contrary, they were among the first things we noticed in our own work and we would expect others whose aims are similar to ours to pick them out quickly as well. We would urge, however, that the search not stop there. Those who move beyond the easily observable may find the categories outlined in this chapter to be a useful guide.

$\backsim$ PART TWO $\backsim$

Becoming Aware of
Moral Complexity
Within a School Setting:
FOUR SETS OF OBSERVATIONS

*I*n Part One we offered two sets of categories that contained things to look for when trying to understand the moral function of a school and its teachers. We also offered a parallel set of suggestions about how to look for those things. The "how" part of that offering did not include specific advice about the techniques of observation but rather emphasized the importance of looking at what goes on in classrooms from a symbolic or expressive point of view. Only in that way, we suggested, can one begin to appreciate the potential impact of qualities such as the teacher's character and temperament or the atmosphere of the classroom in general on the moral well-being of those present.

However, the task of becoming attuned to the moral subtlety of what happens in classrooms calls for more than altering our way of seeing. We must also reflect on what we have seen and persist in turning events over in our mind's eye long after they have disappeared from sight, drawing from our memories of them and from reflecting upon those memories whatever moral significance the events may be found to contain. We shall illustrate that process of reflecting and ruminating on the expressive in this part.

Open Work

The process turns out to be rather complicated. It involves not only *thinking* about what was seen but also *talking* or *writing* about

45

it, and commonly both. The thinking, talking, and writing do
not usually proceed in serial fashion, but neither do they happen all at once. Instead, they get jumbled together in sporadic
sessions that sometimes last for hours and are stretched out over
days or weeks or even longer, the actual length of the process
depending on what we have observed, what our purposes were
for doing so, and how much time is available.

     We can distinguish two phases of the process: one descrip-
tive, the other reflective. The descriptive phase takes place while
sitting in the classroom—which may mean taking a respite from
directing classroom affairs if the observer happens to be the
teacher in charge—and consists of jotting down whatever strikes
one as noteworthy, without worrying unduly at the time about
its potential moral significance. Later, those notes can be expanded, preferably that same day or soon after, in order to fill
in some of the detail that is still remembered but was not jotted
down. It is then that the reflective phase begins.

     Both phases—describing what we witness and later reflect-
ing upon it—involve interpretation. This claim may strike some
readers as odd. Those who feel that way probably look upon
what actually goes on in classrooms as being factual and not
a matter of interpretation at all. The latter, they might insist,
comes later. It is something one *does* to the facts themselves. To
those who hold such convictions we can only say that we strongly
disagree. Moreover, the basis of our disagreement is integral
to an understanding of the outlook we advance in this book.
Because of the way it bears upon our work in general, we will
briefly explain our position before beginning to take a look inside classrooms.

     Classrooms, as we have come to understand them, are
not places whose buzz of activity fits neatly within a single descriptive framework. They are too crowded and too much goes
on within them. Therefore, every description that might issue
from such a complex, crowded environment is a selection from
among many that could possibly have been given. That selection is inevitably the result of an act of interpretation on the
part of the observer regarding what is worth noting and the way
it should be noted. Even when two observers focus on what seems

to be the same event unfolding before their eyes, their reports will inevitably vary, partly as a result of each one's individual perspective, conditioned by past experience, present state of mind, and more, and partly because of the language each uses to describe what was seen. This is not to say that the two accounts will be totally different. There is almost bound to be some overlap in the descriptions, and often the reports may be nearly identical. But particularly when what is being reported upon is as ephemeral as the look on a teacher's face or the manner in which an action was undertaken, the potential for complete agreement is reduced and the interpretive or selective nature of the description is all the more evident.

Why is recognition of this condition integral to an understanding of the outlook we present? It is so because a moral reading of what we see when we look upon the world of schooling seems to work differently than does a flat rendering into words of the ongoing activities or physical objects before our eyes. We say "seems" to work differently because we suspect the contrast to be one of degree rather than kind, although we will not trouble to pursue that suspicion here. In any event, listing the objects in a classroom, for example, or even naming the major activities that might be witnessed there—the sessions of seatwork, discussion, recitation, and so forth—strikes us as quite unlike the job of trying to describe the manner in which a teacher handles a very delicate situation, let's say, or the sense of disappointment that overtakes a class whose privileges have just been curtailed. The difference is not simply that one type of description takes few words and the other many or that what is described in one seems substantial and enduring, whereas the other comes and goes in a twinkling, although both of those dissimilarities may be true as well. The source of the difference lies deeper than that. Some might claim that it has to do with the observer's overall sensitivity to what is going on. But ascribing the contrast to such a vague psychological source seems to us to be equally unhelpful.

The commonest words we find applied to such difference are *objective* and *subjective*. In those terms, descriptions of physical objects and common activities would be called objective, whereas those focusing on the mood and manner of what is seen to occur would be called subjective. One implication of that usage is that the objective description refers to something outside of oneself, something that resides in the external world as a *fact,* whereas the grounding of what is called subjective comes from within and is fundamentally a report on how one *feels* about something, or perhaps an *opinion.* A corollary of that way of speaking ascribes one description to the province of science and the other to art. One purports to describe what is real; the other, what is fictional or imaginative.

In the kind of work in which we have been engaged, the objective-subjective dichotomy turns out to be more of a hindrance than a help. We readily acknowledge that it is much easier to describe the physical layout of a classroom than to talk about how the teacher carries out his or her duties or how the class as a whole responds to the room's ambiance. What we reject about the words *objective* and *subjective* is the implication that one refers to something real and the other does not. We also find the distinctions between outside and inside and between seeing and feeling to be of little value. This is not to say that such distinctions are always inapplicable and of no help to anyone. On the contrary, under certain circumstances they may be precisely the ones to make. It is principally the ontological assumptions underlying them — the belief that one outlook provides a window to reality and truth, whereas the other does not — that we find troublesome and unnecessary.

When we describe a teacher as responding *candidly* to a student's question or as waiting *patiently* for the room to become quiet, we believe that description to be fully as real and objective as the color of the teacher's eyes or the chalk smudge on his sleeve. This is not to say that everyone will have seen the same thing and will agree with our perception. Others who were present in the room may have failed to note the qualities of candor and patience, just as they may have failed to note the color of the teacher's eyes or the chalk smudge on his sleeve. Or the observers, particularly if they are very young students, may lack the conceptual tools that allow them to see candor and patience when they are expressed. But the failure of others to see what we have seen does not by itself discredit our observation or imply that what we have seen is somehow unreal. It would take observers who were looking for such qualities and who were equipped conceptually to make such distinctions to begin to challenge our description.

For us, a more useful set of terms than *objective* and *subjective* for talking about the kind of looking and ruminating in which we have been engaged are *open* and *closed*. The distinction is one that was suggested to us by a recently translated work of Umberto Eco.[3] As Eco uses the terms and as we would like to employ them here, a description or report that is open is one that invites further reflection and commentary; one that is closed does not. The invitation to continued exploration may at times result in a discrediting of what was said or written, which may turn out to have been false or shortsighted or insensitive. But more typically, at least in our experience, the initial statement or document becomes enriched through continued thought. Our understanding of it deepens. We begin to see within it aspects that were not apparent at first. What was said or written may undergo change as well. Not all that gets added in the way of understanding augments what was there at the start; sometimes revisions are called for. In short, the process is an evolving one. It is also one that has no proper terminus. We stop reflecting when we become temporarily tired of doing so or when new ideas are no longer forthcoming. But a fresh start on a different day may yield additional insights and someone else may well find food for thought in material that we had given up on.

We now turn to examine some of the things we saw in classrooms. We look upon our descriptions and the commentary that follows as "open works" in Eco's terms, and we invite our readers to do the same.

The first set of observations was collected over several days in a first-grade classroom. The observer writes:

> It was a typical morning in Ms. Hamilton's first-grade classroom. She was working in the corner of the room by the chalkboard, with each of the reading groups in turn — first the Butterflies, then the Rainbows, followed by the Lollipops, and finally the Stars. She sat on one of the first-grade-sized chairs, facing into the classroom. The children were gathered about her on the rug.

It is obvious from the way this observation begins that the observer has been there before, probably on many occasions. He speaks of it as being a typical morning. Also he apparently knows the order in which the four reading groups will be called to the front. The names of those groups, incidentally, were selected by the children themselves. They are all such goody-goody names. One wonders why. Why no Monsters or Insects? Is it because such choices were never suggested by the students or might the teacher have vetoed (subtly or otherwise) such possibilities?

Notice that the first thing the observer does is to locate the teacher and describe her position. In our experience that itself is a very typical observational move. It underscores the centrality of the teacher as *the* person to keep an eye on in this environment. The children probably sense that as keenly as the observer. The teacher, in turn, positions herself to have the widest angle of vision possible. She needs to see everyone just as everyone needs to see her. This viewing arrangement expresses a relationship of domination and subordination, one that characterizes this and most other classrooms. Yet in this particular situation there is a variation on that typical relationship that deserves comment.

It stands to reason that teachers, when teaching, would want to be in a physical position that enables them to see all of the students in their instructional group, although there are certainly situations where that common arrangement does not hold, such as when a teacher is on television. But in this classroom the teacher positions herself to be able to see even the pupils who are supposedly working at their seats. Why does she do that? There are likely several answers to that question, including the very real possibility that she wants to be able to give instructional help to students who signal the need for it from their seats. But certainly a major reason for the teacher's positioning herself in that way is fundamentally a moral one: she wants to be able to observe any outbreaks of misbehavior or signs that they might occur and to take corrective action from a distance. In short, the angle of the teacher's chair expresses a moral intent.

Speaking of the teacher's chair, is there any significance in the fact that she is sitting in a chair designed for children? Possibly not. It may just be that she uses a small chair because it takes up less room or is easier to move around when the reading sessions are over, or perhaps because it allows her to be closer to the children and thus to speak in a lower voice. At the same time we wonder what having her seated in an adult-sized chair would do to the moral quality of the instructional arrangement. Would it increase her prominence as an authority figure? By sitting in a small chair, is she expressing her acceptance of the diminutive size of her pupils?

The observer continues:

> While she was working with each group, the rest of the children in the class were busily working individually. They had sentences to write and arithmetic problems to solve. Some of the children were also taking turns on the computer at the back of the classroom.

This paragraph invites two brief comments. The first picks up on the dominance of work in what is described. Classrooms are obviously workplaces for both teachers and students. If they were not, a large part of the moral authority of the teacher would disappear. Many of the moral strictures that she enforces have as their goal the maintenance of a working environment and the transmission of a work ethic. That fact will become more apparent as the observational notes continue. The other comment refers to the practice of taking turns at the computer in the back of the room. The need to share resources is common in many classrooms. A willingness to share constitutes a way of life that is fundamentally moral in its outlook. It is also a practice that commonly requires supervision and enforcement.

The observation continues:

> When she called the Lollipops for their reading group, Gary got up from his desk and hopped backwards toward the front of the room. Ms. Hamilton called out, "Gary! Could you walk to the reading group?"
>
> He turned around and started walking.
>
> "That's much better," said Ms. Hamilton.
>
> A little while later, Ms. Hamilton needed scissors from her desk, and she sent Gary to get them. At first he couldn't find them and Chris came over from his seat to help.
>
> "That's all right, Chris," said Ms. Hamilton. "Gary found it, but thanks for helping."

These two small incidents take up only a few seconds all told. Yet each is replete with moral significance and the pair of them appear to be interrelated. First, there is the incident involving Gary's hopping backward to reach the front of the room. Why is he doing that? Does it make any sense to ask? Does it matter? Why does Ms. Hamilton decide that it is improper behavior? Is she afraid that other children will start to copy it? But what if they do? Would it lead to chaos? Or is it only that jumping backward does not fit the work orientation of the setting? (It is easy to imagine a backward-jumping contest on the playground, one that the teacher herself might supervise. So it is not the behavior itself that is judged to be wrong

or inappropriate, but the context in which the jumping occurs.)
And what of the way Ms. Hamilton brings about the change
in Gary's behavior? She asks a rhetorical question whose meaning Gary clearly understands, because he immediately complies
as though a request or a command has been made. Why doesn't
she simply tell him to stop? The answer to that question, which
the observational record itself could not possibly reveal, is that
a direct command would be out of character for Ms. Hamilton.
She seldom gives such commands. Her action, in other words,
reveals something about her teaching style (and something about
the moral climate of the room as well), although there is no way
to know that without having made repeated observations. Ms.
Hamilton immediately acknowledges Gary's compliance with
a word of approval. This too is typical of her dealings with her
students.

Improper behavior → teacher comment → compliance →
approval: this sequence occurs dozens of times every day in most
elementary classrooms, each occurrence lasting for only a few
seconds. Moreover, it not only occurs but is witnessed by everyone present, students and observers alike. This surely is a form
of moral education, even though it is seldom described in those
terms. Its ubiquity is striking.

The second brief incident also involves Gary. This time
he is sent on an errand to the teacher's desk. Is it just a coinci-
dence that the teacher turns to him for help so shortly after the
jumping-backward incident? Has that past action and her response to it been on her mind? Notice how she handles Chris's
attempt to intervene. Her "That's all right, Chris" sounds as
though she might be trying to ward off his help, enabling Gary
to find the scissors on his own. Notice too how she thanks Chris
for helping, even though he apparently did not really do so. He
only tried to help. It's obviously impossible to draw any conclusions from an isolated incident such as this one but at the
same time we cannot help but suspect that such an incident reveals something important about Ms. Hamilton. In the language
we prefer, it *expresses* a stylistic quality. If we were to choose
a single word to capture that quality we would probably say
that, at least in this incident, she behaves in a *kindly* manner.

The observer goes on:

> She continued to work with the Lollipops. On
> the board, she'd written *mad,* and she asked one of
> the Lollipops to read it. Then she wrote *bad* and
> asked a different child to read that. Then she wrote
> *had* and asked Felicia to read it. Felicia was stumped.
>   "Okay," said Ms. Hamilton, pointing to *bad*
> and *had,* "what's the same about these two words?
> What's different about them?" Felicia was just figur-
> ing it out when Ms. Hamilton noticed that Richard
> (who was at the far end of the room from her) was
> talking rather loudly to the girl at the desk closest
> to him. He'd been talking to her about picking out
> a pumpkin for Halloween.
>   "Richard! Richard!" said Ms. Hamilton, "are
> you visiting or helping?" Without a pause, Richard
> said, "Helping."
>   "Could you do it in a quieter voice?"

This brief episode contains much that merits commentary of a moral kind. Perhaps the most interesting feature is
the disruption of the teaching session caused by Ms. Hamilton's
reaction to Richard's loud speaking. The first thing to say about
that event is that it reinforces what was said earlier about the
strategic positioning of Ms. Hamilton's chair. Richard, it appears, was a considerable distance from Ms. Hamilton, all the
way across the room, in fact, yet he was not far enough away
to escape her surveillance. What is especially interesting about
the interruption caused by Richard's behavior is its timing. Not
only is Ms. Hamilton in the midst of a teaching session, but
she seems to be at a very crucial moment within that session.
Felicia is struggling to decipher the difference between *bad* and
had when the break occurs. What, if anything, does the timing
of that event say about the relative importance of instructional
and moral matters in Ms. Hamilton's room? If we assume that
the teacher immediately returned her attention to Felicia as soon
as she asked Richard to speak in a quieter voice, we might want

to say that the interruption was hardly noticeable. Perhaps the children in Ms. Hamilton's room are so used to such interruptions that they pay no more attention than they would to a bothersome fly or noise from a plane overhead.

Are we carrying our ruminations too far by pausing to reflect on such an apparently trivial matter? Perhaps so. The question of when sensitivity to such matters turns into hypersensitivity is one that continually plagues the classroom observer who is bent on teasing out the moral significance of what he or she witnesses. Yet if we become afraid of going too far in the direction of magnifying the moral significance of what we see, we run the risk of overlooking much that later turns out to be truly noteworthy. Such, at least, has been our experience.

Ms. Hamilton's manner of confronting Richard is typical of her. She calls his name with some urgency, but instead of simply telling him to be quiet she asks, "Are you visiting or helping?" The children in her room understand the distinction between those two verbs and are used to being challenged with that query. "Helping" means helping a classmate with schoolwork. "Visiting" means socializing for the fun of it. Sometimes both are permitted, but during periods of seatwork visiting is usually forbidden, whereas helping is not. What makes this particular challenge noteworthy is that Richard does not tell the truth (he is clearly not helping), yet Ms. Hamilton does not question his response. Does she believe it or does she simply overlook his lie in order to return to her lesson and avoid getting entangled in a more complicated exchange? Or might she have some other reason for her action?

Is seems to us that Ms. Hamilton's frequent use of the helping versus visiting question has the effect of inviting her students to take a third-person perspective on their own actions and see themselves objectively, which might be read as the first step toward self-criticism. Moreover, when they answer the teacher's question they are not only put in the position of having to tell the truth or to lie, as Richard chose to do; they are made to do so in front of all their classmates. This means that their social reputations with respect to truth telling are on the

line each time they answer, particularly—perhaps exclusively—
when they are behaving improperly.

Are we arguing that Ms. Hamilton consciously seeks those
effects? Or that her way of questioning is part of her plan for
the moral upbringing of her pupils? The answer is no. One of
the central premises of our investigation has been that the moral
impact of what goes on in classrooms is by no means tied to
the intentions of those in charge. Such intentions are not irrele-
vant, for surely many actions have a greater impact if we know
or suspect that they were done on purpose and that their purpose was what we perceive it to be. Nonetheless, the power of
things done casually and unintentionally cannot be disputed.

At this point, some readers may be wondering whether
we ever bothered to query Ms. Hamilton directly about her intentions. We do, in fact, have fairly extensive testimony from
her about a number of matters, including how she sees herself
as a teacher. However, we never asked her about any specific
actions of hers that we observed. We chose not to do so for
several reasons that we think are worth mentioning before we
return to the observational record.

Our decision not to query Ms. Hamilton was a matter
of policy. We did not question *any* of the teachers about the things
we observed them doing in their classrooms. We limited our
observational activities to what we actually saw and heard within
the classroom itself. One reason for this was to avoid putting
the teachers in the defensive position of having to justify their
actions. We feared that if we did, they soon would not want
us around. We also did not want them to feel that we were evaluating them in any official or professional way, although they
knew from the start, as we did, that as observers we could not
escape making evaluative judgments along the way, no matter
how neutral or nonevaluative we might strive to be. Second,
we often did not formulate our own questions about what we
had witnessed until well after the observation had ended and
our crude notes had been transformed into fuller descriptions,
a process that sometimes took days or even weeks. By then we
usually felt it was too late to question the teachers about what
may have crossed their minds and been forgotten days earlier.

A third reason we did not question the teachers was that we wanted as much as possible to limit our conjectures about the moral significance of what was going on to what was directly observable and audible. We reasoned that such a limitation put our perspective as observers on a par with what the students in those same classrooms could see and hear—since they are normally not privy to their teachers' reasoning and planning—even though we and the students might remain very unequal when it came to our respective experiential backgrounds. By limiting ourselves in this way, we hoped to concentrate on those aspects of school life that had *the potential* of being seen or experienced as morally significant by everyone present, even though not everyone who witnessed them may have regarded them that way.

The observer continues:

> When the Lollipops went back to their seats, the Stars came up front. While they were working, Elaine decided to play a trick on Tara. Elaine scooted up behind Tara and pretended to write Tara's name on the back of her sweatshirt. Tara tried to turn around and see it, but she didn't see anything.
>
> "Oh, I wrote it further down," said Elaine, "you couldn't see it."
>
> Tara was beginning to take her shirt off to see what Elaine had done to it when Ms. Hamilton spoke up, saying, "Tables three and five are being so noisy I can hardly hear the reading group. Please be polite. Act the way you would like other people to act when you're in your reading group."
>
> Tables three and five quieted down, and Elaine confessed to Tara that she was only kidding, so Tara didn't have to take off her sweatshirt.

The brief interplay between Elaine and Tara seems to have escaped the teacher's attention entirely, although she does respond to the heightened noise level at tables three and five, where the two girls are sitting. This small episode reminds us of how much goes on behind the teacher's back and also how much of that unseen activity might elicit a moral comment of some kind if the teacher witnessed it. What might Ms. Hamilton have done if she was watching and listening to the exchange between Elaine and Tara? Or did she actually notice what was going on and decide to forgo comment? Or are her general comments to tables three and five a specific response to Elaine and Tara? Neither the observer nor Elaine and Tara can be sure.

Ms. Hamilton's comments to the children seated at tables three and five contain explicit moral instruction, including a rephrasing of the Golden Rule to fit the specific occasion. The children's compliance with her request raises a number of questions. Are they acting on principle? Do they understand and appreciate the basis of Ms. Hamilton's appeal for quiet? There is nothing in the observational record itself that would answer such questions, but we find it difficult to imagine the children responding chiefly to the rational force of Ms. Hamilton's words. It seems to us more likely that the youngsters settle down because they see that their teacher is upset or simply because she asks them to do so. If she had finished by saying, "Please be polite," the room would probably have quieted down just as readily. Yet an appeal to a principle *is* made and is heard by all the pupils, not just those who were making the noise. Ms. Hamilton's call for quiet and her ensuing remarks are a classic example of our fifth category, spontaneous interjections of moral commentary into ongoing activity. She often voices such appeals. Is it foolish to imagine them sinking in now and again or beginning to do so after a sufficient number of repetitions? We think not.

The observation continues:

Ms. Hamilton returned to the Stars, who were working on pronouns *she, me,* and *you.* They were using the words in sentences when Ms. Hamilton noticed Richard walking around her desk, looking at one thing and another.

"What are you looking for, Richard?"

"Nothing." He had a paper in his hand, which
he put in the basket on the desk.
"Oh, I thought you were."
Richard went back to his seat and sat down.

This is the same Richard who a few minutes earlier was
asked whether he was visiting or helping. We know that he lied
in answer to that prior question. Is he telling the truth here? Does
Ms. Hamilton think he is? She says she thought he was looking
for something yet she seems to take him at his word when he
denies doing so. Or does she? We have the feeling that Ms. Hamilton doesn't quite trust Richard. Is that only because of the way
he behaved in the previous situation? No, there is more to it than
that. It is partly because of the way the observer describes the
situation. He describes Richard as "walking around" the desk,
"looking at one thing and another." The inference is that he is at
least being nosy if not actually looking for something. We suspect that is what the teacher believes as well. Her question, which
sounds like a helping gesture, is probably a decoy for what is
really on her mind, which likely is the question: "What's he doing rummaging around my desk?" She does confront him with
her uneasiness over his presence at her desk but only in a very
benign and watered-down way. She tells him she thought he was
looking for something and leaves it at that. Richard's prompt
return to his seat brings the episode to a close. Yet we are left
wondering about the moral significance of that small drama. It
seems to be of a piece with her handling of the prior situation
involving Richard and also with the way she dealt with Gary's
backward hopping. She seems to work by indirection. She questions, rather than asserts or commands, yet her questions imply
more than they overtly contain. Do we see here in nascent form
something that we might later want to describe as Ms. Hamilton's
teaching style or at least an important component of it?
The observer continues:

Ms. Hamilton was beginning to explain to
the Stars what a pronoun is when she noticed Mark
at the pencil sharpener.

"Didn't I just give you a new, long pencil,
Mark?"

Mark mumbled, "Ummm, uhh—"

"What's happened to it?" asked Ms. Hamilton, who could see that the pencil was by now only
about two inches long.

"Well, maybe I sharpened it too fast," Mark
suggested.

"Well, maybe if you did it a little slower,
maybe it would last longer the next time."

Mark nodded in agreement.

Once again Ms. Hamilton interrupts her teaching in order
to deal with a situation that lies outside of the teaching encounter
itself. Once again we witness her making use of questions to
address an instance of misconduct and possibly prevent its recur-
rence. As before, her questions are clearly rhetorical. We don't
doubt for a minute that she remembers quite clearly that she
recently gave Mark a new pencil and that she now sees with
her own eyes what has happened to it. She also engages in a
kind of playful banter with Mark, even while she is correcting
him. Note how her double use of *maybe* echoes Mark's use of
the word and does so in a teasing manner, making it perfectly
clear that she does not take Mark's expression of doubt seriously
yet at the same time has no wish to force him to disavow it.

Think how different the moral situation would be, however, if she had directly confronted Mark with what she knew
and saw. Suppose that she had said something like "Mark! Let
me see that pencil you are sharpening," and then, "Why, that's
the one I just gave you! Look what you've done to it with all
that sharpening! Now go back to your seat and don't you ever
do that again!" Insofar as the dynamics of the situation are concerned, the two modes of responding lead to the same behavioral
outcome. In both of them the teacher catches Mark in the act
of doing something wrong and warns him not to do it again.
Yet Ms. Hamilton's way of handling the situation is markedly
different from the fictional one we have just concocted. Is hers
the better way? We have no definitive answer to that question,
though we frankly prefer hers to ours.

What seems more important, however, than trying to determine which way is better is to consider the stylistic dissimilarities between the two modes of responding. The point of doing so is not to establish that our made-up version is better or worse than Ms. Hamilton's; its intent is to show that Ms. Hamilton could not possibly have responded as we imagined a fictional teacher doing *and still have remained Ms. Hamilton.* It would be entirely out of character for her. Taking that to be so, we can now begin to appreciate what we spoke of in the last chapter as the expressive manifestation in everyday teaching of a teacher's outlook on moral matters. Ms. Hamilton's rhetorical questions, her reluctance to press for confessions of wrongdoing on occasions when they are all but evident, her attentiveness to the class as a whole, even while working with a small group — these do not come across to a reader of the observational notes as the mechanical working out of a set of techniques learned in a teacher-training course. On the contrary, they seem integral to a way of interacting with others, a personal style, one might call it, whose origin in all likelihood predates the time of Ms. Hamilton's formal training and is broadly expressive of her approach to life in general. What readers of the observational record might also note is how quickly these expressive qualities begin to stand out once we start to attend to and reflect upon the subtleties of the teacher's way of working. What initially appear to be run-of-the-mill classroom actions suddenly take on moral significance.

The observer continues:

> A little bit later, while Ms. Hamilton was still working with the Stars, David came up to her to show her his work. She looked at it, smiled at him warmly, and said, "Gee, that's really great." Then she turned him around and sent him back to his seat.

Here is another interruption in the teaching session, this time occasioned by a student actually breaking into the reading circle rather than Ms. Hamilton noting something going on in the room that has to be attended to from a distance. Yet despite the fact that David interrupts her, Ms. Hamilton responds

approvingly and with some warmth to him before she sends him
back to his seat. David's apparent need for approval takes prece-
dence, at least momentarily, over the ongoing activity. But at
the same time, we discern a trace of impatience in the way Ms.
Hamilton is described as effecting David's return. She "turned
him around," the observer writes, capturing in those few words
the image of Ms. Hamilton placing one or both hands on David's
shoulder and gently but firmly turning him to face in the direction of his seat (smiling all the while, we might equally imagine).

What moral messages are being communicated here? Is
Ms. Hamilton's warm approval of David's work more telling
in moral terms than her apparent, and quite understandable,
impatience over the interruption? What is David thinking on
the way back to his seat? Is he glowing with pride over his
teacher's enthusiastic approval or does the lingering pressure
of her fingertips on his shoulder remind him of her desire to
be rid of him and scoot him back to his seat as soon as possible?
We find it impossible to say. Yet it seems to us incontrovertible
that this situation, like almost all the others the observer writes
about, is imbued with moral significance. Perhaps there is no
way to fathom what such experiences mean to those engaged
in them. All the same, they do seem worth reflecting upon, if
only as a reminder of the complexity to be found within something as simple as David's brief interruption and his teacher's
handling of it.

The observer continues:

> Ms. Hamilton was almost finished with the
> Stars when Chris came up to tell her that he had
> to go to the bathroom, but the pass was gone.
>
> "After Richard gets back," said Ms. Hamil-
> ton. Then she looked at Chris and asked him, "Can
> you wait, or is it an emergency?"
>
> Chris considered for a moment and then de-
> cided he could probably wait, and he went back to
> his seat.

Yet another interruption. Not this time by a child seeking approval but by one who only wants to relieve himself and

finds the means to do so (the pass) lacking. The first thing to notice about Ms. Hamilton's response to Chris is that it signals her awareness that Richard is out of the room. She has obviously seen him depart and taken note of it. This is the same Richard, we remember, who earlier said he was working when he was not and who was seen walking around the teacher's desk, apparently looking for something. Is Ms. Hamilton keeping a special eye on him or does she keep a running check on each child who leaves the room? We have no way of knowing from the information available but it seems reasonable to suspect that Ms. Hamilton is mindful of what all the children are doing, especially the ones who move about, and has not singled Richard out as the only one to keep an eye on. Her expression of concern over whether Chris is going to be able to wait for Richard's return is consonant with the way she handled David's need for her approval of his work. It also communicates something about the flexibility of the classroom rule that requires a pass to go to the toilet. That rule, her question to Chris implies, can be laid aside in cases of emergency. What her full response says, in effect, is that the rule is firm but not inflexible. Its administration will be humane. Chris hesitates, as if reading his own bodily signs, and then opts to wait for Richard's return. (We wonder how Richard would have responded to the same question. Would Ms. Hamilton have bothered to ask him? On the basis of what we have seen so far, we would guess that she would.) Chris's return to his seat reflects his understanding and acceptance of the rule and its exceptions.

The observer continues:

> At the end of the morning, Ms. Hamilton went to her desk and looked over the work that the children had turned in while she had been with the reading groups. Looking at Gary's work, she said, "You know, Gary, you got a lot of work done back there when you were working with Amy, didn't you?"
>
> Gary proudly agreed.

The teacher's singling out of Gary's work for comment (assuming his to be the only work Ms. Hamilton comments upon

when she returns to her desk) raises a number of questions that
the observer sitting in the back of the room or someone who
later reads his notes might quite naturally begin to ask and speculate upon. The first of these is the obvious: Why only Gary?
Does the teacher believe that he needs special encouragement?
She sounds as though she might be genuinely surprised that he
accomplished as much as he did. Is she? Did she privately suspect that he really was not working when he was with Amy and
was only visiting instead? But such questions draw us into the
particularities of Ms. Hamilton's thoughts and intentions in ways
that not only are unanswerable from the observation alone but
that threaten to obscure the moral significance of what happened.
Whatever her reasons for choosing to comment on Gary's work,
it is clear that Ms. Hamilton means her remark to be congratulatory and that Gary accepts it in that spirit. He proudly agrees
with her assessment, we are told. Pride over his accomplishment seems to be the dominant goal and outcome of this brief
exchange. The same was true of the episode involving David,
although there the compliment was sought, while here it is freely
offered. What makes such exchanges moral is the fact that they
entail judgments about good and bad, that they are either sought
after or gratefully received, that they function to affect the self-
esteem of their recipients. They may come and go in a twinkling,
as the two we have just examined seem to have done, but we
must not judge their potential importance by their brevity.

　　Thus ends that day's observational record. What has it,
plus our commentary, revealed about this particular teacher and
her students and, more generally perhaps, about the moral significance of what takes place in classrooms?

　　First of all, it tells us something about the process of observing. It is not clear from the record exactly when the observation began and when it ended, although it seems to have covered the better part of a single morning. It sounds as though
the observer began his notes some time after the reading groups
were under way, which would mean after opening exercises and
whatever else preceded reading, and ended them before lunchtime dismissal or whatever else went on between reading and
lunch. Therefore, the observer was in the room for two hours

or so. His record of that visit, obviously written some time later, covers about two and a half typewritten pages, double-spaced. The events he reports upon fit within a very small fraction of the total time he was in the room. If each event had been captured on film and the set of episodes spliced together, they surely would not take more than a full minute or two to replay.

Between those isolated nodes of reported activity, each covering hardly more than a few seconds, lie vast oceans of observational silence. What, if anything, are we to make of that fact? Can we assume that the events reported upon constituted all that went on during those two hours that was worthy of comment from a moral point of view? Certainly not. All we can glean from the report is that these were the events the observer decided to record. Other observers might have chosen differently. In fact, another observer might have become so intrigued by the moral implications of what was going on within the reading groups that he or she would have paid almost no attention to the interruptions on which our observer concentrated. Still another observer might have chosen to look exclusively at what was going on among the children who were doing seatwork. Such possibilities reinforce what was said earlier about the complexity of classroom life and the selective—that is, interpretive—nature of all descriptions.

What went on in Ms. Hamilton's room that morning? Anyone who chanced to visit would probably agree that Ms. Hamilton spent most of the morning in the front of the room working with one reading group after the other while the remaining children were occupied at seatwork. However, if we asked these same observers, "What happened there that might be of moral interest?" we might expect quite divergent responses. This would not be because the discernment of moral matters is inherently subjective—a figment of each person's imagination—but because there is usually *too much going on* from a moral point of view for anyone to report on all of it and also because we do not all respond to the same moral stimuli. The ultimate test of the insightfulness and verifiability of what each of us sees from our individual perspectives is not whether others have spontaneously seen the same thing on their own, but whether they can be brought to appreciate and understand what we have seen after we have described it to them.

We earlier asked what that one set of observations plus our commentary on it tells us about Ms. Hamilton and her students. The quick answer is: not very much. It takes a lot longer than a morning's worth of looking to arrive at a settled view of a teacher's style or to fathom the pattern of interactions that characterize a classroom. Moreover, even when it becomes settled, such a view must remain open to revision and change, for there is a sense in which we never come to a complete understanding of another person or achieve a total grasp of any of the countless situations in which we find ourselves.

At the same time, we trust that our having lingered over these brief reports as long as we have has contributed to an emerging sense of what Ms. Hamilton might be like as a teacher and an additional sense, though necessarily a vague one, of what the classroom as a whole is like. Ms. Hamilton starts to come across as a considerate woman, patient in her dealings with students and not given to sudden outbursts of anger or annoyance in the face of events that intrude upon her teaching. Her persistent use of questions in the handling of those events strikes us as being somewhat unusual and would seem to merit further observation and reflection. The class as a whole appears to be remarkably self-controlled and well-behaved, if we can assume that the recorded events were the only instances of misconduct requiring the teacher's attention within that two-hour period. In fact, the episodes involving misbehavior were so few and so benign that it is hard to believe that there were not more of them that the observer either failed to see or chose not to record. Here we see how tempting, though misconceived, it is to treat observational records as though they contained accurate time samples of the events they catalog.

What has our set of observations taught us about the moral life of schools in general? This turns out not to be a very good question, even though it sounds reasonable enough at the start. What makes it unattractive is its tacit suggestion that a few hours of observation might be sufficient to teach us something worthwhile about so complicated a topic. It takes a lot more observing than that, certainly, to begin to understand what is going on within a single classroom, and the thought of being able to say something definitive about the moral life of schools in general based on such a short period of observation is almost ludicrous. But there is a further reason for the question not being very good. It implies, without saying so directly, that the outcome of looking in classrooms and thinking about the moral significance of what is seen there ought to fit the designation of "new knowledge," which in turn should be reducible to a set of statements that are readily communicable to the world at large and that contain generalizations that have never been made before.

That conception of the anticipated outcomes of inquiry is ill-suited to a description of what actually happened to us as we sought to understand the moral life of classrooms. We trust that it also does not fit what has happened and will happen to others, particularly those of our readers who may initially have entertained the hope that such an outcome—the treasure of freshly minted knowledge, untarnished by prior use—would soon be theirs. To them we can only express our hope that the benefits of staying with us to the end will at least partially compensate for our failure to fulfill their initial expectations. For what happened to us in the course of our work, as we hope will happen to many of our readers as well, was that we changed in unexpected ways, very few of which conformed to the usual model of knowledge acquisition. Often, however, the change had the *feel* of new knowledge. It had that quality of newness or freshness about it that one associates with an act of discovery.

Our most recurrent experience as we observed in classrooms and later wrote about and talked about our observations was one of affirmation, or reaffirmation. Our observations repeatedly affirmed much that we already knew. For example, we had expected to find teachers engaged in many different kinds of moral activities and we did. What surprised us was the depth and variety of their engagement. But this surprise constitutes a kind of reaffirmation in its own right. For if we were to stop and think about it we would quickly realize that the people we've known, the things we've done, the novels we've read, and so forth constantly reveal new and unexpected moral meanings.

Yet there is a sense in which we seem to need constant reminders of this fundamental fact of life.

At the start of our work we had also anticipated that we would become more sensitive to the moral aspects of schooling as we went along. That certainly happened as well. What surprised us as this process took place were the roles that reflection, writing, and discussion played in bringing these aspects to light. And yet how could we hope to address moral matters *without,* for example, extensive reflection?

Finally, we thought at the start that our informal and exploratory way of working would pay off in the end, although we could not anticipate how. Collingwood reminds us that "most human action is tentative, experimental, directed not by a knowledge of what it will lead to but rather a desire to know what will come of it."[4] Our work began that way as well. What surprised and delighted us was how richly our way of proceeding did in fact yield insight and understanding.

Back to Ms. Hamilton for a moment. The observational record that we have just shared and commented upon is perhaps most striking in its ordinariness. Although it contains a number of unknowns, mostly about what Ms. Hamilton is thinking of when she behaves a certain way or what she intends to do by questioning as she does, there is very little that is overtly problematic about her actions. When pupils get too noisy, she sees to it that they quiet down; when someone needs praise, she doles it out. In other words, although we find a lot in the record to talk about in moral terms, the situations it describes are not themselves morally ambiguous. They do not leave us wondering what we would do ourselves in similar circumstances or whether the teacher's actions are appropriate.

Often, however, we did witness morally ambiguous situations in the classrooms we visited. Ms. Hamilton's was no exception, as the two observational records that follow make clear. Each of them invites further reflection and discussion. The first report goes as follows:

One morning in March, Ms. Hamilton's first graders were working on an assignment that com-

bined arithmetic and art. They had been given a
worksheet with a hidden picture. In order to see
the picture, the children needed to color it. Each
color to be used had been assigned a number, and
the various parts of the picture were coded with addition and subtraction problems, each of which,
when solved, corresponded to the number of one
of the colors. When properly colored, the picture
was supposed to reveal a rabbit.

Wayne finished coloring his picture and
showed it to Ms. Hamilton, who asked him what
it was a picture of.

He said he wasn't sure and guessed, "A turtle?"

Ms. Hamilton said, "No, you must have done
something wrong."

They went over the problem and found the
places where he had made mistakes. When Ms.
Hamilton was sure Wayne understood what went
wrong, she told him to make a note on his paper
before he turned it in. She told him to write, "This
should be blue instead of yellow." Then he should
draw an arrow to show what part of the picture the
note was talking about.

But Wayne wanted to correct the paper.
"Well," he said, "I could color over the yellow part
with a blue marker."

Ms. Hamilton said, "No, that won't be necessary. You can just draw an arrow."

"I could put white-out on it," Wayne said.
"Then I could put blue over that."

"You don't need to," said Ms. Hamilton.

"I could take it home and do that. I don't have
to do it right now."

"No," said Ms. Hamilton, "that won't be necessary. As long as I know that you know what it's
supposed to be, that'll be good enough."

"I don't mind," Wayne insisted. "I can do it —
really."

"It's all right," said Ms. Hamilton, firmly.
"Just write the note."

Wayne finally relented and turned in his
paper, but he still didn't seem convinced that just
a note was enough.

Ms. Hamilton and her pupil, Wayne, are obviously at
odds in this episode, with Wayne wanting to produce a correctly
colored picture and his teacher insisting that a note indicating
his awareness of where he went wrong would be sufficient. The
teacher wins out in the end but the cost of doing so, in moral
terms, may be greater than she suspects. At the very least, her
handling of the situation raises an interesting question about
what to do when a student's standard of excellence or drive for
perfection exceeds what is called for in the teacher's eyes.

The source of the difficulty in this particular instructional
setting seems to be that Ms. Hamilton does not look upon an
accurately colored drawing to be very important at all, except
for the way it reveals the pupil's understanding of arithmetic,
whereas Wayne seems more concerned about the coloring of the
rabbit than about the mistakes in arithmetic that caused his
drawing to go awry. From an academic point of view we can
certainly understand the teacher's position. Learning how to add
and subtract is clearly more important than accurately coloring in the blanks on a workbook exercise, an add-on activity
whose function is largely motivational. But what if the pupil
doesn't see it that way and believes, as Wayne apparently does,
that the point of the lesson is to produce a satisfactory drawing? From Wayne's point of view, his teacher is trying to talk
him out of doing his best and seems unmoved by his persistent
proposal to rectify his error.

What are we to make of Ms. Hamilton's behavior in this
situation? Should it be read as insensitivity? Or might she have
a good reason for discouraging Wayne from spending more time
on the drawing? If so, would it have helped for her to have made
that reason clear to him? Or would that have been a further
waste of time? And what has happened to Ms. Hamilton's
strategy, which we saw in the earlier observational excerpts, of

using questions to lead her pupils to an understanding of their own actions? Have we been premature in so designating her actions during the morning reading time? She easily could have used that strategy here. When Wayne suggested coloring over the yellow to make it blue, she might have asked him if he thought it was necessary, instead of bluntly telling him that it wasn't. Even if he had said yes at that point, she could have queried him further to find out why he thought so, and she might have brought him by steps to see that a simple note on his paper would suffice. But such a strategy would probably have taken more time. Is that why she chooses to behave as she does? Or *does* she choose to do so? That is, does she consciously weigh alternative ways of responding to Wayne and then act on one of them, or does her reply to his suggestion occur too quickly for that to be a possibility? The brevity of the record supports the latter interpretation, but perhaps there were pauses between responses that the observer did not note. If not, should we read Ms. Hamilton's manner of reacting to Wayne as a sign of impatience? Was that how the observer himself read it? Was that why he chose to write about it? Or was he more taken by the ambiguity of the situation than by its status as an example of a particular moral posture?

This spate of questions reveals not only the moral ambiguity of the situation as it was recorded but also the way in which that ambiguity almost inevitably broadens to include the intentions of the recorder. We say "almost inevitably" because the observer might have chosen to clarify his intentions in the record. If, for example, he intended that particular episode to be an illustration of the moral ambiguity to be found in classroom events (as we have used it here and as we happen to know were his actual intentions), he could easily have said so. Lacking such an explanation, we are led to conjecture about it as part of our own efforts to resolve the ambiguity. This phenomenon occurs frequently in the arts, where the reader or the viewer, confronted by a work whose meaning is not obvious, is led to ask about the artist's intentions. Our own experience as classroom observers leads us to believe that ambiguity, in the form of uncertainty about what things mean and particularly about what they mean in moral terms, is a far more common attribute than might be assumed by the clarity of most portrayals of what goes on there.

Here is a second example of such ambiguity. The observer writes:

> One morning in Ms. Hamilton's first-grade classroom Cheryl came up to me and asked if I could help her get her coat off—the zipper was stuck. Belinda wandered back to see what was going on, and she asked Cheryl what was wrong. Cheryl told her the zipper was stuck: "And Ms. Hamilton couldn't get it opened either." While I was tugging at the zipper, a girl came into the classroom looking for Ms. Hamilton. When she found the teacher, she said, "Cheryl took my pencil and she didn't give it back."
>
> Cheryl overheard and broke in, "I did too. I gave it back on the playground."
>
> "No, you didn't," said the girl, whose name was Farida.
>
> "Did too."
>
> Before the argument went further, Ms. Hamilton intervened and asked each girl to explain what had happened. They repeated their claims without adding much detail. They agreed that Farida had given Cheryl a pencil, but not about what had happened after that.
>
> So Ms. Hamilton had them tell their stories once again.
>
> "Cheryl took my pencil," said Farida, "and she didn't give it back to me."
>
> "Farida gave me her pencil," said Cheryl, "and I gave it back to her on the playground."
>
> "Go on," said Ms. Hamilton to Cheryl. "What happened when you gave it back to her?"
>
> Cheryl screwed up her eyes as if she was trying to see the event at a great distance. Then she

said to Farida, "I remember I gave you the pencil back and you put it in your mouth."

Farida said, "No, I didn't."

But Cheryl insisted, "Yes, you did. Because I remember you were playing with Emily, and I went over and Emily was pulling on your jacket, and I remember you had the pencil in your mouth, and Emily was pulling on your jacket."

Suddenly, Farida remembered too: that was what had happened. Cheryl was vindicated, though the location of the pencil remained something of a mystery.

Unlike the situation involving Wayne, this one centers on an obvious injustice or at least the suspicion of one. To that extent it is more clearly a moral situation in the standard sense of the word than was Wayne's worry over the correctness of his drawing. In bare outline it treats a circumstance that teachers of young children encounter frequently: one child believes herself to have been mistreated by another and goes to the teacher for help; the teacher adjudicates the dispute and the conflict is resolved. What is noteworthy in this instance is the form of the teacher's intervention. All Ms. Hamilton does, apparently, is to have the two girls tell and retell the story. During the second telling Farida remembers that Cheryl did indeed return her pencil and, therefore, her accusation had to have been false. But why does Ms. Hamilton ask for the story to be retold? And why does she specifically ask Cheryl to try and remember what happened when she returned the pencil? Does she anticipate that this will reveal the truth? She can't possibly know that. The successful outcome of her handling of the situation has to be a stroke of luck. Yet Cheryl's fortuitous recollection might not have taken place if Ms. Hamilton had not urged the girls to reexamine their memory of what happened. Should we read Ms. Hamilton's action as a form of trust, an expression of her confidence in Cheryl's truthfulness, perhaps? Or might it go even deeper than that? Might her seemingly casual and offhand request for a retelling of the stories express her faith not just in Cheryl's veracity but in the fundamental goodness of children in general, in their basic honesty in most situations? This may sound like too grand a reading of such a fleeting and mundane event, and we certainly would not push for its acceptance without a lot more thought and discussion and much more observation, but it is precisely around questions having to do with the moral significance of seemingly trivial happenings that the swirl of ambiguity typically revolves.

II

The next set of observations we shall examine was gathered in a Catholic high school for boys. The teacher, Father Maran, is a Franciscan priest with twelve years of teaching experience. As the observer describes him:

> Father Maran is of medium height and solidly built. He is always impeccably attired and groomed. He wears either a long brown Franciscan robe belted at the waist with a white cord, or else dark slacks with a tan sweater and white neck-collar. He writes clearly and by the end of each lesson the blackboard of his room is usually covered with numbers and equations all written in his neat hand.

The observer goes on to describe where Father Maran sits at the beginning of each period and how he reacts to those entering his room:

> He is typically seated at his desk going through some papers. Students pause to hand in work before heading to their seats. While pointing to the spot where they should place their exercises, Father Maran glances around the room. Silently, he takes roll and continues to go through materials.

Each class begins with a brief ritual, which the observer describes as follows:

> Once the boys have filed to their seats, one of them steps to the front of the room and turns to face the class. The students rise from their seats as he does so. The boy who is leading the exercise

makes the sign of the cross, at which point his classmates and Father Maran (also now standing) do
the same. Together they recite the Lord's Prayer.
Then the boys ease back into their seats. A bunch
of them go to sharpen their pencils, in anticipation
of the writing to come. Father Maran makes a last-
minute check of his materials and walks to the front
of the room.

The instant impression that emerges from this description of Father Maran and the first few minutes of class is one
of rather striking formality and seriousness, with perhaps a trace
of coldness present as well. Father Maran comes across as a man
of reserve and dignity. It is noteworthy that in his description
of Father Maran the observer chooses to speak first of the priest's
height and build. "Medium height" and "solidly built" are the
words used, both being somewhat vague and nondescript and
yet certainly conveying the image of substance. Nothing is said
of Father Maran's facial appearance (Is he clean-shaven or
bearded? Does he wear glasses? Is he usually smiling or grim?),
though we are told how he typically dresses in class. His manner of dress and his grooming are the first signs we come upon
of the teacher's presence as a person. They establish the sense
of psychological distance and the air of formality that will be
intensified by what follows. Not only does Father Maran always
wear a badge of his religious office (either a full monkish robe
or a clerical collar), which distinguishes him from his students
as well as from other adults who are not members of a religious
order, but he also dresses in somber colors and his grooming,
we are told, is impeccable. The overall impression, based solely
on the initial paragraph of the observer's description, is one of
an authority figure who seeks to stand apart from the flow of
activity that surrounds him.

The description of Father Maran's behavior before class
adds to the sense of formality and distance. We see him busy
at work when the students arrive; another teacher might have
been at the door to greet them or might have already been standing at the front of the room. Father Maran apparently exchanges

no words with those who enter, not even those who come to his desk to drop off homework assignments. Instead, he merely points to where the assignments should be placed and continues with his work. Even his taking of the roll is done silently. The reciting of the Lord's Prayer at the start of each class adds a final note of solemnity to the mood created by his physical presence and initial posture.

The record continues:

> By the time Father Maran has stood up and walked to the podium the class has become silent. His students, many of whom were chattering, teasing, or joking with one another moments before, now give him their full attention. They have cleared their desks of everything save for the math books, pencils, and papers they'll need.

The students' behavior supports the air of seriousness implicit in the observer's description. This seems to be a class whose participants get down to business quickly and whose teacher dislikes distractions.

Now the lesson begins. The subject is eleventh-grade algebra. (The words in capital letters indicate a raised voice.)

> Father Maran writes in the upper left corner of the board "Class #22" and then the date. He turns to his class and says matter-of-factly, "Now, let's continue reviewing factoring for the quiz coming up. Any questions from your review or from your homework?"
>
> Several hands go up.
>
> Father Maran calls on a student in the first row, a boy who does poorly in math and who has been assigned a front seat in order to receive the teacher's special attention. "Okay, Mr. Bailey."
>
> "My situation, you see, is that when I try—"
>
> "—MR. BAILEY, GIVE ME A *PROBLEM*!"
>
> "Well, I have two here, I'm—"

"—GIVE ME *ONE* PROBLEM!"

Mr. Bailey looks down at his exercise sheet, then looks up and dictates a problem. Father Maran writes the problem on the board. Before he can turn back to the class, a forest of hands goes up.

Father Maran calls on a student, who offers a step-by-step solution to the problem on the board. "That is *exactly* correct," says the teacher. "Did you follow that, Mr. Bailey?"

"Yeah, I got stuck on the middle one in workin' it out."

"The middle what?"

Mr. Bailey looks disconcerted. Some hands instantly fly up again. Mr. Bailey remains non-plussed. Father Maran repeats, "The middle what, Mr. Bailey?"

Silence prevails. Hands begin to waver, some slowly sink back down into laps. Father Maran brings his right hand to his chin and looks intently at the floor. He is standing right in front of Mr. Bailey.

The boy screws his face up as he looks at the problem above him on the blackboard. Suddenly he sees the light. "Oh! The middle *term!!!*" The hands that were in the air collapse like punctured balloons.

"RIGHT," replies Father Maran. "The middle *term*. Now, what is your second problem?"

The first noteworthy move in this brief description is Father Maran's writing the date and the number of the class on the board. Why, we might wonder, does he bother to write the class number? If he is interested in having the students copy the information on their own papers to identify them later, surely the date alone would suffice. Who cares, in other words, whether it is class no. 22 or 23? The answer is that Father Maran obviously cares, and this provides an additional clue to the kind of moral climate that is being constructed here. This is a classroom in which exactitude matters a lot, even when there appears to be no ostensible reason for it. It is also one in which the teacher's definition of what counts as important is not to be questioned.

The plight of the first student called upon reinforces what has just been said. Bailey (the teacher calls him "Mr." Bailey, yet another sign of formality) barely opens his mouth before being informed that he has said the wrong thing. Father Maran is looking for a specific problem to put on the board and is not interested in hearing Bailey's description of the trouble he is having in trying to *solve* a problem. Moreover, Father Maran wants only one problem, not two. But what is puzzling is that he did not ask for a problem at the start. He began by asking whether students had any questions from their review or from their homework. It sounds as though that's what Bailey is beginning to provide when his teacher interrupts him.

What are we to make of the teacher's raised voice? Is it a sign of impatience? There is certainly no need for him to shout, with Bailey right in front of him.

When another student gives the correct answer to the problem that Bailey was having trouble with, Father Maran emphasizes its correctness by calling it "exactly" correct, again underscoring the importance of precision and exactitude. He then turns back to Bailey to find out if he has followed the correct solution. Bailey promptly runs into trouble again, this time for referring to the middle term of the equation on the board as the middle "one." Father Maran adopts a posture of gravity while waiting for Bailey to find the right word — his right hand on his chin, his eyes on the floor. There is a clear note of theatricality about his pose, but for whom is it being struck? For Bailey, to whom it is conceivably threatening? For the rest of the students, who might be amused by their teacher's mock gravity? For the observer, who may be pondering its meaning even while dutifully describing it? Here is moral ambiguity of a somewhat different type than was encountered in Ms. Hamilton's classroom. The silence is broken when Bailey remembers the correct word and Father Maran asks him for his second problem.

What are we to make of the episode? What does it reveal about Father Maran and about the moral climate of the room as a whole? We have already said that there is an air of formality and seriousness about the encounter, perhaps even solemnity, reinforced by the prayer at the beginning, by Father Maran's dress and demeanor, and by his use of "Mr." in addressing the students. His insistence that Bailey follow the routine by naming a problem rather than discussing a difficulty adds to that formality. We might almost think that Father Maran only cares about seeing the problems worked out correctly and is not at all interested in hearing about his students' trials as they grapple with their assignments. Also, the subject matter itself, advanced algebra, contributes to the dominant mood. Not only does it serve to justify Father Maran's emphasis on exactitude, for if any subject requires this it is certainly mathematics, but it also adds to the air of formality and psychological distance through its depersonalized signs and symbols that bear only a scant and arbitrary relationship to things in the real world.

Here is another brief glimpse of one of Father Maran's classes, in this case, ninth-grade algebra.

Father Maran begins to write a problem on the board: $b^2 - 36$. Before he finishes, a bunch of hands go up. After momentarily surveying the class, Father Maran nods, "Okay, Mr. Robinson."

The student proceeds, with the teacher writing each step on the board.

"Two parentheses." (   )(   )
"b, b." $(b$ $)(b$ $)$
"6 and 6."

Father Maran freezes, his chalk six inches from the board. Keeping his body rigid, he turns his face halfway to the class and, eyebrows raised and mouth set firmly, looks out of the corner of his eye at Mr. Robinson.

Several hands go up. Mr Robinson stares intently at the board.

"Oh! *Plus* and *minus!*"

Father Maran relaxes his posture, tilting his head up slightly as he turns to write the signs next to the numbers.

Once again, the emphasis is on a step-by-step procedure, with Father Maran serving as a secretary for the student, Robinson, who is dictating a solution to an exercise in factoring. As soon as the student takes a false step, the transcribing stops abruptly and Father Maran stands with chalk in midair as though he were a manikin whose inner workings had suddenly become jammed. The way he keeps his body rigid while turning only his face, plus the expression he adopts in looking at Robinson, bring to mind the theatricality of his grave posture while waiting for Bailey to correct his mistake.

Here are two more episodes containing similarly dramatic postures and gestures.

> "*What* do I do with the *2?*" Father Maran asks a student in an amazed tone of voice. But the boy who had been narrating a solution says nothing. He stares at the problem on the board, then down at his exercise sheet, then back at the board.
>
> Watching him, Father Maran steps away from the board and stands near the podium. He places one hand on it, bringing the other to his chin. He slowly bows his head and closes his eyes. He remains motionless.
>
> Meanwhile the other students either watch their teacher or glance over at their classmate, who is still trying to find his mistake. A half-dozen or so raise their hands, although they do so in a leisurely manner, which seems to say that they know Father Maran is going to take his time.
>
> Finally the teacher looks up and directs his question in a soft voice to the whole class: "What do I do with the *2?*" A student gives the desired answer, after which Father Maran loudly affirms, "RIGHT! YOU TAKE *OUT* THE 2 AS A COMMON FACTOR!" The errant student shakes his head in dismay, exclaiming "Dang!" as he hastily erases what he has written on his sheet. Then he promptly looks up and proceeds with the next step.

The second episode is as follows:

> During another lesson Father Maran calls on
> a student who wants to finish a problem. But the
> fellow immediately errs on a step the class has al-
> ready completed. Father Maran interrupts him with
> the familiar question: "*X* is what, Mr. Green?"
>
> Green stares at his worksheet. Father Maran
> repeats the question as he walks nearer, now stand-
> ing directly in front of the student. Meanwhile
> several of the students who are seated nearby are
> encouraging Green to come up with the desired an-
> swer. "Come on, man!" they urge. Father Maran
> repeats, "*X* is *what*, Mr. Green?" at the same time
> literally hopping off the floor toward the boy as he
> bends over him, as if willing him to come up with
> the answer.
>
> "Oh!" the student suddenly says, "Twelve!"
>
> "Aaaaaah," Father Maran sighs as he straight-
> ens himself. Turning back to the board he says,
> "Please continue!" and Green does so.

In commentary on his own notes the observer mentions
Father Maran's "raised eyebrows, his suddenly frozen postures,
his booming voice, his demonstrative gestures." He speaks of
how alert the students are to these signals and how promptly
they respond to them. But the question we need to ask is what,
if anything, such histrionics tell us about the moral character
of the teacher or the climate of the room as a whole. How should
we read them?

Father Maran does seem to be more "on stage" as a teacher
than was Ms. Hamilton; that much is clear. His impeccable
grooming, his "costume" (i.e., his religious garb), his studied
manner, his grand gestures (e.g., silently pointing to where the
homework is to be deposited), his delayed stage entrance (i.e.,
his slow and deliberate move from his desk to the front of the
room), his dramatic posturing during the lesson itself—all of
these have the mark of someone who is acutely aware of his own

presence and its effect on others. Do they bespeak an attitude of self-pride as well? Possibly.

Father Maran's one-on-one exchanges with the three students featured in the episodes we have reviewed amplify the aura of theatricality that his behavior creates. Each of these students shares the stage momentarily with his teacher as might a volunteer called up from the audience by a showman of some kind — a tuxedoed magician, perhaps. The remainder of the class looks on as a theater audience might do. Some wave their hands, indicating their willingness to have a turn at being the showman's assistant.

What does all this on-stage behavior have to do with morality? Does it connote artificiality or insincerity on the part of the teacher? On one level it certainly must. No adult watching Father Maran could fail to see at least some of his facial expressions and postures as studied and "put on." In that sense at least they are artificial and insincere. Do his students see matters that way? We obviously cannot answer that question on the basis of observation alone. Yet their evident involvement in the lesson seems to imply that they take what Father Maran does quite seriously. Furthermore, we would have to acknowledge that despite his dramatic posturing, or perhaps because of it, Father Maran succeeds in capturing the attention of his students. He also seems to be fully engaged and absorbed by what he is doing. It is as though his playacting is subservient to some larger goal or mission, such as helping his students learn math, while at the same time teaching them to attend to the details of what they do. Father Maran comes across, in other words, not simply as an actor, but as a *serious* actor, one who does what the role calls for, rather than one who only seeks the plaudits of the crowd.

What shall we say about the air of formality in Father Maran's teaching style — for example, his beginning each class with a prayer, his careful numbering of each session, his insistence on the correct use of terms, his use of "Mr." when addressing his students, and the impersonal routine of analyzing problems? Viewed sympathetically, all of those practices are consonant with the subject being taught. Algebra is itself a formal subject, one whose content is severe in its simplicity, like the Lord's Prayer or a priest's collar. Did Father Maran plan it that way? Did he think about such things when he worked out the way his class would run? It's hard to believe he did, any more than Ms. Hamilton did in the previous record we examined. More than likely, Father Maran's chosen way of working is an expression of the man himself—a well-groomed, impeccably dressed, and serious-minded person, or so it would seem on the basis of the look afforded by these brief observational records. Might such a person exert a positive moral influence on the young men with whom he associates daily, even those, like Bailey, Robinson, and Green, who occasionally feel the sting of his quizzical looks and threatening postures? Undoubtedly. We ourselves are certainly convinced of Father Maran's potency as a moral agent.

III

Our third set of observations comes from a second-grade classroom in an independent school, where we see the teacher, Mr. Jordan, interacting with his students in a variety of settings. The first record, which covers a period that extends from late in the morning through the lunch hour, is a bit lengthier than the ones we have presented so far.

Late one morning in February, Mr. Jordan was working in his second-grade classroom with a reading group. The children in the group took turns reading the story aloud, with Mr. Jordan encouraging them, asking an occasional question, and invariably saying, when they'd finished, "Very, very nice"—regardless of how much they'd stumbled or how confused they'd been. Twice he had to interrupt the oral reading in order to tell Jim and Lisa to be quiet. The second time he said to them, "Jim and Lisa, I'm asking you not to talk. Do you understand why?" They nodded their heads and he said, "Is that clear?" Again they nodded.

Later, when Mr. Jordan sent the children from the reading group back to their seats, he called Jim and Lisa to join him. He told them they'd been playing around and making too much noise. "We don't have that kind of time in here. We went outside to play. Now it's time to work."

Just before lunchtime, Mr. Jordan called the class to the rug. He had a few questions about the morning activities, and he also wanted to tell the children what they would be doing during the afternoon. Lisa was sitting near the back of the group, and instead of sitting up straight, she was leaning

back against one of the desks. Mr. Jordan motioned
to her to sit up straight, but she didn't, and a minute
or so later the desk noisily slid a few inches because
of her weight leaning against it. Mr. Jordan glared
at her and said, "Sit up, Lisa," then he continued
with his review of the afternoon schedule.

As always, the children ate lunch in their
classroom, and as always, Mr. Jordan joined them.
Today he sat with a group of girls at a table near
the blackboard. Among other topics, he talked with
them about "playing kitchen" with his niece. While
they were talking, Mr. Jordan noticed that Lisa
(who was sitting at almost the opposite side of the
room) was unwrapping a cream-filled cupcake. Al-
luding to his legendary love of cream-filled cup-
cakes, Mr. Jordan called out, "Lisa, do you want
me to eat that for you?"

She shook her head, he nodded his, and she
shook hers again, and he nodded again. He returned to the conversation at his own table, but
then, when she was still struggling with the wrap-
per a little while later, he said, "Lisa? Please Lisa?"
With a big smile, she continued to refuse him.

Meanwhile, the girls at Mr. Jordan's table
had begun to talk about their fathers' first names.
Mr. Jordan knew the names of most of their fathers,
but there were a couple he wasn't sure about. Finally, one of the girls asked him what his father's
first name was, and he said, "Daddy." The girls
laughed but seemed satisfied with this answer. They
were done eating by this time, and after cleaning
up the remains and putting away their lunch boxes,
they went off to play games or work on projects until
the end of the lunch period. Mr. Jordan was the
last one to finish eating, so it was up to him to get
the sponge from the sink and wipe off the table.
While he was doing this, he passed by Lisa, who
had finally unwrapped her cupcake and taken the
first bite out of it.

"Oh," said Mr. Jordan rapturously, "that cream in the middle, that's the best." With the cupcake still in her now-smiling mouth, Lisa very deliberately turned away from Mr. Jordan, as if to show that she was still not going to let him have any of it.

About five minutes later, Mr. Jordan rang the bell, indicating that the children were to put away their games and projects and line up at the door to go to gym. Emily had been working on valentines, and she continued working, even after the other children had put their things away and lined up. Finally, Mr. Jordan said to her, "If you're wondering whether there's a temper hidden in this room, there is; and if you want to find it, just keep writing, Emily." Emily hurriedly stuffed her valentines in her desk and joined the other children in the line for gym.

As was true in our two previous sets of observational records, the teacher is the key figure in this series of episodes as well. What do the observations reveal about him? Before trying to answer that question it may be worthwhile to say a few things about the question itself. The first is that it is the most natural question in the world to ask within a classroom setting. It is the uppermost question in the minds of students of all ages on the first day of class (and often beyond that as well). It recurs every time the teacher is absent and is replaced by a substitute. It is also a moral question. For what we want to know about any teacher is what kind of person he or she is. Will she be kind? Will he be tough? Will he be "easy"? Will she be "hard"? What makes these questions moral is that they concern, among other things, the dispersion of praise and blame. They ask about a teacher's character as lawmaker and dispenser of justice, and they touch on the question of how much student effort will be called for, which deals with matters of will, endurance, and perseverance—all moral matters. Finally, because they boil down in the end to the question of whether the student will like or dislike the teacher, they become entangled with the fundamental moral attitudes of love and hate.

Asking what an observational record reveals about a teacher presupposes that it will inevitably reveal something. How sure can we be of this? We have already quoted Emerson's answer to that question. He took a strong line, as readers will recall. He believed that everything we do reveals the kind of people we are. Here again, is the way he put it: "Character teaches above our wills. Men imagine that they communicate their virtue or vice only by overt actions, and do not see that virtue or vice emit a breath every moment."[5] Few can fail to be impressed by the poetic power of Emerson's words, but how seriously are we to take them? Do virtue and vice really emit a breath every moment? With respect to teachers in particular, are they always expressing some aspect of their character in everything they do? With that question at the forefront of our thoughts, let us consider the report on Mr. Jordan.

The report opens with Mr. Jordan working with one of his second-grade reading groups. As each child finishes reading aloud, Mr. Jordan dispenses the same words of praise ("Very, very nice"). Do such fleeting comments from a teacher constitute examples of Emerson's breaths of virtue? Possibly so. It does seem that the praise Mr. Jordan gives will be welcomed by those who receive it. The observer also describes Mr. Jordan as being encouraging throughout the session. Thus, on the strength of this information alone we might want to begin thinking of him, at least tentatively, as a helpful and supportive teacher, one who encourages a lot — all qualities that are widely thought to be among the teacherly virtues.

But what about the fact that Mr. Jordan apparently says the same thing to every pupil who reads, no matter how well or how poorly he or she does? His lack of discrimination would seem to diminish the worth of his praise, but what does it do to his virtue? It certainly tarnishes it somewhat, for the uniformity of his "Very, very nice" makes us suspect that he does not really mean what he says. His response is so automatic that he may not even be aware of what he is saying. Does that mean that he is being insincere? Maybe. Can one be helpful and supportive, but insincere? There is nothing to prevent it. But what kind of person is insincerely helpful? Presumably, one who is less attractive, from a moral standpoint, than one who is sincerely helpful. If Mr. Jordan tailored his praise to each student's performance, saying things like, "That was very nice, Billy, but you need to work on words that begin with *t,* don't you?" or "Excellent, Sarah! I particularly liked how you clearly pronounced each word," we (and the observer) probably would have been more impressed than we were with his helpfulness. So our initial impulse to applaud Mr. Jordan for his apparent helpfulness has to be restrained.

At this point some people are almost sure to object to the speed with which we are making moral judgments. "After all," they might point out, "you have barely begun to examine the observational record and here you are talking about Mr. Jordan as someone who seems to be helpful but insincere. And all of this on the basis of his repeated use of the three little words: 'Very, very nice.' Now really! Isn't such a conclusion just a bit premature?"

Indeed it would be, if it were a conclusion. But all we are doing here, perhaps with a touch of insincerity on our own part, is testing within the context of teaching the truth in Emerson's remark. Our point is not that Mr. Jordan should be thought of as helpful or insincere on the basis of such skimpy evidence. We want only to point out that if we are willing to ponder the meaning of such seemingly insignificant events, even something as apparently trivial as the way a teacher nods to his students or gives them a verbal pat on the head after a recitation can be seen as reflecting enduring moral qualities *or at least can trigger the thought that this might be the case.* In that sense at least, Emerson seems not to be so far off the mark. We can look upon almost everything a person does as revealing something about him or her. Using this single instance as a guide, Emerson also seems to have been right in his talk about character teaching above our wills. This recalls what we said in our discussion of Ms. Hamilton's class — a point that we also addressed implicitly in our remarks on Father Maran — which was that a teacher's actions can have moral consequences *regardless* of his or her own intentions.

Another point emerges from this discussion. It is that our looking at another person in these terms — that is, as being a certain *kind* of person, as possessing a certain *kind* of character — is not only possible, but natural. This is particularly so when that person is in a position of authority, as teachers are. This should come as no surprise. The character of our superiors is especially important to us because of the power they have to make our lives pleasant or miserable. Does this mean that the students in Mr. Jordan's reading group were conscious of his repeated use of "Very, very nice" and pondered its significance as a clue to their teacher's character? Certainly not. But it's a fair guess that every child in the room had an *opinion* about Mr. Jordan's character, one that began to be formed on the first day of class or perhaps even earlier, through remarks they may have overheard on the playground or at home. It is also reasonable to suppose that their opinions of Mr. Jordan were contributed to unconsciously by the same kinds of everyday, fleeting remarks that we have been attending to here.

The report as a whole centers on Mr. Jordan's interaction with Lisa. We first find him telling her and Jim to be quiet during the reading session and later speaking to them privately about their behavior, expressing his disfavor over their actions and pointing out the distinction between work and play. His conversations with them emphasize the rationality of his request for less talking and less playing around. Some time later in the morning Mr. Jordan has another exchange with Lisa, this time because she is leaning against one of the desks rather than sitting up straight. His motion for her to correct her posture is ignored and a minute later the desk she is leaning against moves, making a noise, which causes Mr. Jordan to glare and command her to sit up.

Nothing about Mr. Jordan's actions on these two occasions seems at all unusual. Nor does Lisa's behavior seem particularly noteworthy. Her misbehaviors, if that is the word for them, are certainly minor and Mr. Jordan's response to them is correspondingly low-key. Then it comes time for lunch and Mr. Jordan begins teasingly to ask Lisa to share her cupcake with him under the pretext of having a particular liking for that kind of cake, all of which takes place while he is having lunch with a group of girls at another table. He asks her not once but three times to share the cake with him and does so in a way that makes Lisa smile and finally join in the teasing game by deliberately turning from him as he passes by.

What should we make of these lunch-hour maneuverings? Mr. Jordan seems to go out of his way to play his teasing game with Lisa. Is he trying to make amends for the mild scoldings he gave her earlier that morning? Or has he already forgotten them and is he only responding to Lisa the way he would respond to any other child in the room who might have taken out a cream-filled cupcake, which is said to be one of his favorite desserts? Either way, he certainly seems to bear no grudge toward Lisa for the way she acted that morning. Is that the message he is trying to get across? If that is so, how does it modify, if at all, our initial impression of the kind of person Mr. Jordan is? Does he now begin to look more caring than before, contradicting, perhaps, the image implicit in the scolding manner he displayed earlier? And what are we to make of the playful banter overheard in his exchanges with the girls at the table? How do *those* snippets of information add to or subtract from our emerging impression of Mr. Jordan as a teacher?

Instead of addressing that spate of questions head-on, we might briefly step outside the observational record once again and examine our questioning process itself. For there is something both natural and unnatural, both reasonable and unreasonable, about our form of commentary. Let us try to figure out why.

In light of what was said earlier about the character of a person being revealed in seemingly trivial and inconsequential acts, it seems perfectly reasonable to scrutinize every fragment of a teacher's actions with an eye to what it might tell us about that person. We earlier contended that it was not only possible but natural for us to want to come to such a judgment. At the same time there seems to be something wrong, something too intrusive, perhaps even unfair, in doing what we have been trying to do with the record of Mr. Jordan's interactions with his students. We have been behaving as though a tally sheet is being kept whose entries consist of each and every movement Mr. Jordan makes and whose bottom line will yield our final evaluation of the man. What's wrong with doing that? Why does it make us feel uneasy?

One reason is that it is an unnatural thing to do, even though we have just said that it is perfectly natural to want to judge those who are in positions of authority. What is unnatural, however, about the way we have been proceeding here is that we normally do not scrutinize what others do as carefully as we have been attending to Mr. Jordan's actions. But then, sitting in the back of a classroom taking notes — whether it happens to be someone else's classroom or our own — is not a natural thing to do either. So the whole process in which we are engaged has something odd about it. It is not something we typically do in the course of our everyday affairs.

Of course there are occasions when we do scrutinize people's actions as carefully as we have been doing with Mr. Jordan's. One such occasion would be when we have some reason to doubt their character, when we suspect them of keeping something from us or of possessing traits that they may want to hide even from themselves. So at least a portion of our discomfort here may be attributable to our feeling that we are somehow spying on Mr. Jordan, who has certainly done nothing to deserve such intense scrutiny.

But there is more than this to the sense of unnaturalness in what we are doing. For even if we were suspicious of Mr. Jordan and had reason to assess his character, we probably would not go about it this way. Rather than pausing to consider every single thing he did, we would be looking instead for selected actions, ones that had a telltale quality about them, behaviors that might give him away such as a crucial slip of the tongue or a violent outburst that could not be contained. So it is not just our spylike scrutiny that makes what we are doing feel odd. We are acting strangely, even for spies.

If our attention to the details of Mr. Jordan's conduct is so out of the ordinary, why, then, have we proceeded this way? Our chief reason has been to show that everything Mr. Jordan does — everything *any* teacher does — lends itself to the kind of questioning we have been subjecting it to here. We do not commonly choose to give it that kind of attention, however, because we rarely have occasion to do so and because weighing the moral significance of every act would consume so much time and energy that we could not get on with other things we might want to do. The way of looking we are enacting here, therefore, constitutes a departure from our normal, day-to-day perceptual habits. We step into this way of looking, as it were, although in actuality the process is not as simple as the metaphor "stepping into" may imply. We will continue to illustrate what we mean by this as we proceed, and we will also have more to say about it in Part Four when we discuss this way of looking in more general terms.

Having said all that, we still must ask about the benefits of this kind of scrutiny, using the case in point. Has our mode of questioning either (1) altered our perception of Mr. Jordan in some important way or (2) deepened our understanding of how moral considerations permeate the things we observe in classrooms?

It seems to us that our pausing to question Mr. Jordan's actions in the way we have *has* made a difference in our perception of him (as happened in our ruminations on Ms. Hamilton's and Father Maran's classrooms). Having begun to wonder about the moral significance of Mr. Jordan's doings — what he might have meant by his actions, and what moral messages they might wittingly or unwittingly convey — we start to see the man himself in a more full-bodied or, let us say, more textured way. The two-dimensional image of Mr. Jordan contained in the observational record begins to rise from the page. It starts to take on a third dimension, almost like a bas-relief, whose emergence seems a function of our having paused to speculate on the meaning of his actions. And this remains true no matter what the outcome of our speculations, and even if we fail to answer the questions they raise. This last point is worth underscoring, for it helps explain the difference between the process of questioning in which we have been engaged and the running tally of good and bad deeds to which we compared it earlier.

To think about a person in moral terms, to begin to wonder what kind of person he or she might be, is to bring that person to life imaginatively. We need not pause in this process to tally up a subtotal each step of the way. For what animates our image of that or any individual is less our final judgment or the provisional ones leading up to it than it is our close and continued attention to what he or she says and does, added to the speculation that accompanies this attention. And the same conditions seem to hold whether the person we are speculating about is someone we are actually looking at and listening to or a description created by someone else, as is the case with Mr. Jordan.

As we stated in the introduction to Part Two, the kind of descriptions and commentary that we have included in this book are to be looked upon as *open* rather than *closed*—open in the sense of inviting continued speculation and questioning on the part of our readers. Acceptance of that invitation, which means the willingness to continue searching for the moral significance of all that we encounter, is itself a moral act, requiring patience, tenacity, fairness, and above all a sense of caring about whatever it is we are looking at and thinking about. John Dewey identified a similar set of qualities lying at the heart of all inquiry. "Open-mindedness," "whole-heartedness," and "responsibility" were his terms for them.[6] He called such qualities moral and referred to them as "traits of character." Dewey's "open-mindedness" and Umberto Eco's "open works" dovetail rather nicely within the present context. They both refer to moral qualities and they both come into play in every attempt to make sense of what is going on in classrooms. We will have more to say about these matters in Part Four.

The observation continues:

> One morning, early in October, the fire bell rang. Without a word from Mr. Jordan, the second graders stood up and formed a double line at the door. The line leaders led the way out of the room, down the stairs, and out the front door to the sidewalk. Mr. Jordan brought up the rear, helping Joel, whose leg was in a cast.

From the standpoint of the observer, the key words in this brief report are "Without a word from Mr. Jordan." What seems to have impressed our onlooker is the fact that when the fire bell rings the youngsters line up and exit the room on their own, without their teacher's guidance. As a matter of fact, Mr. Jordan lags behind and brings up the rear (giving help where it is obviously needed, we might note). Though we as readers might likewise be impressed by the report of the students' behavior, it is not immediately apparent what their independence signifies from a moral point of view. Does it show the youngsters to be well disciplined? That seems to be the most obvious interpretation, but what should we make of it? Should we credit Mr. Jordan with that accomplishment? It seems we should, unless we want to leave open the possibility that the students learned to behave that way the year before, under the tutelage of some other teacher. But so what? Let's suppose that Mr. Jordan himself trained his students to line up mutely and march smartly out of the building whenever the fire bell rings. Is that an unusual accomplishment? Also, what is the important element here? Is it the students' ability to act independently in such a situation or their sheeplike obedience in following the rules established by their teacher or some other authority figure?

Could this be an example of the observer having made a bad choice? In instances like this the observer's motives and intentions may become even more important than those of the teacher himself. The fact that he wrote this brief report makes it evident that the observer wanted us to gain an insight of some kind from it. What was it? What seems important is less the teacher's behavior than his lack of behavior, his failure to act in a situation in which one might have expected him to do so. Is that it? Is the observer trying to get us to see that what the teacher *doesn't* do may be as revealing of the moral climate of the room as what he *does?* With that possibility in mind, let us move to the next section of the observational record. It too consists of a single paragraph.

> Above one of the blackboards in Mr. Jordan's room the alphabet is displayed. But it is not a commercially prepared illustration of proper penmanship. Each of the letters, on its own piece of construction paper, was designed and colored by one of the children in his class.

This time we are shown neither the teacher nor his students. Instead, all we have is a brief description of the letters of the alphabet displayed above the blackboard, the important

point apparently being that instead of coming from the usual
commercial display, each of the letters was designed and colored
by one of the pupils in the room. We begin our speculation by
wondering why Mr. Jordan chose to have his pupils engage in
such a project. Certainly, from the standpoints of both neatness
and legibility, the commercially prepared letters would have been
superior. They would have saved time as well. What was gained
by having the children work on such a project? Well, for one
thing, each child was given a chance to contribute to a common project and to do so in a manner that would be visible to
all. How to be one among many without losing a sense of
identity—that is the problem for which the handworked alphabet
appears to be a solution. Were such thoughts on Mr. Jordan's
mind when he assigned the project? Does it matter? Does the
alphabet's instantiation of *e pluribus unum* have anything to do
with the independent way the children marched out of the room
during the fire drill? Do they both exemplify a second-grade
version of what it means to shoulder responsibility for one's actions? And how do these two observational fragments fit with
the first report, the one featuring the interaction between Mr.
Jordan and Lisa? Do all three have something in common? Possibly. They all speak to the importance of being a cooperative
member of a collective undertaking. When Lisa disturbed that
undertaking—first by talking and later by leaning against a chair
that made a noise—she was admonished for doing so. But later
Mr. Jordan went out of his way to be friendly with her, as if
to assure her that he bore no ill feelings over her misconduct.
Is that to be read as his effort to keep her in the fold?

　　Instead of trying to answer that question, let us hold it
in abeyance as we move on to the next excerpt from the observational record.

　　　　After coloring a picture for about fifteen min-
　　　　utes, Peter took his finished work to Mr. Jordan,
　　　　who was helping another child. Peter waited. When
　　　　Mr. Jordan finished with the first child, he turned
　　　　to Peter, who held up his picture and said, "Mr.
　　　　Jordan, do you like this?"

"Wonderful!" said Mr. Jordan, after he'd
looked it over for a moment. "Reminds me of you."

From a moral perspective, the most salient aspect of this
brief report is the exuberance and warmth of Mr. Jordan's response to Peter. We don't know what Peter drew, but we might
reasonably assume that it was not a self-portrait or even a drawing of another person and, therefore, that Mr. Jordan's "Reminds me of you" refers not to the actual content of the drawing itself but to its quality, which he describes as wonderful.
Peter, in other words, receives a double-barreled compliment.
He is told his drawing is wonderful and so is he, and all within
the span of five words. Though the observer doesn't tell us so,
we can also imagine that Mr. Jordan wears a broad smile as
he speaks to Peter. Two compliments, plus a smile. What more
could Peter ask for in the way of approval?

We also should note the form of Peter's question. He does
not ask whether his drawing is well done, nor does he seem interested in how it might be improved. What he wants to know
instead is whether Mr. Jordan likes it. He is seeking his teacher's
approval of what he has done. Such a request is common among
second graders and therefore does not convey much information about Mr. Jordan himself. It does remind us, however,
of how important their teacher's approval is to pupils of this age,
which underscores the potency of Mr. Jordan's enthusiastic response. His "Wonderful!" must be a bracing tonic to all who
receive it.

What can we say of a teacher who enthuses over a child's
drawing (and the child himself) in that way? What about his
sincerity? Do the drawing and the child deserve what they get?
Is Mr. Jordan handing out false praise? We have no way of knowing from the record itself, but something about the way the situation develops — its casualness, perhaps, plus the way Peter
frames his question — makes us think that the issue of who-
deserves-what is not particularly relevant here. This does not
mean that Mr. Jordan is free to say whatever he likes about
the drawing. He does take time to look it over, which contributes to the impression that he is making an accurate and fair

judgment. But what the situation obviously calls for is not a finely calibrated assessment of the drawing's merits. Peter wants approval and that's what Mr. Jordan gives him. The spontaneity of his response leads us to believe that Mr. Jordan would say just about the same thing no matter what the drawing looked like and perhaps no matter who drew it. His doing so would not make him insincere, unless we wish to define insincerity in a most picayune and legalistic way. In short, when someone asks us for approval of something they have done or something they own, social custom dictates that we be liberal, perhaps even lavish, in the praise we give, which is the way Mr. Jordan seems to respond to Peter.

What makes Mr. Jordan's response interesting from a moral point of view is not what it says about his sincerity or insincerity in an overall sense but what it reveals about the supportive environment that teachers, especially those who work with young children, are constantly called upon to create and maintain. They are practically required to cultivate a way of responding to the world around them that is at once positive in tone and enthusiastic in delivery. This does not mean that teachers must always rave over their pupils' slightest accomplishments or gush at everything they see and hear, but it does require a readiness and a willingness to interpret what their pupils say, and to do this in at least a favorable light, if not the best one possible.

The need to maintain a positive orientation is also felt by observers who are out looking for the moral good that teachers and the classroom environment as a whole might be doing. They, too, must be constantly on the alert for personal and environmental qualities whose virtue can only be faintly perceived or is only partially realized. Observers need not respond to what they see with quite the same enthusiasm that teachers use with their pupils, but a willingness to give teachers the benefit of the doubt when the situation is morally ambiguous is no less crucial for them.

The observation continues:

> One morning in April, during snack time, Louise was talking to Mr. Jordan about her "manners class," which she had recently completed.

"At the end," she said, "we had a cocktail party."

"Oh?" said Mr. Jordan.

"Hm hm. We had to small talk, but not with anyone we knew." Louise took the last bite of her fruit roll-up. "It was boring."

"Did you learn any manners?"

Louise shook her head. "No."

What's going on here? Why did this observer think this brief conversation worth recording? Was it only for its obvious humor? One thing that makes the vignette more than simply humorous is the subject under discussion: a second-grade youngster's experience at a "manners" class. Broadly interpreted, manners make up a subdivision of morals (Dewey calls them "minor morals").[7] Therefore, a course devoted to the teaching of manners could be looked upon as a form of moral education, though not the kind we usually think of when the term comes up in ordinary conversation. The image of a roomful of seven-year-olds participating in a simulated cocktail party is also a bit unusual, to put it mildly. Some might find it laughable; others, disturbing. The ability to engage in small talk with a stranger is indisputably useful in many social situations, particularly among the cosmopolitan well-to-do. But the practice of enrolling young children in classes where such skills are systematically taught raises a host of questions about what our society thinks valuable, what today's parents want for their children, what education is all about, and so forth. Louise's use of "small talk" as a verb serves as a symbol of the linguistic precocity that such manners classes seek to develop.

But as we disapprovingly ponder what our world is coming to when children of Louise's age are taught to be adroit small-talkers, we slowly begin to realize that the conversational fragment we have just read could almost have been lifted directly from an actual cocktail party! There is Louise nibbling on her fruit roll-up, the juvenile equivalent of a canapé, while chatting with her teacher during snack time, the ubiquitous break in the school day (at least in the lower grades) that serves to relax and refresh, much as cocktail parties are supposed to do for adults. Mr. Jordan is not a stranger, true enough, but he could as easily be one, given the content of the conversation. *Now* how do we feel about Louise's lessons? Are we still as disapproving as before? We may well be. But, having noted the resemblance between the content of the conversation and the conditions of its enactment, we are in a position to ask whether or in what sense Mr. Jordan's classroom could also be looked upon as a "manners class" for all of the children present and possibly even for Mr. Jordan himself.

When Lisa is chided for talking in class and later when she is spoken to for leaning against a desk, isn't she being given a lesson in manners? And what of Mr. Jordan's behavior following those two episodes — his playful conversation during the lunch hour and his repartee with Lisa about the cupcake? Aren't those too a pair of living lessons about how to behave in public? Or, at least, we might imagine that to be the way his students are inclined to read his behavior. In the same way, we might say that the classrooms of Ms. Hamilton and Father Maran also feature a form of ongoing manners classes.

Might we look upon what goes on in Mr. Jordan's room as comprising a set of lessons for him as well as for his students? We could if we saw Mr. Jordan as someone who is still in the process of learning how to become a teacher or how to improve on the teacher he has become. Is he that kind of person? These snippets from the observational record leave us wondering. Yet they do not leave us totally in the dark. Having watched Mr. Jordan in action, even as briefly as these anecdotes allow, we have begun to form an opinion of him as someone who cares for his students but does so without sentimentality — a bit stern at times, but also quick to forgive, a teacher who is not above small talk when the occasion allows, but who also knows when it's time to get down to business. The handmade alphabet above his blackboard may stand for the kind of teacher Mr. Jordan has become so far, one who respects the individuality of his students but does so reservedly, allowing the uniqueness of each child to find expression within the constraints of a common task.

IV

The final set of observations to be introduced in Part Two describes Ms. Walsh, an English teacher in a large public high school. The observational record opens with some general remarks about Ms. Walsh's appearance and her behavior at the start of the class. It then moves to a set of brief vignettes that serve to concretize the generalizations made at the start.

It is not unusual to observe Ms. Walsh's students absorbed in watching her. She seems always on the move. She is tall, with dark hair and hazel eyes, and always comes to class fashionably dressed. At the bell announcing the start of class, she typically corrals her students' attention by rapidly calling out their names, by smiling at them, by teasing them, by joking with them.

"Okay! Papers! Papers!" she announces one morning to her ninth graders as she strides from her desk to within a foot or two of the first row of seats. Surveying the rows of students, she continues with a smile: "Great papers, wonderful papers, papers that will make me happy and not ruin my weekend!"

In her speech class, she reins in a suddenly rambunctious debate by raising her voice: "Please! You're upperclassmen! I *like* upperclassmen! Please prove me right that upperclassmen are mature!"

She goes from group to group in a class she has divided into foursomes to prepare for a discussion. Placing her hand on the back of a chair and leaning over a group, she asks, "Do you need me?

Are you okay?" And to another she asks, "You know what you're doing? Do I need to worry? Because I *do* worry."

She prepares a class for her absence the next day by saying: "You don't really need a substitute, you can do the practicing [of speeches] yourselves. But I will be *crushed* if I hear any bad reports about you!"

Ms. Walsh is a commanding presence in the classroom. All eyes focus on her. From the start of class she occupies center stage with her flair for the dramatic. Dress is important to her. She is described as always coming to class fashionably dressed. In all of these ways, she reminds us of Father Maran, who was also a commanding presence and a theatrical figure, as well as being "impeccably groomed." But there the resemblance seems to stop. Ms. Walsh is portrayed as "smiling," "teasing," and "joking" with her students, ways of relating that fit poorly with the image we have of Father Maran. Also, Ms. Walsh addresses her students in a much more personal way than he did. We cannot yet tell whether she uses first names or "Mr." and "Miss" in addressing them, but even without knowing that, we sense a vast difference in the intimacy of the approach these two teachers take to their students. There is a noticeable difference in emotional tone as well.

Ms. Walsh pleads with her students to act as she wishes and she does so in a very personal way. Her appeals contain references to how *she* will feel or what will happen to *her* if her students do not behave as expected. She says she will be "crushed" or will "worry," and asks that they not "ruin" her weekend. How seriously are we to take these dire proclamations? Will she really feel that way or is there more than a touch of irony and even humor in her words? We opt for the latter interpretation. It seems to us unlikely that a teacher as confident and as experienced as Ms. Walsh will have her weekend ruined by a set of student papers that are not up to par. We also doubt that she will really be crushed to learn that her class misbehaved while she was away. Disappointed? Maybe. Annoyed? Almost certainly. But crushed? No.

The hyperbole in Ms. Walsh's speech, combined with the appeal to her own feelings and state of mind, elicits two reactions. The first is that her way of talking makes her sound a bit like a high school student herself. Adolescents are known for their exaggerations and for their tendency to magnify the emotional impact of their experiences. With her talk about being crushed and ruined, Ms. Walsh begins to sound like one of them. This point recalls our observation in Part One that it is not just teachers of the very young who speak to their students in a different voice than they use with others.

There is also something alluring, almost flirtatious, about Ms. Walsh's manner of speaking. The observer initially says that she "corrals" her students by "smiling," "teasing," and "joking," and later that she "reins" them in by raising her voice. Eight exclamation points are used to capture the excitement and urgency in her voice. The combined effect of the language and the punctuation brings to mind the call of a siren from some legendary shore.

And yet, having said all that, we still must acknowledge the evident sincerity that undergirds Ms. Walsh's hyperbolic and somewhat frenetic way of speaking. Perhaps she won't be crushed or have her weekend ruined by the way her students behave or the kind of papers they hand in, but who can doubt that she really cares about such things, even if the degree of her caring does not quite match the pitch of her voice and the power of her words? We certainly can entertain no such doubts. We suspect her students would have trouble doing so as well.

The observation continues:

> One morning Ms. Walsh begins a lesson by reviewing issues raised the day before about the play the class is reading. Suddenly the principal's voice explodes out of the loudspeaker above the door, warning late students they are about to be "swept" (i.e., cited and penalized for being tardy). His booming, jarring voice seems literally to knock Ms. Walsh

almost off her feet. She spontaneously reels away from the loudspeaker, clasping one hand with notes in it to her heart, and with the other reaching for something to support her.

At the same instant, her ninth graders erupt in laughter. Ms. Walsh, blushing crimson, begins to smile herself.

A split second later the students stop laughing almost as one. They watch her quietly, no longer smiling. They all sit expectantly.

Ms. Walsh straightens her back and then executes a mocking bow toward the loudspeaker. Still flushed, she promptly picks up the thread of her review. Her usually exuberant class remains completely quiet and attentive.

Ms. Walsh's reaction to the interruption created by the principal's voice coming through the loudspeaker reveals again her penchant for exaggeration and her flair for the dramatic. There can be no doubt that the announcement issuing from the loudspeaker comes as a shock to everyone in the room. The observer's use of the words "explodes," "booming," and "jarring" is enough to convince us of that. But observe how Ms. Walsh behaves in response to the sudden noise. She reels away, one hand clutching her heart, the other reaching out for support. As the observer puts it, she behaves as though she almost has been knocked off her feet. The students laugh. They know that her reaction is exaggerated, but they also know that she is truly upset by the interruption. Her blush reveals that the sense of shock, which she acts out by her feigned stumble and the clutching at her heart, is not entirely put on. That may be why the class quiets down so rapidly.

Ms. Walsh's "mocking bow" in the direction of the loudspeaker provides a fitting touch of irony to the situation that the students must also have appreciated, even though we are not told they did and, had the observer stopped to query them, they likely would not have been able to say why they felt as they did. It is at least very unlikely that they would have mentioned irony. What makes the bow ironic is the way it embodies a reversal of what bows ordinarily mean. Ordinarily, we bow to those we respect. But in this instance the gesture of respect is directed toward someone who has just behaved disrespectfully, or so we might interpret the principal's auditory intrusion into the privacy of the classroom.

Is there a moral lesson embedded in the teacher's mock gesture of servility? There surely is and it is one of the most ancient lessons in the history of morals. It is the one Socrates sought to teach Callicles in Plato's *Gorgias*. It is also the lesson that the Reverend Martin Luther King, Jr., preached to his followers in our day. Essentially, its message is this: if persons behave respectfully to those in power who mistreat them, then they, the less powerful, become the masters, at least in moral terms. They occupy the morally superior position. Seen in this light, Ms. Walsh's bow to her invisible intruder is far more than a simple grace note at the end of a solo performance. It is more like the attitude of mock deference that many of today's non-violent protesters have learned to adopt.

Ms. Walsh's sense of propriety and the importance she attaches to manners and rules of etiquette are remarked upon at several points in the observational record. Here are four such comments.

Ms. Walsh often calls out "Please!" in response to spontaneous outbursts of laughter or talking (one reason she has to do this so frequently is because she does not insist that students raise their hands).

Ms. Walsh responds swiftly to breaches of etiquette and violations of school rules: "You're chewing gum, Robert!"—"Philip, off with the sunglasses, please!"—"Felicia, unless you are *truly* freezing, would you mind taking off the winter coat while in class?"

To a girl who she notices is not wearing her student ID (required of all students in the school), Ms. Walsh says: "Angelica, I know it won't match

your outfit, which is very pretty, but please, your
ID!" The girl grins as if she's heard this counsel before and promptly fishes her ID out of her bookbag.

Ms. Walsh halts a discussion she had begun
and directs a pupil to open the classroom door to
admit a girl who is tardy (the door is locked to outsiders after the last bell has rung). To reach her seat
the latecomer starts to walk nonchalantly between
Ms. Walsh, who is standing at a podium, and the
front row of students. "*No,* Marcia," Ms. Walsh interrupts, "walk *behind* me, please." Nonplussed at
first, the girl stops, then turns and walks around
behind the podium to her place. Ms. Walsh waits
with arms crossed, her eyebrows knit and her mouth
set firmly. The class watches silently.

The observer's remark about the class watching silently
as the latecomer wends her way to her seat deserves special emphasis because the same comment could probably have been
made about each of the preceding events. The class, or a significant portion of it, was probably watching each of those events
as well. What makes this observation noteworthy is that our concentration on the interaction between the teacher and the offend-
ing student commonly leads us to forget or overlook the fact
that these one-on-one exchanges are actually being performed
before attentive audiences. This means that their potential impact is far greater in scope than we might customarily allow and
it may also be rather differently apportioned than we might suspect. Let us briefly say why.

Ordinarily, when we think of a student being reprimanded
by a teacher we imagine him or her to be the central and perhaps
even the sole recipient of whatever moral "lesson" the reprimand
entails. Thus, in the situation we have just examined we might
think that the latecomer alone was the one who was taught the
lesson: "Never walk between the teacher and the front row of
students when the class is in progress and you are required to
take your seat." It takes only a moment's reflection, however,

to realize that those who are witness to this small drama may stand to gain as much from it as the offender. Indeed, if we stop to think about what is going on in such a situation we may begin to suspect that the spectators are better positioned to learn from it than the student who is being reprimanded. They, at least, are not pinpointed by the spotlight of attention and thus are not encumbered by self-consciousness or the sense of embarrassment such a predicament might induce.

Beyond leaving us with the impression that Ms. Walsh tends to carp quite a bit about dress codes and minor breaches of conduct, what else does this set of observations tell us about what she is like as a teacher or what life is like in her classroom from a moral point of view?

Consider for a moment the four offenses for which students were reprimanded (leaving aside the latecomer). These included: chewing gum, wearing sunglasses to class, wearing a winter coat in class, and failing to wear the required identification tag. Is it probable that any of those were first offenses, in the sense of being the first time the student in question ever behaved that way in *any* class, not just Ms. Walsh's? Not likely. It seems more reasonable to suppose that each of the students has behaved that way before, perhaps in the classroom he or she has just left. It further seems likely that from time to time these students have gotten away with these infractions of the rules without receiving a reprimand from their teachers. They may even have done so in Ms. Walsh's room on occasion, although that seems less likely. At the same time, their failure to complain or to protest Ms. Walsh's interdiction — or at least the absence of such complaints in the record — suggests an understanding of the rules and a willingness to comply when they are enforced. What, then, does all this say about Ms. Walsh?

The easy inference is that she is stricter than some teachers, and possibly stricter than most. We would not be at all surprised to hear her described that way by her students. But what does it mean for a teacher to be strict? What does strictness entail from a moral point of view?

It means, first of all, that she is probably more attentive than most teachers, at least when it comes to infractions of the rules. She has an eye out for such things, or so it would appear. This must also mean that she cares about them, that they are important to her. But why should a teacher care whether a student wears sunglasses to class or keeps on her coat in a well-heated room? What difference does it make if someone chews gum in class or walks in front of the teacher on the way to her seat?

There are several possible answers to such questions. A by-the-book kind of teacher might simply insist that rules are rules, period. They are meant to be obeyed and the teacher's job is to monitor transgressions and enforce compliance. But somehow that answer doesn't seem to fit Ms. Walsh's manner of handling infractions. Her actions are anything but wooden and mechanical. An answer more in accord with her style and with the rest of what goes on in her room would be one that focused on the *expressive* significance of behaviors like chewing gum or wearing sunglasses to class, on what they proclaim about the actor's relationship to what is going on. Let us ask what these behaviors might express.

They have the capacity to express many things, depending on how we look at them. To the adolescent who is wearing sunglasses or nonchalantly chewing gum, the expressive intention of these actions might be summed up in the single word: *cool*. To his classmates, looking on, the same actions might signal defiance or toughness. His teacher, however, might read them quite differently. She might see in them an attitude of disrespect and disengagement from the activity at hand. The latter appears to be the interpretation Ms. Walsh puts on behavior of this kind. She seems quick to detect and respond to any of her students' actions that could be taken as an affront to the seriousness and importance of the instructional setting. This includes, of course, any and all assaults upon her personal dignity as a teacher.

Yet she does not respond angrily to such actions. Instead, she either issues curt but polite commands or reminders ("You're chewing gum, Robert!") or teasingly badgers or cajoles the students into compliance, as she did with the two girls who were improperly attired. She remains good-natured, in other words, even while correcting behavior that she deems to be offensive. What do *her* actions express to those who witness them? Again, as was true of the students' behavior, they are capable of being read in many ways, though not in any way we wish. Our own reading of them is already evident in our use of words like "good-natured" and "teasingly badgers." To these we would add that it looks to us as though Ms. Walsh genuinely likes the students in her class, even those who cause her trouble and who have to be corrected from time to time. Perhaps it's the other way around. It may be more accurate to say that *because* Ms. Walsh deals so good-humoredly with the students who cause her trouble, *because* she seems to like even these troublemakers, it stands to reason that she must like all of the rest of her students as well.

This reversal of the usual line of reasoning about a teacher's handling of misbehavior (i.e., her treatment of the extreme case taken as an indicator of her attitude toward others, rather than as revealing the limits of her tolerance) accords with common sense. In everyday affairs the litmus test of how good-natured a person is is usually his or her ability "to take a joke," which means being made fun of in some way. It should come as no surprise to find those same dynamics at work within classrooms. Though none of the four students whose actions we have just observed could be said to have been making fun of their teacher, they were certainly testing the limits of her tolerance, whether they intended to do so or not. Her capacity to take such treatment without becoming angry reveals her to be someone who remains even-tempered under trying circumstances. That type of person, we might reasonably infer, will be even jollier and better-tempered when conditions warrant.

In the next observational fragment we see Ms. Walsh on stage again, this time transforming an incidental query about the meaning of a word into a small piece of theater.

"Only seven of Aeschylus' plays are extant," Ms. Walsh informs an upper-level class during a lecture on Greek theater. She suddenly interjects, while leaning forward into the circle of faces, "'Extant' . . . e-x-t-a-n-t. What does that mean?" "Exist-

ing," replies a student promptly. "Yeah," affirms
Ms. Walsh in a deep, almost conspiratorial voice.
Simultaneously she sweeps her gaze around the entire class as if to ensure that they have all shared
in this knowledge. For an instant her students return her gaze with equally engrossed expressions
on their faces.

Ms. Walsh's guttural "Yeah," delivered in a tone that is
"almost conspiratorial" and accompanied by an all-encompassing
gaze, contrasts sharply with the formality of the pedagogical drill
that preceded it. After her no-nonsense maneuver of pronounce-
it, spell-it, ask-it, which teachers the world over learn to perform in their sleep, we might expect Ms. Walsh to follow up
with a bland "Yes!" or "Good!" in response to the student who
blurts out the correct answer. Instead, she behaves like the neigh-
borhood gossip sharing a deep, dark secret over a rubber of
bridge. Even her dialect becomes slangy, sounding less like an
English teacher, as she shifts to a mood of intimacy. What does
such a shift signal from a moral point of view? To us it calls
to mind an initiation ceremony of some kind. The lowered voice
and the conspiratorial look create the impression that the group
has just been let in on something that heretofore had been kept
from them.

Here is another episode in which a similar exchange takes
place, though without the aura of secrecy that we saw exhibited
in the preceding account.

Ms. Walsh asks her ninth graders what language Cicero was speaking when he was overheard
by one of the plotters against Caesar. "Greek!" a
few call out spontaneously. "That's right!" replies
Ms. Walsh. "Have you heard the expression, 'It's
Greek to me'?" "Yeah!" many students respond.
"What does it mean?" "It means you don't understand!" replies one boy with alacrity. "Right!" Ms.
Walsh quickly acknowledges, again surveying her
whole class. "And this is where the phrase originates

from, 'It's Greek to me,' here, right *here,* in Shakespeare's play." She leans forward while stressing the
point, smiling and speaking in an excited, almost
breathless voice. As she does so, many of her pupils
focus intently on her. Some look down at their open
texts to the passage itself.

Again we have the teacher leaning forward as if information of great importance is about to be imparted, the smile, the
animated voice ("excited, almost breathless"), and again the outcome is a deepened understanding of something that is already
familiar to at least some of the students. Many have heard the
expression "It's Greek to me"; now it is revealed to them where
the phrase comes from. As before, the psychological dynamics
and the emotional tone of the exchange are essentially those of
an initiation ritual — the young, who have finally come of age,
are being inducted into the secrets of the tribe.

There is a sense, of course, in which all schooling might
be said to fit within the framework of an initiation rite. The
young are perpetually being readied by their teachers to become
full participants within the larger society. That total process
might be thought of as a form of initiation. But Ms. Walsh's
behavior stands apart from what one might observe of this process in many other classrooms. What is notable about her enactment of the initiation ritual, at least in the two snippets of observation that we have just read, is the drama she manages to
infuse into what might otherwise be a rather routine dissemi-
nation of information. The rapt attention that the students give
their teacher when she behaves this way does not escape the observer. The students "focus intently," we are told; they have "engrossed expressions" on their faces. They, too, behave as though
something of great moment is taking place.

Here she is again, injecting an element of mystery and
drama into what might otherwise be a straightforward explanation of a passage from Shakespeare.

In a discussion of *Julius Caesar,* several boys
ask what Cassius means when he says he will be

a "mirror" to Brutus. A girl promptly responds that it has to do with the friendship of the two men and how they relate to one another. Ms. Walsh affirms her point, then asks the boys if they've ever discovered their own feelings or thoughts about something through noticing their friends' reactions to things they have said or done. The boys remain puzzled, however. Several students speculate aloud about the meaning of the idea. After listening for a moment along with the rest of the class, Ms. Walsh suddenly interrupts: "*Look* at yourselves." She pauses for a moment as the chatter ceases. "Try to *see* yourself." She pauses again, as her class regards her wonderingly. A few students actually bend over and look at their navels before snapping their heads up quickly, some with embarrassed looks. "You can't!" Ms. Walsh exclaims, taking a step forward. "You *can't* 'see' yourself! So Cassius is saying he'll be a 'mirror' to Brutus, he'll let him use him to talk and think with, he'll do this because he is a friend and can be trusted." The students regard her closely.

If we stop to analyze Ms. Walsh's behavior in this situation from a purely expository point of view — that is, from how well she manages to get her point across — we might conclude that her sudden inspiration to have the students try to look at themselves is not a very good idea. After all, there is a sense in which we *can* look at ourselves, as the students who stare at their navels clearly demonstrate. But the point Ms. Walsh wants to make is figurative rather than literal. So she simply has to declare — contrary to the immediate experience of those whose behavior proves otherwise — that such a thing is impossible, that we *can't* see ourselves. And so far as we can tell, the students accept her assertion without further questioning.

The actress in Ms. Walsh stands out in the following episode as well. As usual, she performs before a rapt audience.

While instructing her ninth graders on how to deliver their readings of the play from the front of the room, Ms. Walsh spontaneously acts out the procedure. "Don't read like this," she states, holding her opened textbook inches from her nose. "And don't get all bunched up here!" she emphasizes, while hunching her shoulders in a way that evokes a tightly closed circle. "Don't lean on things," she adds, quickly striding over to her desk where she turns and leans against it, while once more hiding her face behind the book. Meanwhile her students watch silently, some shifting in their seats to follow her movements.

There is nothing at all unusual about a teacher acting out various common mistakes when trying to instruct students on how to read in public. It seems like a very natural thing to do, which is probably why the observer describes Ms. Walsh as behaving "spontaneously." It is also an easy way to add a note of levity to an otherwise routine set of instructions. The only thing that makes Ms. Walsh's performance noteworthy is the reported silence of her students. Why aren't they laughing? Do they take her exaggerated actions *that* seriously? Or is it simply that they are so caught up in what their teacher is doing ("shifting in their seats to follow her movements") that they forget to laugh? In the light of all the other observational reports on Ms. Walsh, the latter seems the more likely explanation.

In this final excerpt we once more observe Ms. Walsh serving as a visible standard of conduct, a person to whom students' eyes automatically turn, even when she is seated in the back of the room.

During a session of her eleventh-grade speech class, one of the students is up at the podium recounting problems in the city's crowded prison system. He describes how an inmate who was prematurely released promptly robbed a woman on the street, at the same time breaking her nose with a blow from a bottle. Hearing this, many students audibly gasp. Several girls immediately turn and glance at their teacher, who is sitting in a back corner of the classroom. Ms. Walsh's face displays both shock and anger as she continues to focus on the speaker. The girls turn back to the front, still with disquieted faces as they shift in their seats a bit, a few letting out breaths of consternation. They rejoin the others who remain attentive to what the speaker is saying.

The girls have obviously turned to Ms. Walsh to see how the account of the mugging registered on her. Their teacher's apparent "shock and anger" seems to jibe with, and thereby legitimize, their own feelings. They are satisfied, in other words, that their teacher feels as they do. But how should *we* read Ms. Walsh's pained expression? Is any of it put on for the benefit of those who are watching (including the observer, of course) or does she really feel as upset as she looks? We obviously cannot answer that question with the information at hand, but having seen how dramatically she has behaved in other situations, we cannot help but raise it. It also provides a fitting start to a final barrage of questions directed toward these observations as a whole.

From a moral point of view, what are we to make of this stately, well-dressed, flamboyantly dramatic, and enthusiastic teacher, this high priestess of ninth-grade English? We have said that she is good-naturedly tolerant of misconduct, but also strict; we have likened her performance to that of a tribal elder initiating the young, but we have also observed that her use of hyperbole and her infectious enthusiasm come close to resembling the youthful spirit of the adolescents with whom she works. Are these contradictory judgments or do they fit together somehow? Or is it perhaps that Ms. Walsh herself is a bundle of contradictions? Does she give off moral messages of a contradictory kind?

She seldom loses her audience. That much is clear. Whatever her students might think of her as a person, they rarely take their eyes from her when she is in front of the room and some of them appear to have difficulty doing so even when she retires to the rear. She has what theatrical people sometimes refer to as "a commanding presence." But what does she command, besides attention? What do her actions communicate, above and beyond the content of English as a school subject?

Perhaps the most important thing they communicate is that Ms. Walsh likes being where she is and doing what she's doing. She more than likes it; she thinks it important enough to worry about, to get upset over. We earlier doubted that Ms. Walsh's weekend would be ruined by the receipt of a batch of weak papers from her class, despite her claims to the contrary. We stand by that suspicion. At the same time, we have no difficulty imagining her being distressed by such an event, even though her discomfort might not be severe enough to make her cancel social plans. The only thing we question, in other words, is how literally to take her words. We never once have doubted the fundamental sincerity of her expressed concern over the quality of her students' work.

Here, then, is a teacher who cares a lot about performances, about her own as well as those of her students. She expresses that concern in a variety of ways, from her manner of dress to the looks she gives to those who misbehave. Yet her caring is not exclusively of a worrying kind. She also takes delight in the artful execution of almost anything, from Shakespeare's eloquence to a ninth grader's prompt answer to one of her questions. "Yeah," she says appreciatively to the student's quick display of knowledge, adding her own artfulness to the situation.

What about the students who make up her audience? Do they appreciate the moral significance of her performance? Are they aware how much she cares about what she and they are doing? The signs of rapt attention that the observer so often commented upon provide only a hint of a positive answer to those questions. Yet it is hard for us to believe that such qualities go entirely unnoticed by those who are present, even those who seek to affect a cool or callous demeanor. They may not speak of Ms. Walsh's manner of teaching in the same terms that we have used here. But surely many will remember her in years to come. We certainly will.

Attending to the Moral

Having completed our commentary on four sets of observational records, each drawn from a different classroom, we are now in a position to reflect back on what those records, plus what we have had to say about them, have revealed about the process of becoming sensitized to the moral dimensions of classroom life. We started out with a broad claim, which said that only by looking at what goes on in classrooms from a symbolic or expressive point of view can we begin to appreciate the moral potential of qualities such as a teacher's character or the atmosphere of the classroom. Another way of putting it would be to say that only by believing in the existence of such qualities and by being on the lookout for them can we begin to bring them into focus as either a firsthand observer, a commentator reacting to the observational record, or a reader of both the record and its accompanying commentary. Now we must ask whether that claim has been substantiated, or at least buttressed, by all that has followed.

Such a question is properly addressed to our readers themselves, for they alone are in a position to judge how convincing the procedures exemplified in Part Two have been. However, it will not hurt our case, we trust, to say a few additional words on behalf of our initial claim while at the same time highlighting one or two points for readers to mull over in coming to their own conclusions. What follows, therefore, is both a summary and an extension of our underlying argument.

We first must reiterate that from the start of our observational work we had no interest in making use of classroom observations to establish the obvious fact that some teachers are kind and considerate in their dealings with their pupils, whereas others are not, or that some are routinely patient and fair, whereas others (few, we would hope) are just the opposite. Nor were we interested in how many of each kind could be found, even assuming that they could be properly identified. (We can easily envision someone asking this question but it would call for a very different kind of study than ours.) We did not compare the teachers we were observing, asking, for example, whether

Mr. Jordan is more honest than Father Maran or less honest than Ms. Hamilton. Finally, we had no desire to show that it is better, from either a pedagogical or a moral point of view, to be kind and considerate or patient and just, rather than their opposites. That also struck us as being too obvious to warrant investigation.

Our concern has rather been with the question of *how to see* the moral or the immoral not only in what teachers say and do but in other features of classroom life as well. Our aim, in other words, was never to establish the good moral intentions of the average teacher or to find out whether the particular teachers with whom we were working were basically good people. We assumed both conditions from the start. Our aim was to discover how to go about discerning those moral properties of teachers and of classrooms in general, properties that we were confident were there to be disclosed.

With that as background, we come to the question of why such a task should prove difficult, as it did for us. For if the existence and even the pervasiveness of qualities like honesty and patience are taken for granted and, further, if the teachers with whom we were working were assumed to possess such qualities in at least average amounts, as "basically good people" would be expected to do, what work would remain for a team of observers, beyond taking note of all those admirable qualities whenever they were exhibited? As we sat perched in the back of classrooms with morally significant happenings going on all around us, what was to prevent us from simply reaching out and catching morality on the wing? That question is one this chapter has sought to address by offering multiple examples taken from our observational records and then commenting upon them.

What that process should by now have made clear is the interpretive character of attaching significance, moral or otherwise, to what is witnessed in classrooms at either first or second hand. For the observer seated in the back of the room and confronted by the cacophonous buzz of classroom life, or for the teacher who momentarily steps out of the flow of activity to become an observer, the first question is what to focus on and report. What is going on here that might be worth remembering and later reflecting upon from a moral perspective? That is the question that must guide observation and note taking. For the subsequent reader of the written record, who may or may not be acquainted with either the observer or the setting itself, the secondary question is what to make of what has been reported. What is morally significant about it? Why might it have been selected as being worthy of someone's scrutiny? The answers to both sets of questions, as we have seen, include many interpretations, for there is nothing at all obvious about the moral significance of much that goes on within classrooms, nor, it follows, is it always obvious why a particular event was reported upon, particularly if the observer offers a straightforward description (albeit an interpretive one) of what went on without adding any comment about its moral significance.

The latter practice, incidentally, typified our way of working for a variety of reasons, not all of them of our own choosing. Even when we sensed something to be of moral significance and therefore worthy of reporting, we often were unclear in our own minds about what made it so. A vague impulse, hardly more than a hunch, was often all we had to go on. We learned, however, to trust our initial impression and to take notes on the events that interested us even if we could not say for sure why they did. This was because, having taken the gamble a few times, we soon discovered that the moral significance of what we had seen and written about often came into focus with the suddenness of a developing photograph once we distanced ourselves sufficiently from the event itself and had a chance to reflect upon it.

The fact that this process seldom missed, which is to say that we almost always found something worthy of reflection in the notes we had taken, was not as welcome an outcome as one might imagine. For one thing, it aroused the suspicion of self-delusion. Perhaps we were seeing moral significance where there was none, spurred on by intuition alone, plus the understandable desire to salvage the time and effort that had already gone into our observations. During the course of our observational work our chief means of overcoming that suspicion was by reflecting on our individual notes and holding regular discussions among ourselves about the possible moral content of what we had seen. We now invite our readers to decide for themselves the legitimacy of the inferences we have made.

Another question that our seeming success brings to the fore is whether we could have missed if we tried. Might what goes on in classrooms be so chock-full of moral significance that its manifestation would be seen no matter where we looked or what we recorded? The brevity and seemingly inconsequential quality of many of the excerpts that we have treated in this chapter could possibly be taken as additional evidence that the task calls for little in the way of human judgment. Indeed, given the apparent ubiquity of what we were looking for, the reader might reasonably wonder why we used human observers at all. Perhaps a mechanical device, such as a tape recorder or video camera rigged to go on and off at random intervals, would have done just as well!

As to why we think that would not have worked, we can only report that during our observations we seldom, if ever, felt the urge to note everything that was going on around us. Instead, some events, and many aspects of the situation that did not qualify as events, invariably struck us as being noteworthy in moral terms, whereas others did not. We do not claim that our judgment was infallible, or that we never allowed noteworthy happenings to slip by unnoticed. Quite the contrary: this must have occurred frequently. But we believe that not *everything* must be held up for inspection, the way a tape recorder or a camera would do. A search for the morally significant calls for human judgment, which is far from infallible, but absolutely necessary.

Having claimed that there is much going on in classrooms that does not need to be seen as moral, as well as much that can be, we should also point out that the distinction between the two does not reduce to the difference between the dramatic and the mundane. This, too, is something that the observations discussed in this section should have helped to make clear. It is an especially important point to make within the context of today's rejuvenated interest in moral education, for in many current discussions of that topic what is considered to be moral is presented in terms of "problems" or "dilemmas" or "situations" that the individuals involved are expected to solve. Typically, the situations under discussion are fictional and the circumstances surrounding their problematic conditions are fraught with human drama and emotion, such as the much-discussed case of the man who had to decide whether to steal medicine for his ailing wife. No one could possibly deny the occurrence of such microcosmic melodramas, for much that goes on within the lives of most of us, including much that deserves to be thought of as moral, has that kind of bounded, situational character about it. It is also the case that in real life many such situations turn out to be quite memorable, which only makes them stand out all the more.

What our observations cause us to doubt, however, is the adequacy of coverage that such a framework of discussion allows. For if our classroom observations reveal anything at all about where to look for information about moral states of affairs, it is that no type of event, activity, or physical object is constitutionally incapable of conveying information of a moral kind.

As our observations have made clear, even something as. seemingly trivial as the way a teacher enters the room or the way he or she stands about while waiting for the class to come to order can be morally revealing to those who attend closely. The same is true of the way students behave, of course. With them, too, the slightest gesture or turn of the head can speak louder than words, and its message is often decidedly moral in both tone and substance. The physical environment sends out its moral messages as well. The dog-eared display on the bulletin board speaks of neglect, the flourishing plants reveal a history of care, the room as a whole gives off an atmosphere of diligent effort or of confusion and chaos, and so on. The attentive classroom observer is surrounded by moral signals of all kinds. The trick in seeing them resides chiefly in a readiness to do so and a willingness to ponder painstakingly the significance of matters that are commonly overlooked.

The observations featured in this part have focused on the teacher. Who is this person? What is he or she like? What kind of moral environment is being created? We have sought to answer these underlying questions by musing on the significance of what was reported. Our justification for that focus, should any be called for, would simply be that the teacher is the most important person in the room, bar none, from both an instructional and a moral viewpoint. He or she sets the tone of the verbal exchange that takes place throughout the day and establishes the atmosphere of calm or vexation that characterizes the room as a whole. Students also contribute to those ends, of course, and conceivably there may be situations in which their influence surpasses that of their teacher. Normally, however, and certainly in all four of the classrooms from which the observations in Part Two were drawn, it is the teacher who leads the way in such matters by dint of ascribed status and acknowledged authority, not to mention the possession of superior social skills.

Our focus on the teacher has in each instance yielded mixed results. In place of a straightforward answer to the question "What is this person like?" we have usually come away with a heightened sense of puzzlement. On one hand, we invariably have wound up with the feeling of having come to know the observed teacher at least slightly; on the other hand, we have often been left wondering why he or she behaved in a certain way or what a particular piece of behavior expressed in moral terms. Thus, our emerging judgments have often been tinged with doubt.

This ambiguity of interpretation and the accompanying feelings of ambivalence are hardly surprising in light of the small number of observations on which we have had to base our judgments. But it is not just the scantiness of the observations that accounts for the uncertainty of our conclusions and their tentative nature.

Our acquaintance with another person often grows irregularly rather than building up brick by brick, like a wall of masonry. Each encounter may add something to what we knew before, but it may also call for *subtracting* something that we hitherto believed. Today's experience forces us to revise what we thought yesterday; tomorrow's may do the same. That process of gradual modification took place as we worked our way through each set of classroom observations in this section. Although the final result in each case has been an increased sense of familiarity with the teacher in charge, the change seldom occurred in anything like a linear fashion.

The inconclusiveness of our commentaries also has to do with the fact that people are themselves inconsistent and sometimes even contradictory in their actions. Teachers, of course, are no exception to the rule. This is not to say that general characterizations of what they are like as people — calling them trustworthy, honest, and so forth — are always inapplicable. But even a teacher whom we confidently describe as being a generally honest or trustworthy person may surprise us from time to time. Indeed, such a person may turn out to be honest in some respects and dishonest in others, trustworthy under some conditions but not under others. In addition, as we have seen, the same act may yield competing interpretations, depending on the observer's point of view. Should we call Father Maran solemn or serious as he stands before the room with his head bowed? Or might he be neither? Could he only be putting on an act? Questions such as these are usually resolved by continued observation, but a residue of doubt may linger for quite a while and may even increase over time. In the extreme case we may never be able to make up our minds.

We began this chapter by saying that we hoped it would illustrate the process of reflection and rumination by which the expressive dimensions of the teachers' actions and the classroom environment as a whole gradually become known to us. We end it by stressing the unending nature of that process. There will always be further questions to ask, new observations to make. No matter how long we look or how many questions we ask, we will never fully fathom the expressive significance of all that lies before us as we gaze upon the classroom world. Nor will others easily exhaust the possible meanings of the reports we bring back. This is what we meant in our introduction when we characterized our descriptions and commentaries as "open works," invitations to further questioning and thought.

Having said all that, however, we also must acknowledge that the same conclusion could be reached about the world outside classrooms as well. There too the expressive abounds, its nuances remaining inexhaustible for those who are willing to look and to question what they see. This leads us to wonder how to decide when to terminate or even to begin such a process. Rephrasing the question to keep it within the confines of the topic at hand, when does it make sense to go looking for the expressive dimensions of a teacher's actions — or a whole classroom, for that matter — and when might we be better off overlooking such matters and trying to adopt a more matter-of-fact perspective? Also, in acknowledgment of what has just been said about there being no natural end to the process, when is it okay to quit?

With respect to our own work, the answer to those questions has not been all that difficult. We began looking almost before we knew what it was we were looking for. Therefore, we never did make an explicit decision to set off in search of the expressive dimensions of the teachers' actions. The importance of such qualities slowly became evident to us during our repeated visits to the classrooms. As for the decision about when to quit, that was more or less made for us by economic considerations. Basically, we stopped when we ran out of research funds, although we must also say that by that time (some two and a half years after starting), we had begun to feel that our overall perspective on the topic had solidified and that further observations likely would not alter the major points we believed our work permitted us to make. Chief among those points was our conviction that the expressive dimensions of what teachers say and do are fraught with moral significance.

So much, then, for our own decisions, or lack thereof, about when to go looking for such matters and when to stop doing so. But what about the advisability of others adopting the same outlook? If we assume for the time being that our own observations plus our commentary on them have succeeded in convincing our readers that the moral dimensions of teachers' actions really do exist and that those actions frequently convey moral messages of many different kinds, what do our readers (or anyone else, for that matter) stand to gain by going off to look for such things on their own? Won't their doing so simply confirm the conclusions offered here?

At this point, the difference between our research project and more conventional research efforts comes into play. The goal of most research is to produce a set of findings about some phenomenon that increases our understanding of its attributes or the way it relates to other aspects of the observable world. Our inquiry shares that goal in at least one important respect. We, too, wish to call attention to one or more aspects of teaching, and of classroom life in general, that are customarily overlooked or do not receive the full attention due them. In this sense, our gradual "discovery" of the importance of the expressive dimension of teaching might be classed a "finding," much like those of conventional studies.

However, when the outcomes of our work are viewed more expansively, its central "findings" are seen to have as much to do with *how* teaching and classroom life in general might be looked upon — namely, from an expressive point of view — as with *what* they are like as phenomena, though the two questions turn out to be inseparable, as our work also revealed. So it is true that we *are* advocating a practice, a way of looking at teachers and classrooms and a way of reflecting on what is seen and heard. Therefore, questions about when to apply that way of looking and when to cease doing so are indeed relevant and need to be addressed. To rephrase the question about when to begin (as the general reader might ask it): What are the circumstances under which a teacher or anyone else should consciously choose to become sensitive to the expressive goings-on within a classroom?

One difficulty with the rephrased question, which was also true of its previous versions, is that it implies a capacity to engage or abandon voluntarily the way of looking that we have been discussing, to turn it off at will. This implication is at least partially at odds with our own experience as both observers and commentators. While it does seem to be the case that we may consciously decide to be more or less attentive to the expressive dimensions of our experience, which would include our experiences in classrooms, it is also true, or has seemed so to us, that once we have adopted such a point of view there is no turning back, no way of abandoning it completely. Once the expressive dimensions of teaching — or anything else, for that matter — have come into focus and been kept there for a time by continued questioning, there seems no way of returning, at least not permanently, to our prior innocence — that is, to a view that overlooked such matters. To the extent that this is true, the question of when to adopt such a point of view is in some sense academic. It only needs to be asked once and the chances are that even that is unnecessary. For to ask the question "Should I cultivate expressive awareness?" implies that we already know what such a point of view entails, which would mean that it has already been adopted. However, since it remains true that we may be more or less attentive to the expressive dimensions of our surroundings and since the process, once embarked upon, can consume a considerable amount of time and energy, the question of when to commit ourselves to that kind of looking still must be addressed.

It may not be a very helpful answer to that question, but the best one we can come up with is to say that we should adopt the kind of orientation demonstrated in this part whenever we wish to become more than casually or superficially acquainted with a teacher or a classroom environment. Why should we wish to do that? There are countless reasons, but the two that come most readily to mind are those connected with being either a teacher evaluator or a student. Students obviously have a built-in reason for wanting to get to know their teachers and their classrooms as completely as possible. Their fate depends on such knowledge. Teacher supervisors and others who may be offering teachers advice about how to improve their work also have a vested interest in wanting to get to know the teachers with whom they work. Those who find themselves in either of these two positions would be well advised to pay particular attention to the expressive dimensions of what is going on around them.

There is a third group, however, for whom such an outlook is also crucial, one that is fully as important as the two that have been mentioned and possibly more so. It is made up of teachers themselves and of those preparing to teach. Such individuals are invariably called upon to become better acquainted with particular teachers, students, and classrooms. They need to learn how to view people and situations expressively, not because they risk suffering the consequences of failing to do so, as do students, or because they are responsible for evaluating or otherwise supervising the teachers they might chance to watch or read about, but because their performance on the job depends upon their ability to probe beneath the surface of classroom phenomena. This means, in a nutshell, coming to appreciate the expressive subtlety of much that lies before them, waiting to be interpreted.

In this part we have sought to illustrate, through the presentation of many brief observations followed by extended, impromptu commentary, the process by which an expressive understanding of classroom life might be developed. Our focus throughout has been on the teacher as the embodiment of a particular set of moral attributes. In Part Three, we will continue to use observation plus commentary to explore the moral significance of teachers' actions, but we will expand our focus of concern to include thoughts about the physical environment and about the overall experience of the students in each of the classrooms. We will also look more closely at some of the moral ambiguities and tensions that lie beneath the surface of teaching.

⮦ PART THREE ⮧

Facing Moral Ambiguity and Tension:
FOUR MORE SETS OF OBSERVATIONS

In this part we continue the practice of offering brief vignettes from our observational records, followed by commentary. As before, these observational materials have been chosen because, in our view, they say something important about the moral environment of the classroom from which they were drawn. This time, however, we will allow ourselves to roam a little more freely than before in the kind of reflection and questions that the observations occasion in our minds. We also will encourage our readers to do the same by presenting them with questions from time to time that point beyond the limits of our own speculations. An alternative way of proceeding that some readers might prefer would be to pause after each observational excerpt in order to formulate questions of their own and then ruminate on them for a while before proceeding to our commentary. That way they may avoid having their thoughts prematurely influenced by the range of interests and concerns that guide our remarks. This procedure will permit only a partial degree of freedom, of course, for the observer's decision about what to report inevitably sets limits on the reflections the observation itself occasions.

What distinguishes Part Three from Part Two is more, however, than just the range of our reflections. Having demonstrated our point of view and revealed some of the ways in which teachers embody positive moral attributes, we now want to show the inexhaustibility of our expressive perspective and the un-

fathomable complexity of moral life. As we move to this deeper
level, readers will discover a somewhat more negative tone in
the commentary, in that we raise disturbing moral questions
about pedagogical actions. This shift in tone is a direct result
of our digging deeper, not a judgment on the teachers we describe. Like the teachers observed in Part Two, all four of the
teachers described here have spent many years in classrooms
and are well established within their profession. At the time we
observed them each enjoyed an enviable reputation in his or
her school. Moreover, we ourselves came to respect and admire
each of these teachers for some of the qualities that show up
in these observations and for others that do not appear. But even
the best of teachers have weaknesses as well as strengths. In that
respect they are like us all. Those we are about to describe are
no exception to that rule. We could easily have presented only
flattering portrayals of each of them, much more easily, we suspect, than for many teachers within the same schools. Our goal
in this book, however, is neither to praise nor to blame individual teachers for what they do. Our sole reason for including
glimpses of a few of their less than admirable actions — unflatter-
ing snapshots, one might call them, the kind that make us laugh
or frown when they get passed around among friends — is to show
how morally complicated teaching becomes when our gaze is
brought down to within inches of its warp and woof, as the outlook we are discussing here tends to do.

I

The first set of observations begins with comments about the physical environment of the Catholic high school for boys in which we observed. It then proceeds to describe a ninth-grade English class in that school, taught by Mrs. Johnson, a well-dressed woman of motherly disposition, who is nearing retirement and who has spent most of her teaching career (over twenty-five years) as an elementary teacher in the public schools. Mrs. Johnson has been working at the Catholic high school for the past three years.

On one side of the corridor outside Mrs. Johnson's room is a set of a dozen or so 11" × 16" posters celebrating the lives and careers of successful African American scientists and inventors [the entire student body of the school is African American]. However, unless the passersby are as tall as basketball players they must crane their necks to read what the posters say, for the latter are positioned well above eye level, atop the rows of student lockers that line the hall.

On the opposite wall, across from the classroom door, hang maps of African countries drawn by Mrs. Johnson's students. Some of the drawings are elaborately and carefully executed, using many different colors to represent topography, crops, mineral resources, and so forth. Others look as though they had been dashed off in seconds. One map of Sierra Leone, for example, consists of little more than a blue penciled, peanut-shaped outline in whose center the country's name appears in misshapen letters. On the left side of the peanut are the words "Western Province" and on the right side,

"Eastern Province." That's all there is to it. Yet this
crudely drawn "map," if that's the word for it, is
as prominently placed as the ones over which other
students have obviously labored.

This brief description of the posters in the corridor gives
rise to a number of questions that anyone interested in the moral
environment of schools can hardly avoid pondering. Let's start,
as the observer did, with the ones depicting the achievements
of African American cultural heroes. We have no difficulty imagining the reasoning that gave rise to their being there. A teacher
or a school administrator or possibly a committee of mixed mem-
bership, maybe even including a few students, probably thought
that it would be a good idea in a school serving an all-black student body to surround the students with as many positive role
models as possible, which would include bringing to their attention the achievements of prominent African American men
and women throughout history. The row of posters above the
lockers is the result of that line of reasoning.

The most obvious question to ask about these posters is
the one implied in the observer's comments—that is, why are
they placed so high on the wall that it takes someone with the
height of a basketball player to read them? The quick answer,
which is that they can't be placed any lower because the student lockers are in the way, is not very satisfying, for if they
are so hard to read one naturally wonders why they were put
up at all. Might their out-of-the-way placement be an indirect
expression of the school's indifference to the goal of providing
adequate role models? Or is it, rather, that whoever is responsible for their being there believes that the sheer number of
posters (close to a dozen), plus the obvious fact that each depicts
the achievement of an African American person, should be
sufficient to have a positive role-modeling effect even if passersby
cannot read the print that explains how the featured individual
earned his or her fame? The latter possibility may not be as outlandish as it may at first seem, particularly if we consider the
typical placement of portraits, statues, busts, and other commemorative depictions of cultural heroes that we commonly

encounter in public buildings, which also may be placed well above eye level.

Having raised the question of what moral functions might be served by the likes of these posters, we are led to wonder about a host of related issues having to do with the moral significance of decorative and artful portrayals of famous people. Think, for example, of Peale's unfinished portrait of George Washington that used to be ubiquitous in the classrooms of our nation and is still to be found in some of them. What, if anything, does such an object accomplish from a moral point of view? For those who bother to look at it and who recognize the person portrayed it certainly serves as a constant reminder of what Washington was supposed to have looked like, and it may also trigger a number of random thoughts about the man himself—that he was our first president, led our nation's troops in the Revolutionary War, was spoken of for a time as the father of his country, and so on. Might it also cause the viewer to reflect on the fact that after more than two centuries we continue to honor the man and his deeds? Possibly so, although such thoughts are more likely to be the outcome of a teacher-inspired activity, such as a social studies lesson or a program on Presidents' Day, than to arise spontaneously.

It is also curious that such portraits are usually to be found only in public spaces, such as schools or courthouses, rather than private ones. Very few of today's homes, we would wager, contain portraits of Washington or any other political leader or war hero. Yet many contain pictures (usually photographs) of family members. Does this happen because pictures of public figures belong in public places and those of private citizens in the privacy of their homes? That would seem to make sense. Yet we also know that American adolescents commonly hang pictures of movie stars and sports figures in their rooms and they are certainly public figures. It seems that certain kinds of public figures— "serious ones," let's call them—are legitimately displayed in places like schools, whereas others, like rock idols and movie stars, are much less likely to be found there.

Returning to the pictures of the African American heroes hanging in the corridor, we are left with the impression that

they are not to be taken very seriously, even though the reason
for having them there was clearly a serious one. Does their placement trivialize that serious purpose? Would it be better if they
weren't there at all? We leave those questions to our readers,
trusting them to see beyond to the important educational issues
that such questions foreshadow.

The student-drawn maps on the opposite side of the corridor raise a different set of issues, but ones that are also fraught
with moral significance. There is first the question of what such
an exercise, the actual drawing of the maps, might be expected
to accomplish. The second question is what the display of those
drawings might yield. And, finally, there is the issue that seems
uppermost for the observer, which is the inclusion of poorly executed drawings in the display.

We pass quickly over the question of what Mrs. Johnson
might have had in mind when she assigned the map-drawing
exercise or what she might have hoped it would accomplish, for
there seems nothing about the exercise per se that gives rise to
moral questions, although we might wonder about the appropriateness of such a task for high school students, a question that
does have moral overtones and one to which we shall return.
Nonetheless, asking students to draw maps of the countries they
study is such a routine assignment that we will not pause here
to query its educative value. The fact that the drawings are of
African countries seems to go hand in hand with the character
of the pictures on the opposite wall. Presumably school officials
or at least some of the school's teachers give special emphasis
in their instructional program to the geographical and cultural
heritage of African Americans.

The question of why such drawings are on display is also
hardly worth intensive scrutiny, given the pervasiveness of such
a practice throughout today's schools. The display of students'
work is a common feature of classrooms everywhere. However,
the question of what such displays are supposed to accomplish
does entail some assumptions that are explicitly moral in character and, therefore, worth considering. The most obvious reason
for putting students' work on display is to provide an opportunity
for the students to be proud of their accomplishment. A drawing

or written document that is available for everyone to see bears an implicit stamp of approval from the person responsible for the display, which usually means the classroom teacher. "Good work" is the unspoken label that all such displays carry. What makes that a moral judgment is an additional understanding, also tacit, that good work is done by good students. Thus, the map or the drawing on the wall — which is almost always signed, so that the person who made it can be identified — entails a double commendation. The first is for the quality of the work itself, and the second is for being the type of person who does good work.

There is something a trifle odd, however, about a display of objects like maps or spelling papers that are not themselves pleasant to look at, with little or no redeeming aesthetic value. We can understand how a teacher might wish to commend a student for work well done. And if the object is intended to be aesthetically pleasing, such as a painting or drawing, we can also understand its public display. But why display, for days and sometimes for weeks or months, objects whose only value is that they are examples of good work? The answer to that question, though not a very satisfying one, rests in the commonly held belief that, at least within schools, good work, in and of itself, requires or deserves a kind of lavish praise and acknowledgment that it would not receive elsewhere. Do we assume that children and adolescents require this kind of praise if they are to be properly acculturated to the role of student? But if teachers and other adults recognize that such objects are truly not worth looking at in their own right, might there not be something disingenuous and perhaps even condescending about such a practice?

It is with those questions in mind that we turn to the observer's remarks about the poorly executed map of Sierra Leone. It seems rather evident from the details of his description that he was surprised by the crudeness of the drawing and was puzzled or perhaps even annoyed by its inclusion in the display. What seems to be at issue here is the principle of restricting such displays to examples of good work, rather than extending them to include work in general or, in the extreme case, as seems applicable here, to cover poor work as well. In short, if every student's drawing is to be put on display, regardless of its quality, does that not vitiate the idea of using such a practice to reward and encourage good students? Moreover, from a moral point of view, is it not in some ways *unfair* to those who worked hard and did a good job to have their work displayed alongside that of students who seem almost to have flouted such standards of excellence?

It is possible, of course, to imagine a set of conditions under which the display of the poorly drawn map would make ethical and moral sense. Let's suppose that the student who drew it was handicapped in some way — visually impaired, perhaps, or even mentally retarded. We might then judge such a drawing to be very good work under the circumstances and not at all a flouting of commonly held standards of excellence. The observational record does not allow us to determine whether such unusual conditions held in this particular circumstance, but it certainly occasions reflection on a range of moral issues having to do with the display of student work.

The observation continues:

> The classroom is bright, with three banks of fluorescent lights overhead. Opposite the door are large windows, extending from desk level to the ceiling. They look out over the playing fields of the school, and beyond to a high wire fence that separates the grounds from an old brick apartment building.
>
> The teacher's desk is just inside the doorway, turned at an angle that requires everyone entering the room to steer around it to take a seat. It is covered with books, papers, photos, baskets containing student writing, and various folders. Even its drawers look crammed.
>
> The desk's clutter plus the highly personalized character of the room's decorations signals a single adult occupant. Unlike most high school teachers in public schools, Mrs. Johnson does not have to share her room with colleagues.

The back wall of the room has a wide bulletin board covered with commercially produced prints of scenes from an African village: men and women working, dancing, singing, children playing, tending goats or cattle. Above the board, in 9" black letters that stretch almost across the whole wall, is the message, "Today Is the First Day of the Rest of Your Life!" In the corner by the windows are two file cabinets filled with stacks of poster paper of various colors and sizes as well as various writing instruments.

On the wall opposite the windows, and just to the right of the door as one enters the room, are pictures of Martin Luther King, Jr., and Harold Washington [then mayor of Chicago]. There are also some newspaper clippings about the school and about the education of black youth.

To the left of the doorway is a collage made of photos cut from magazines. Most are of young men and women, a few of whom are instantly recognizable (e.g., Michael Jackson). The rest seem to be models cut from advertisements or articles. At the bottom is a picture of a professional basketball player dunking a ball. Next to the collage is a blackboard that extends the length of the room. On the board, in three columns, are the names of several well-known American and English poets, mostly white. The board is empty except for these names, which are a bit smudged and look as though they have been there for some time. Across the top of the board are pictures of several of the poets on the list. Above those pictures and almost reaching the ceiling are posters with nature scenes. One shows a forest lake, deep blue and shimmering beneath a pale blue sky dotted with cumulus clouds.

Along the front wall is yet another blackboard. Between it and the corner of the room nearest the door, the wall is covered with pictures of famous

black Americans, including one of Harriet Tubman.
On the far side of the blackboard are more posters.
Four of them are identical. They show a photograph
of a smiling black adolescent. Below each photograph, in bold print, are the words "YOUR MOVE,"
plus the name of the school, "ST. NORBERT's." To the
left of the words "YOUR MOVE" on each poster, Mrs.
Johnson has appended a message. On one it reads,
"To like yourself"; on another, "To be an 'ordinary'
person"; on a third, "To improve your grades"; and
on the fourth, "To relate to others." Below three of
these posters is another one of a Franciscan monk
dressed in the traditional brown robes. He is pour-
ing from the spout of a watering can a shower of
little red hearts onto a blond-haired girl. The back-
drop is a green field, a few trees, and a blue sky.
In blue letters at the bottom are the words, "Love
Is Our Business . . . . . . The Franciscans."

Above the center of the blackboard is a television that is sometimes on just before the start of
class, particularly if it follows one of the teacher's
free periods.

The observational record contains further description of
the room's physical condition but since the observer next turns
to the description of a particular teaching practice, this seems
like a good place to interject some commentary. The central
question, of course, is what to make of all the pictures and posters
displayed about the room, not to mention the teacher's cluttered
desk and the views from the tall windows that look out on the
school grounds and the neighboring buildings. The room seems
to be exceptionally busy from a visual perspective. What does
that busyness add up to from a moral point of view?

The most noteworthy feature of the majority of the room's
visual messages is their blatantly moral tone and content. They
exhort their readers or viewers to start afresh, to like themselves,
to love others, to work hard, to improve their grades, and so
forth. They also contain plenty of reminders of what a virtuous

person might accomplish. These reminders mainly take the form of pictures of people whose fame has rested on their adherence to a demanding moral code of one kind or another, whether achieved in artistic or public spheres of endeavor. Even the nature scenes and the pictures of the African villages might be said to broadcast a moral message, though not as blatantly as the others. They speak of an earth that is serene and beautiful, filled with loving and caring people — a peaceable kingdom. They say, "Regard this earth and the beauty it contains. See its people at work and play. Be thankful for these things and seek to preserve them." In short, the room overflows with moral advice and exhortation. In fact, it rather resembles the teacher's desk in that regard. One might almost speak of it as being "morally cluttered."

Beyond offering a variety of moral messages of a generic nature, applicable to everyone, many of the photographs and posters are also chosen to address an audience of young men of high school age who also happen to be African Americans. The focus on youth in general and on black culture in particular — its heroes, its geographical origin — stands out as blatantly as does the overall moral tone of much of the material. In short, the room's decorations are obviously designed to speak with special force and directness to its young inhabitants. Another way in which the posters and pictures respond to the local audience is by their focus on Saint Norbert's itself and on the moral values of the Franciscan order whose priests and brothers run the school.

But what does all this particularizing mean? Are these the kinds of messages that today's young African Americans take seriously? Do they even notice them? Or are these appropriate questions to ask? Might the *expressive* significance of all the posters and signs have little or nothing to do with their explicit message?

Consider this possibility: imagine that what the signs and posters truly express is Mrs. Johnson's worries about the future of these young men, her hopes for their success, and her best guess about how to address that state of affairs. Why else would anyone go to such lengths to decorate a classroom in that manner? Seen in this light, the big message of Mrs. Johnson's room goes something like this: the teacher in charge of this room obviously cares a lot about her students, for she has gone out of her way to surround them with messages of encouragement and support.

But other messages can also be derived from that same set of conditions, not all of them as positive as the one just imagined. For example, by focusing on the kitschlike quality of many of the displays, we might conclude that what they express above all is an excessive degree of sentimentality, a kind of pie-in-the-sky optimism, ill-suited to the interests of high school students and to the realities confronting many of today's African American males. From this point of view, the equivalent big message would proclaim: the teacher in charge of this room is out of contact with the psychological makeup of her students. She surrounds them with decorative material better suited to a third- or fourth-grade classroom than to a roomful of teenagers. (In this regard, we might recall that Mrs. Johnson spent most of her career as an elementary school teacher.)

These two readings are not incompatible, of course. It is quite possible that Mrs. Johnson cares a lot for her students but does so in ways that are developmentally inappropriate. It may also be the case that what at first appears to be ill-suited to a particular group of students is later seen to be appropriate when more is known about the students themselves and about other things that go on in the room. Either possibility prompts us to return to the observational record for more information about what Mrs. Johnson is like and what goes on in her classroom.

In the corner next to the front windows are more file cabinets. They contain stacks of binders, one for each of the students in Mrs. Johnson's five English classes (two ninth and three tenth grades). The binders, some of which lie on top of the cabinets, contain all the written work (mostly compositions and poems) and exercises (grammar, spelling) the students have turned in so far this year. (These become each student's property at the end of the school year. Until then they are free to inspect their binders anytime they wish but they cannot

remove them from the room without the teacher's
permission. Mrs. Johnson likes to make sure that
her students don't lose any of their work.)

Mrs. Johnson often gives me some of the
binders to look through. They contain many corrections of grammar and spelling in red ink. Beyond an occasional "good" or "very nice," there are
no comments on the content, form, or structure of
the compositions.

The binders sometimes contain a short letter or two from her, addressed both to the student
and to his parents or guardians. One letter that
warned a student that he was falling behind con-
cluded: "It's important you know how much I care
about you." Another that praised a student's work
ended: "I'm so proud of you, you have it all together
this year."

There is also a large binder on top of the file
cabinet that contains letters and cards to Mrs. Johnson from students, parents, fellow teachers, and administrators esteeming her and/or thanking her for
some service she has rendered. The first few cards
are from three years ago, when Mrs. Johnson began to teach at Saint Norbert's.

Mrs. Johnson's practice of having her students collect all
of their graded papers in individual folders that are taken home
at the end of the year brings to mind the "portfolios" currently
being advocated by many of today's experts in educational evaluation. As the experts describe them, these portfolios, containing samples of students' work, are designed to replace standard
evaluation procedures based solely on test scores. However, our
purpose here is not to applaud Mrs. Johnson for keeping up
with the latest developments in the field of educational evaluation (assuming her to be aware of those developments), but to
reflect on what the student folders might contribute to the room's
moral environment. How should we interpret their use in expressive terms? Is it to be read as an extension of the teacher's

concern for her students, one more sign of how much she cares about them? Or should we see it as something else, a means of self-aggrandizement, perhaps (remembering the uppermost binder, full of accolades to the teacher), or a way of impressing parents and classroom visitors with the sheer amount of work undertaken in the course of the year?

A part of what we need to know in order to answer those questions is how Mrs. Johnson makes use of the folders, if she does at all. But even with that knowledge, the laudatory comments contained in some of the folders, plus the fact that Mrs. Johnson, we are told, "often" gave the observer a set of folders to look through (did she force them on him?), make it rather apparent that the folder project as a whole is a source of pride for the teacher. In her eyes, at least, it expresses something good. But is it a *moral* good? It is to the extent that it bespeaks an attitude of caring on her part, which it almost seems designed to do. (Recall the written comment to a faltering student: "It's important you know how much I care about you.") However, having acknowledged that to be so, we must also voice some misgivings about the moral worth of the project, based on other things the observer says.

Why, for example, do the papers in the folders show grammatical and spelling corrections but little or no substantive criticism of the written work? Are the former simply a lot easier to make than the latter? If so, we might begin to wonder how much Mrs. Johnson truly cares about helping her students improve in their work. At the same time, if she is teaching five classes a day, totaling more than a hundred students, could she reasonably be expected to be any more thorough in her corrections than she is? All we can do is register a doubt about this matter.

The most puzzling element in the account of the folders is the presence of the separate binder devoted to letters of praise honoring Mrs. Johnson. That item is not really part of the student folder project per se, but since it lies on top of the cabinet that houses the folders, it was grouped with them in the observer's report. We can readily imagine a teacher who is beloved by many, as Mrs. Johnson appears to be, cherishing the letters and cards written to her over the years and wanting to preserve them in a scrapbook or folder of some kind. The only thing that makes such a folder unusual in Mrs. Johnson's case is the prominence of its display. There it sits, out in the open for all to see. "Well, why not?" a friendly voice might inquire. "She is obviously proud of the abundant praise she has received." "Yes, and justifiably so," might come the reply, "but isn't it a bit unseemly to flaunt that praise as she seems to be doing? Doesn't it signify immodesty at the very least and perhaps a trace of insecurity as well?"

The difference of opinion contained in those hypothetical reactions calls our attention to the potential difficulty of trying to come to an agreement about the moral significance of an item as enigmatic as Mrs. Johnson's scrapbook. Actually, it is not the scrapbook itself that is enigmatic. Rather, it is its *placement* that raises eyebrows and explains why the observer bothered to mention it at all. If the scrapbook were kept in a desk drawer and only brought out and examined in private or shared on occasion with a few intimate friends, its moral significance would alter dramatically. But placement alone is not the key to understanding, as the remarks of our hypothetical commentators reveal, for one of them sees nothing at all wrong with having the scrapbook where it is, whereas the other interprets its prominence as an act of immodesty and wonders whether it might also express some basic insecurity on the teacher's part. Which of them is right?

The answer we would give is that neither one is right in any absolute sense. The placement of the scrapbook contains no fundamental moral truth that one of the onlookers sees and the other misses. However, our two hypothetical observers inhabit different moral worlds; they speak different moral languages. The first believes that it is perfectly acceptable to boast of one's accomplishments; the other does not. The first subscribes to a moral code whose tenets call for awards and honors to be displayed with pride, along with badges, titles, and any other insignia of status and accomplishment to which one may have legal entitlement. The other belongs to a community of belief whose members look upon the majority of such displays as being in poor taste. In the latter community the place for most letters of commendation and insignia of honor is the family strongbox or the proverbial attic chest, full of mothballs and memorabilia.

In our view, such differences are cultural, even though the people they separate may live next door to each other or may be members of the same family. Indeed, they may even be the same person, for who has not struggled from time to time with the question of which code to follow? Our calling them cultural only signifies that each embodies a coherent perspective on the question of what to do about such matters. It does not mean that the two views, placed side by side and examined carefully, will turn out to be of equal worth. And it certainly does not prevent or even discourage the adherents of one perspective from arguing with those of the other over the relative merits of their respective points of view.

Returning to the folder full of congratulatory messages on the file cabinet in Mrs. Johnson's room, we are left with the question of what to make of it from a moral point of view. Should we read it as a sign of immodesty, or do we look upon it as perfectly acceptable and inconsequential, about as significant in moral terms as the rows of diplomas and certificates that typically adorn the walls of doctors' offices? One thing is certain: it seems pretty clear that Mrs. Johnson herself has no doubts about leaving the folder where it is. She apparently does not think it immodest to keep such material in a place where it can be readily examined by others. Moreover, it is doubtful that any of her students find its placement to be morally offensive or in poor taste. Why, then, do we bother with the possibility of an alternative interpretation?

We do so because we ourselves were surprised to find such a folder virtually on public display in the classroom. At first glance, we felt it to be of questionable taste, even though that judgment created a sense of guilt. Our guilt arose because the contents of the folder reveal Mrs. Johnson to be a person deeply revered by many who know her, including a goodly number whose knowledge of her is far more intimate and solidly based than any classroom observer or commentator on those observations could achieve. Indeed, during the course of the Moral

Life of Schools Project, we came to like Mrs. Johnson a great deal (and vice versa, we believe). In the face of all that praise and in the light of our own feelings, it may seem rather petty, if not downright disloyal, to call such a practice into question.

Yet our goal here is neither to extol Mrs. Johnson's virtues nor to find fault with what she does. Instead, our goal is to illustrate a process, a way of looking at classrooms, and in so doing to reveal some of the confusion and conflict that often attends that process. The truth is that no teacher is morally perfect, no matter what perspective on his or her work we might choose to adopt. Nor is anyone else, quite obviously, including classroom observers and those who comment on the observers' notes. It is inevitable, therefore, that those who look carefully at what is going on within almost any classroom are bound to see actions by the teacher that appear to be of questionable moral value or that they think they would do differently under similar circumstances. The thing to do when that happens is to avoid jumping to the conclusion that the observer or commentator is right and the teacher wrong. What to do instead is to take note of these misgivings, reflect upon them later, and seek to integrate them with an emerging sense of what is going on within the room as a whole.

With that caveat in mind, let us return to the observational record.

There are thirty movable desks in Mrs. Johnson's room, arranged neatly in five rows of six desks each. Each desk has an armrest on which to write and, beneath its seat, a wire basket to hold books and papers. The largest of Mrs. Johnson's five classes contains twenty-three students.

Hanging from the bank of lights nearest the window is a row of haikus written by Mrs. Johnson's students. Those on display change every few days, which ensures that every student will have his work exhibited. Each haiku is written on a sheet of poster paper strung from a coat hanger. Most are covered with collages of pictures cut from magazines.

Interspersed among the pictures are the words of the haiku. Some reflect considerable effort; others look as though they were made in a hurry. One of the posters features a farmland scene with birds. These pictorial fragments surround the words: "Green fields and meadows, happy flying birds." Another has drawings and cutouts of several rainbows, interspersed with the words: "The rainbow shows the colors of our spirit."

For two more paragraphs the observer's comments remain concentrated on the physical setting. Why did he bother to mention the number of desks, their features, and their physical arrangement, together with the statistics revealing that there were seven more desks than were needed in the largest of Mrs. Johnson's classes? Is he only trying to help us imagine what the room looks like or might he be inviting us to wonder why the desks aren't arranged differently or why Mrs. Johnson retains more of them than are needed, thus making the room unnecessarily crowded? We surmise that both questions crossed the observer's mind, although whether they did or not is less important than the question of how we should respond to them here. Should we pause to reflect on their significance? Are they *moral* questions in any way?

We have suggested repeatedly throughout the preceding sections that there is practically no aspect of classroom life that is completely devoid of moral significance. To find that significance, we have suggested, all we need to do is to look at things from the proper angle or ponder them sufficiently. The way desks are arranged in classrooms and the overall aura of spaciousness or crowdedness conveyed by the presence or absence of furniture are surely not exceptions to that rule. Desks lined up in neat rows convey a greater sense of order and control than those that are more haphazardly or informally arranged. Crowded environments, especially if they have a lot of superfluous and unused furniture, create the impression that a room was designed for some function or group other than the one that is using it. Both of those interpretations resonate with moral overtones. The room's formality or informality relates to the way authority is exercised. Its spaciousness or crowdedness, particularly as they relate to the activities going on within the room, speak to the planning or lack of it that has gone into the room's design. That, in turn, says something about the degree to which the planners have taken the needs of those who are present into account. However, there are lots of reasons why a room may have more furniture than it needs. Similarly, there are reasons beyond those of wanting to be neat and orderly that would explain why classroom desks would be lined up in rows rather than arranged in some other configuration. Thus, without adding a great deal to the observational record, about all we can do with the information contained in this brief paragraph is to file it away for further reference. These facts may become more pertinent as we proceed.

The description of the illustrated posters containing haiku is a rather different matter, for it contains echoes of the observer's comments about the hand-drawn maps of African countries displayed in the corridor. Once again we are presented with a contrast between works that are painstakingly done and others that seem to be hastily put together. We are also given to believe that every student's work will ultimately be displayed. Furthermore, based on the examples given, readers who know something about haiku might begin to wonder what the students in Mrs. Johnson's class have been taught about this form of poetry or at least what they have come to understand about it. Do they believe that any combination of scenic phrases, such as "Green fields and meadows, happy flying birds," constitutes haiku? Finally, the description once again raises the question of developmental fit. How appropriate is it for a group of teenage boys to spend time leafing through old magazines and cutting out pictures to make posters of this kind? What is the educative function of such an activity? Doesn't it seem a bit more suited to elementary pupils than to high schoolers? Such questions may sound as though they had more to do with strictly educational matters than with moral ones. What gives them a moral cast is their linkage to issues of intellectual honesty and personal integrity.

The question of what students are taught and how well they are taught it is always, at heart, a moral question. This is so because education is a moral endeavor. Education's over-arching goal is to make its recipients better than they were when they began the process. It seeks to improve them in some way. This means that shortcomings in the delivery of educational services — giving students less than was promised them, for example, or less than they require to meet life's basic demands — are a form of consumer fraud, a way of shortchanging those being served. Giving students less than they are capable of handling, failing to challenge them, and treating them in ways that are better suited to much younger students are only variants of the same thing.

We certainly do not know enough from what has been described to accuse Mrs. Johnson of any such shortcomings. However, the suspicion that she might be demanding less of her students than they are capable of delivering, "babying" them, so to speak, is definitely aroused by what we have read so far. Is it fair of us to harbor these suspicions on the basis of such skimpy evidence?

One of the things we have learned from this form of inquiry is that it is always better to acknowledge, at least to ourselves, our tentative impressions about a classroom or a teacher than it is to deny them or brush them aside on the grounds that they are premature or hastily drawn. Moreover, it is essential to do this, we have found, no matter what the evaluative cast of those early impressions — that is, whether they are basically positive or negative. What makes this acknowledgment essential is that by bringing such biases to the fore, by facing them directly, we become alert to the possibility of their covert influence on our thinking. We position ourselves to counteract them by leaning hard in the opposite direction and being on the lookout for evidence that might contradict our initial judgment. In that way our immediate response becomes a tool for determining what to look at and listen to when we are observing or for deciding what questions to ask next when we are perusing the observational record.

Mindful of the advantages of that way of operating and having candidly stated the direction of our own biases so far, we now return to the observational record. This time we will follow the record to the end before adding our commentary.

Within seconds after the bell rings, announcing the end of first period (one of Mrs. Johnson's free periods), ninth graders begin entering the room.

Mrs. Johnson hovers about them. "Danny Jones! Take that coat off," she barks at a confident-looking fellow strutting to his seat. "Don't walk into my class with a coat on." Danny wheels about with an annoyed look on his face and heads out to his locker.

"Dion!" The teacher addresses a boy with thick glasses and a mischievous grin. "Put those shoes all the way on!" He complies while taking a seat.

"Tuck your shirt in, Wayne," she says, while giving the lad a gentle push toward his seat. "Put the hairbrush away, Anthony," she grins at another boy striding by. "Why, Robert," she says, while putting an arm around a thin youngster's shoulder, "how are you feeling today? You oughta take a spoonful of honey every day, that would stop you from getting all those colds."

A nearby laugh catches her attention. The laugh stops abruptly. "You really think you're cool, don't you, Andrew?" Mrs. Johnson coos at a tall, lanky boy. He brings his hand to his forehead in embarrassment. Some classmates, most of them settled in their seats by now, chuckle and grin. "With your fancy sweaters"—she strokes his arm—"and those silk socks"—some fellows guffaw at this—"but you weren't so cool when we had your father in here last week!" Andrew smiles good-naturedly as he seats himself amid laughter from his classmates.

Some boys are chattering and teasing as they position themselves in their seats; others are quiet and begin taking out pens and paper.

"Now, you *listen!*" the teacher calls out, gazing over them. "We're getting near to the fourth

quarter [of the school year]. I expect you to *know*
all those things I've taught you so far! Let's get our
act *together!*"

The class is still not fully settled. A few students exchange last words; others shuffle through
bookbags.

Mrs. Johnson continues her warnings. The
whole group now seems to be paying attention.
"When you were in elementary school, you probably thought very little about skipping school, any
old little thing would keep you home. But in high
school it's *different, any* day you miss can really put
you behind, so you have to really *try.* You need to
think about all the things you do."

"You really don't know yourselves yet at all,"
Mrs. Johnson continues. She surveys her students,
all attentive now, save for a few boys fiddling with
pens and papers. "That's what we're doing, and
that's what we're going to do today." She pauses dramatically. "Who am I?" she asks, a sudden frown
on her face. "Who AM I?"

Her voice turning gentler, she moves slowly
away from the desk. "Who am I? Like when you
enter school, you take off your earring [to follow
school policy]." To the amusement of many of the
boys, she mimics slowly the twisting out of a single earring. "Do I want to be cool? Do I want to
be a con [thief]? If I see a nice shirt in the gym,
and say 'Oh! that would look so *good* on me!,' do
I try to find a way to get it? Do I want to be a drug
user? A pusher? How does smoking marijuana
make me feel?"

A few boys in the back row have a daydreaming look on their faces; one is doodling with a pen,
another leaning his head on an arm staring out the
window. Most of the other boys are watching the
teacher.

"When I see Mr. Roberts [the school disci-
plinarian], do I try to slink up the stairs? Do I want

to get out of his way? What about William here?"
she suddenly says, walking over to a slight-looking
fellow seated by the window. She puts her hand
gently across the top of his head. "He's so sweet,
all the teachers say that, but we heard him last
week, sometimes he gets tired of that role, sometimes he curses, lashes out." She lifts her hand from
William's head and moves toward her desk. "So
which of these characters do you want to be? Who
are you now? Who do you want to become?

"What about Dion?" Mrs. Johnson continues.
"He used to do *nothing*, just *nothing*, all the time. Now
he can't stop working." Dion looks around at his
neighbors. "That's right," he says with a nod. "Yeah,
that's *right*," echoes the teacher. The boys murmur
and chuckle, trying to catch Dion's eye in order to
tease him.

"And you, Paul, you're a lover," she smiles.
A couple of boys grin. "I know you like girls, and
I know they like you. You're a ladies' man!" Paul
looks down at his hands on the desk. He seems to
be trying to keep a straight face. A few chuckles
are heard. A boy sitting next to Paul bops him good-
naturedly on the arm.

"And you too, Maurice, I saw you at the
dance. You held on to one girl like a leech, you held
so tight!" This brings a chorus of guffaws.

"Now, after you've decided on one of these
roles, write it down and tell me about it. But write
on just one. You're torn apart because you're trying to be so many people."

The boys begin to get paper and pens arranged. Some have already done so in anticipation
of being asked to write a composition in class. A
few begin writing straightaway.

"But don't write what you think I want to
hear," Mrs. Johnson interrupts. A few students look
up at her. "This is English class, you can write
whatever it is you want, I just correct your *grammar!*"

She smiles broadly at one boy in particular while saying this. He nods his head and turns to his paper.

The teacher sits down at her desk. She puts on reading glasses and begins perusing some papers. She soon pauses to write a note. "Clifford," she says quietly. The boy named, who is seated two chairs away, looks up. "Take this to Father Daniel in the office." Clifford takes the note, grabs the wooden pass off the front blackboard, and leaves the room.

A few moments later Mrs. Johnson looks out over her reading glasses: "Andrew, come here." Andrew, the tall boy who was singled out earlier because of his fancy clothes, struggles out of his seat and shuffles to the teacher's desk. He has to bend over to hear her while she talks in a low voice. She is pointing at what looks like homework. Andrew nods his head and shuffles back to his seat, taking a long look out the window while slowly easing back down.

Most of the boys are writing. Some look as though they were thinking about what to write. The classroom is quiet. After a while, those who seem to have finished their assignment begin to do other things. A few take out grammar exercises, one boy begins reading a paperback, another examines some papers in a small binder. A boy in the back puts his head on his arms.

"Are you finished, LaBradford?" Mrs. Johnson asks a boy near the front. "Bring it up here." In the next few minutes other boys bring their papers to Mrs. Johnson's desk. She reads through them and begins to read aloud from a few of them while seated at her desk. "'I am too complex to describe: arrogant, conceited, but also strong,'" she reads. Some boys are watching her; others are still writing. "'It's like a beach, all those grains of sand. I have knowledge of so many things, but I'm not a brain. I can be great like the beach, or small like one grain.' That's very nice," she smiles at Clifford. She turns back to the class: "Isn't it amazing what you can write once you start!"

She reads from another. "'I don't want to know who I am. I am mysterious and want to be that way to others.' I love it!" cries Mrs. Johnson, looking up at the class. "I just love it!" She continues reading from the papers, occasionally repeating "These are just beautiful!" or "I love this! I love it, I love it!"

Soon most of the boys seem to have finished. Looking up from her reading, Mrs. Johnson searches for Maurice. "What *would* you tell your mother, Maurice, about this girl you like? You should try to find the right time to tell her." This remark seems to invite commentary from others.

"I'd like to tell my mother," William blurts out, "that I don't like school as much as I did, there are other things." He is the boy Mrs. Johnson had mentioned earlier who had lost his temper in class the week before.

"Your interests have expanded, William. I've seen that in you," responds Mrs. Johnson.

"I don't like to be a goody two-shoes," another student complains. "I have to be a momma's boy all the time, but I'd like to *do* some things, some other things!"

The teacher's gaze sweeps the classroom. "Can't you all just *feel* what he's feeling just by look-ing at his face? *Can't* you?"

Other boys speak up rapidly:

"Yeah, my mother's always *checking up* on me, I don't like that."

"Well, for me, I'm talkin' on the phone, you know, and she'll always ask, 'Who is it?' Man!"

"I can take care of myself, but she never thinks so," says Paul. He grins, "She even kisses me good night still!" A couple of boys laugh.

By this time many of the boys are chuckling
and laughing with each other. Remarks about girls
and mothers fill the air. Mrs. Johnson looks wist-
fully back at Paul. "I know why she kisses you good
night, Paul," she says. "I do this even with my own
twenty-six-year-old son." There is sudden silence
in the room. Mrs. Johnson continues, "See, parents feel you slipping away. This is hard for them.
And parents are concerned, because there's so much
going on out on the street. They're worried you
might get in with a bad bunch, and they'll destroy
everything they've tried to do. So you see, you need
to remember this side of it."

The class is quiet for a time, but the buzz
picks up again as Mrs. Johnson continues to read
the compositions partly aloud, adding her own comments from time to time as well. She repeatedly says
how much she "loves it" (meaning some comment
she has just read) and that it is "amazing" and "wonderful" what one can write once one starts. As the
period nears its end the class has become boister-
ous. Several boys joke and tease about the comments they overhear their teacher reading. A few
whose papers have not yet been read call this fact
to the attention of their teacher. A couple of strag-
glers hand their papers in with an eagerness that
seems to say, "Read this one next."

Mrs. Johnson continues reading until the
bell. When it rings the boys spring to their feet,
packing up bookbags and tucking in shirts. They
wind their way out of class, calling out "Good-bye"
and "So long" to the teacher, while the next group
of ninth graders winds past them on its way in.

Coming to grips with the moral implications of a class
like this one is no easy task. Indeed, so much that went on during the session has such an explicit moral cast to it — Mrs. Johnson's intimate exchanges with her students, her reflections about

the importance of hard work, the self-descriptions asked for in the writing assignment, and so forth — that it is hard to know which of those elements to comment on first. However, far more pressing than where to begin our probings is the question of what to say about the apparent emptiness and triviality of the session from a purely academic point of view. For that negative judgment about the educational worth of the session thrusts itself upon the reader and begs for commentary even more insistently than do the obviously moral overtones of many of the exchanges.

What should we make of a high school class in which the entire period is devoted to the writing of a brief description of oneself, an activity that receives scant guidance at the start and one whose products are subsequently gushed over indiscriminately by the teacher? What is all that supposed to accomplish? And what of a class whose teacher announces, "This is English class, you can write whatever it is you want, I just correct your *grammar*"? What are the students being taught? If this class is typical of what goes on in Mrs. Johnson's room, wouldn't any fair-minded judge have to conclude that her students are being cheated of what is due them — academically shortchanged, shall we say?

The idea of being shortchanged connects with our earlier worries about the haiku posters hanging from the ceiling and the hand-drawn maps of African countries lining the corridor. Those worries were twofold. First, we were concerned that inferior works, including ones that seemed to have taken no effort at all, were displayed side by side with those that appeared to be painstakingly done. What worried us about this arrangement was that the inferior works were given as much honor and attention as the superior ones. Second, we wondered about the developmental appropriateness of both projects. Were they, we asked ourselves, better suited to much younger students than to boys of high school age?

Our current misgivings about the writing project resemble those earlier concerns. Again we wonder about the fairness of distributing praise uniformly to one and all. Though the writing project may not be better suited to elementary students than to high schoolers, we are once again struck by how undemanding the assignment seems to be. "Shouldn't their teacher be challenging them a bit more?" would be a polite way of framing the question. This apparent lack of challenge is what gives substance to the harsher accusation about the students being shortchanged.

However, returning to the subject of fairness, how fair is the accusation itself? After all, it is based on our reading of a single set of observational notes, covering one fifty-minute class period from among the hundreds of such sessions that constitute a year's teaching for Mrs. Johnson. Perhaps this was just a bad day for her or maybe the rationale for the writing assignment would make a lot more sense if it were placed within a larger context, if we could see, in other words, what came before it and what was to come after. The possibility of what statisticians refer to as "sampling error" seems far too great to sustain such a harsh judgment.

There are other worries as well. The order in which the notes are written, with the observations about the hall displays and the room decorations coming before the description of what went on during class, makes us begin to wonder if the observer might not have had his own suspicions firmly fixed even before the class began. His description of the maps in particular makes him sound puzzled and annoyed by the equal prominence given to all the drawings, good and poor alike. "That's all there is to it," he dismissively says of the crudely drawn map of Sierra Leone. Could that annoyance have carried over and affected his account of the class session? This is not to suggest that he made up any of what he reports having seen and heard. The detail and verisimilitude of the record satisfies us that this was not the case. But it is possible that another observer or even the same one under different circumstances might have given us a rather different portrayal of the same set of events.

Does this mean that through another pair of eyes, or the same pair focused differently, the poorly executed maps and posters might have looked like works of art and Mrs. Johnson might have come off as an intellectually demanding teacher after all? No, it does not. But it does imply that if the description of the class had been framed in a different way, if it had not been preceded by the remarks about the maps in the hall and the posters hanging from the ceiling, not to mention the details about the wall decorations within the classroom itself, our worries about the intellectual rigor of the assignment might never have been aroused or at least might have taken a back seat to some of the other features of the session that were also noteworthy.

Consider, for example, the playful banter between Mrs. Johnson and her students, which is reported in such loving detail and which reveals her acquaintance with her students' family life, their love interests, their pride in their clothing, and more. If we wanted to understand the moral impact of a teacher like Mrs. Johnson, might this not be a far more profitable focus of thought than the question of whether her students are being adequately challenged from an academic point of view? Or think about the praise she seems to lavish so indiscriminately on whatever her students hand in, good drawings or poor ones, hackneyed self-descriptions or ones bearing the stamp of originality. "I love it! I love it! Amazing! Wonderful!" she enthuses over the students' writing. And before long the young men in her room are practically lining up, self-descriptions in hand, to bask in the warmth of their teacher's admiration.

Think of that effusiveness in the light of Mrs. Johnson's many asides about drugs and crime and poverty and other forces as well (including girlfriends!) that threaten to lure her students away from their studies. Might more be asked of those students than the kind of wishy-washy assignment that dominates this particular lesson? Quite possibly so, and it may be, as we have said, that harsher demands are more typical of what goes on in Mrs. Johnson's room than this report of a single class session would have us believe. But even if it turned out not to be so, we still might wish to restrain our criticism. For one way of interpreting what is going on in Mrs. Johnson's room is to look upon her generous ladling out of praise as a kind of rescue operation, one aimed at kindling fresh interest in academic matters and at salvaging whatever interest is already there. And all of this, we must remember, is undertaken with young men who might otherwise fall by the wayside and perhaps even give up school entirely. What stands out in the observer's report is the personal touch Mrs. Johnson brings to her dealings with her students, a kind of motherly caring that is perhaps reflective of her days as an elementary teacher.

With our thoughts turned in this direction, we recall the folder full of praise that sits atop the file cabinet in Mrs. Johnson's room, the one containing letters and cards from her many admirers. What can we now say of that puzzling object? "We receive as we give" is one thought that such a look backward might occasion. For it certainly seems as though Mrs. Johnson has been treated in kind by her former students and friends. But, once again, why does she allow that praise to remain on what almost amounts to public display? Might it be because Mrs. Johnson, in her own way, is as needful of admiration and support as the students she serves? Is it possible that it takes such a person to behave as she does, to be as sensitive and responsive as she seems to be to her students' appetite (or is it also a need?) for praise and approval? If Mrs. Johnson did not feel natural behaving as she does, if her enthusiasms were not genuine, would they be as effective, would she have her students calling out to have their assignments read? Those questions lead to a host of others having to do with the sincerity of teachers and with the relationship between a teacher's personal needs and his or her capacity to serve the needs of others. We leave all such ponderings to the future delectation of our readers, although we cannot resist adding the hope that as they grapple with these kinds of questions they also think about the danger of making a summary judgment about any teacher on the basis of too little evidence and too little reflection.

Finally, does an appreciation of Mrs. Johnson's responsiveness to the needs of her students forestall any further questions or criticisms of the seemingly low level of the intellectual demands she puts before them? Certainly not. In all that has been said there is nothing to stop anyone from following up on those concerns and thinking about their moral implications as time and interest allow. Anyone who chooses to pursue them further, however, would do well to keep Mrs. Johnson's previous teaching experience in mind. Though we may continue to wish for more substance and higher standards in the curricular fare she offers her adolescent boys, we should not find it surprising to discover that a transplanted teacher of the very young, someone who has worked for twenty-five years or more in an elementary school, persists in old habits and continues to keep her classroom rather "elementary"-looking in both decor and intellectual content. This observation is not offered as an excuse for Mrs. Johnson's failure to challenge her young men more than she seems to do. Short change is still short change, no matter who gives it or how they do so.

II

The next set of observations describes a fourth-grade classroom in a public school. Its teacher, Ms. Morton, a neatly attired woman approaching middle age, teaches science to several sections of fourth graders. She also has one of those sections as her homeroom class. The first section of the record contains a lengthy description of a test-taking situation in one of the science classes, a situation that contains a lot worth thinking about from a moral perspective. The description is preceded by a short paragraph that sets the stage for the action to follow. Here is the entire section:

> One afternoon in December, Ms. Morton gave a science test to one of her groups of fourth graders, warning them beforehand that the test was "very difficult. In the past most classes have had to take it twice," she told them.
>
> A week later, she announced that she was giving the test again that day. "Obviously," she said, "there's something wrong with the test." She went on to suggest that perhaps the assignment was not well organized and maybe the material was too difficult. Also, she reminded the students that they had had to take the test in two parts — the first half on Monday, the second half on Thursday — which may also have helped to explain their poor performance. Finally, she posed the possibility that she hadn't taught the lesson properly. All of these were reasons, she said, why they might not have done well. "This is a smart classroom, and there are a lot of smart people in it," Ms. Morton said. Nevertheless, there had been only two A's and two B's, and, as she put it, "the rest of you got something you don't even want to know about."

In fact, though, they did want to know about it. Carlos raised his hand and asked, "Are we going to get the papers back?"

"Not now."

Several of the children began to call out, "Please! Please! Please!" but Ms. Morton was adamant. All she was going to do, she said, was to read the names of the people who had received A's and B's. Those with an A would not take the test again; those with a B could choose to take it again or not. Ms. Morton explained that she would throw out the lower grade of the two tests, because, she said, "I don't think the bad grades are entirely your fault."

After she read the names of the four high-scoring students, the two with B's decided they would rather not take the test again. The rest of the children, meanwhile, again began to plead to have the papers returned. Without hesitation, Ms. Morton refused. "I said I would return the first version when I return the second paper, because I don't want you feeling bad," she explained.

She walked around the room, pausing at each table to pass a stack of papers to one student whose job it was to give a copy to each of the others at his or her table. At table 5, she gave the tests to Paul. Before Paul could pass them out, however, Gordon stood up, reached across the table, and grabbed a test. Ms. Morton immediately told Gordon to stand up, walk to Paul, and give back the test. When Gordon had done that and returned to his seat, Ms. Morton said, "Paul, please pass that paper to Gordon."

As Ms. Morton was about to begin preparing for the test, Harold raised his hand to explain that he had no pencil.

"Your responsibility," said Ms. Morton, "is to walk in the room ready to work." She then went on with the preparations for the test, while Harold was left on his own to find a pencil as discreetly as he could.

The first step in taking the test was for the children to write their names on the test paper. They were then to put their pencils down. After that was done, Ms. Morton began to review the test. She moved from item to item, discussing each in a manner that almost gave away the answer. The particular wording of the answers was important, she insisted. "You can't be a good scientist unless you are very, very accurate."

Four times during the review, she noticed a student with a pencil in his or her hand, and each time she called the student's name and asked, "Why are you holding a pencil?"

At the end of the review, several students had questions, which Ms. Morton patiently answered. She had just told one of the questioners that his question was a good one "because it shows you're really thinking," when she noticed that the boys at table 4 had nearly finished with their test papers, even though she had not yet announced that they could even begin. They had obviously been writing their answers during the review. Ms. Morton immediately took the test papers, announcing that all four boys would receive a zero. "That is the same as cheating!" she said. "I wanted everyone to have an equal chance."

A few minutes after the rest of the children had started on the test, Sam (one of the boys from table 4 whose papers had been taken) raised his hand. Ms. Morton walked to him, and he pointed to table 5, saying, "Gordon started too."

"Are you tattling?" She turned around and walked back to her desk. But about five minutes later she strolled over to table 5 and examined Gordon's paper.

It is hard to comment on this segment of the observational record without sounding critical of Ms. Morton. She comes across in the report as a fairly stern and unforgiving woman who seems more absorbed with tests and grades than one might imagine a fourth-grade teacher would need to be. This is surprising for those of us who know Ms. Morton to be a reflective teacher, deeply committed to treating her students fairly. "Why design a test for fourth graders that is so difficult that most of the children who take it receive unsatisfactory grades and have to take it over again?" is the question that comes immediately to mind. Ms. Morton's various explanations for the initial poor showing of her students are not very convincing, perhaps because she offers too many possibilities and seems unsure of all of them. If there is "obviously" something wrong with the test, as she avows at the start, why does she continue to make use of it? Is it because it was so hard to construct that she cannot bear the thought of trying to make up a new one? Or could it be that this was a commercial test of some kind that Ms. Morton was obliged to use whether she wanted to or not? But even if the latter were the case, what shall we make of how she announces the grades — by reading the names of the four top students and then telling the others that their grades were so poor that they wouldn't want to know what they were? And what of her response to the boy without a pencil and her treatment of the boys at table 4 who begin to fill in the answers to the test questions before being given the signal to do so? Doesn't each of those actions leap out as being at least questionable, if not reprehensible, from both a pedagogical and a moral point of view?

We might begin responding to Ms. Morton's handling of her class by wondering if we are being fair in coming to a negative judgment so quickly. This line of questioning is similar to the doubts that troubled us regarding Mrs. Johnson and her seemingly undemanding curriculum. When we introduced our vexation in that situation we spoke of it as a statistical problem, having to do with sampling. The same worry intrudes here. What the question boils down to is whether Ms. Morton *typically* behaves as we see her doing in the test situation. If the

observer stayed around for a long time, might he see her behave the same way again and again?

That question is clearly pertinent if our goal is to come
to a conclusion about what kind of teacher, or even what kind
of person, Ms. Morton is. But that is *not* our goal. What we
are interested in is learning how to think about the moral environment of classrooms. We should be asking, therefore, not
what kind of person Ms. Morton is, but rather what it might
be like from a moral point of view to spend a day, or a year,
in her room. Yet those questions, as we have already seen in
our analysis in this and the previous section, are so closely intertwined as to be inseparable. Moreover, the speed with which
we jumped to a conclusion about Ms. Morton's handling of the
testing situation shows the priority of the more personal of the
two queries over the "cooler" and more intellectual formulation.
It seems that we just naturally rush to judgment when we witness an episode like the one reported above. We are quick to
see that Ms. Morton handled the situation poorly or at least
in a manner that could easily be improved upon. But what does
that tell us about moral matters as they pertain to classrooms,
beyond reminding us perhaps that some teachers don't behave
as well as they might? Is there any way of moving past our negative judgment to a more analytical, more insightful, and perhaps
even more charitable rendering of what the observer saw?

One way of doing this might be to ask what was wrong
with her behaving the way she did in each of those instances.
What rules were being broken? What code of ethics was being
violated? When we asked that question of someone who had
read the above portion of the record, her quick reply was: "Common sense!" Others would surely agree. We do ourselves, which
is why, in voicing our own sense of alarm, we spoke of what
"any sensible person" would do. But to accuse Ms. Morton of
lacking common sense is not a very satisfactory answer to the
moral questions; in fact, it is no answer at all. Though it may
leave us feeling satisfied as an expression of our impatience with
what we take to be her pedagogical faults, it certainly does not
advance our understanding of what is wrong and how to correct it or prevent it from happening elsewhere. Nor is it enough

to say that this or that aspect of her overall behavior should have been eliminated or done differently. The question is one of principle. What we want to know is what, if anything, was lacking in Ms. Morton's performance *in moral terms*. What kind of moral climate did her actions serve to establish? Or, in order to finesse our prior worries about statistical representativeness, perhaps the question should be phrased: What kind of moral climate would Ms. Morton's actions serve to establish if she persisted in behaving in a similar fashion throughout the school year?

Looked upon expressively, what seems to be lacking most in Ms. Morton's performance is a sign that she is sensitive to the psychological state of her students and cares about how she makes them feel. Her apparent insensitivity in this regard is evinced by several of the things she does. She administers a test that is admittedly too difficult for most of her students to handle; she tells the students that their first performance was too poor to report; she harshly penalizes a group of boys for what might have been an honest error; she accuses one of those penalized of tattling when he proceeds to point out that someone at another table behaved as he did, an action that could be taken as an expression of his sense of having been treated unjustly; she shows a complete lack of sympathy for the student who came to class without a pencil; and she carps about the premature picking up of pencils, which may only be a sign of the students' eagerness to get started.

When recited serially in that fashion, Ms. Morton's insensitivity appears to be blatant and severe. A year of living under that kind of authority would not be a very pleasant prospect from a moral point of view. What we must be careful of, however, is the intensification of the effect created by that kind of itemized summary and, indeed, by the observational report itself. We must remember that each of the actions that has aroused our concern was initially part of a larger context of activity within which the reported items were fragments. We also must not lose sight of aspects of Ms. Morton's performance that the observer glossed over rather quickly in order to concentrate on what doubtless struck him as being a set of rather questionable practices. For example, the review process alone must have consumed a lot of time. We are told that Ms. Morton reviewed each test item, one by one — in a way that "almost gave away" the answers, reports the observer — and that she "patiently answered" questions when the review was finished. Compared to the amount of time that total process must have taken, her sporadic admonishments about the pencils and even her reaction to the boys at table 4 probably used up no time at all. Yet they are what the report concentrates upon to the relative exclusion of the review. And understandably so, we might add. Our purpose in calling this imbalance to our reader's attention is not to criticize the report as being unfair or inaccurate, but to open the door to a new line of questioning. The fact of the imbalance prompts us to puzzle a bit over what the report might be saying about the salience of moral wrongdoing (or what might pass for it in the eyes of many) and the corresponding lack of saliency, if not invisibility, of certain kinds of virtue.

If we sat with a stopwatch in this class and counted the minutes during which Ms. Morton exhibited signs of patience and impatience — assuming that we could detect either attribute with equal ease — would there be any question of the results? We doubt it. We are confident that Ms. Morton, on average, would turn out to be far more patient than impatient. Moreover, if we could go a step further and divide all of her actions throughout the day into three broad categories — harsh, neutral, or kind — each pertaining to the quality of her relationship with her students, we think we know how that would turn out as well. Our guess is that the results would reflect favorably on Ms. Morton, at least in statistical terms. We suspect that far more of her actions would be judged neutral or kind than would be judged harsh.

But what would such an accounting come to? Would it prove that, in the final analysis, Ms. Morton was a patient and kindly teacher rather than an impatient and unkindly one? Certainly not, for we typically do not ascribe virtues or vices on the basis of such a tally. A single act of cruelty might be sufficient to label a person cruel, even though he or she was a model of kindliness most of the time, and this might be true of Ms. Morton as well. Following the rules that govern ordinary discourse, we may choose to describe her as harsh or impatient depending on a handful of things we see her do, no matter what the results of such an imaginary survey might show. But pinning a label on Ms. Morton is not what we are about here. Indeed, it is exactly what we have been trying to avoid doing. What we want instead is to imagine what it might be like, from a moral perspective, to live under her tutelage for a year or so.

The first thing we might imagine is that the day-to-day quality of life in Ms. Morton's room would vary greatly, depending on how frequently a student was the target of one of her complaints or criticisms. The youngster who was an A student and who always followed directions would likely have one type of experience; his or her opposite, quite another. But this does not mean that the inhabitants of the room can be neatly divided into those who are on their toes intellectually and who therefore escape Ms. Morton's admonitions and their hapless, slow-witted classmates who do not. For it is not always easy, even for those who listen carefully, to discern what their teacher wants. Consider the following episode involving a student named Naomi.

> Most of the students had finished an assignment and were killing time, waiting for the rest to be done. Ms. Morton stood behind Naomi, who was working on a handicraft project she had brought from home.
> "Put it away, Naomi."
> "But you said I could."
> "No, I said you could work on something. You knew what I meant."

Did Naomi know what Ms. Morton meant? We can't tell from the record itself, but it's easy enough to imagine that she might not have known, or at least that she was uncertain. And even if Naomi did understand Ms. Morton's explanation, we ourselves are left to speculate on how sensible this rule is. If the teacher really said, "You can work on something," as she admits doing, what's wrong, one wonders, with working on a handicraft project? Isn't that "working on something"? Ms. Morton apparently intended that students should work on school-work during their idle moments, but that restriction is not made clear in the wording that appears in the report.

So in response to the question of who experiences what in Ms. Morton's room, about all we can say on the basis of the evidence available to us is that though some of her students may feel their teacher's wrath or annoyance more than others (indeed, it is hard to imagine any classroom in which that does not happen), it also seems likely that very few entirely escape her admonishments and disapproval. For one hypothesis that begins to emerge from our perusal of the record is that Ms. Morton is frequently unclear about what she wants from her students. Moreover, her way of making her wants known sometimes complicates the matter rather than clarifying it. Consider, as an instance, her behavior in the following episode. No one is admonished, but an element of uncertainty is there all the same.

> One afternoon in December, the children from Room 101 came noisily into class. Ms. Morton said nothing, but walked from the blackboard at the east side of the room toward the windows on the north side, where she sat on the edge of a desk used for storage. After a few moments, she surveyed the children, who were still talking with one another, and said (without mentioning that she was quoting from Shakespeare's *Twelfth Night*), "She sat like Patience on a monument." About a week later, the same situation recurred. Again the children from Room 101 came in noisily, and again Ms. Morton walked deliberately from the blackboard to the desk by the window. There she sat and waited, though this time without the quotation.

This is a particularly noteworthy episode from a moral point of view because in it Ms. Morton likens herself to a statue of patience in order to communicate her obvious *im*patience with the students' noisiness. The use of a quotation from Shakespeare compounds the complexity of the message conveyed by her move to the far side of the room because it seems likely that no one but the observer understood the allusion. Why did she bother to mention it? Was it simply a reflex action or could she have believed that some of her students would know what she was referring to? Might she have been trying to impress the observer? The fact that she omitted the quotation the second time around leads us to choose the "reflex" explanation, but no matter why she said what she did, the pattern remains the same: talking or explaining things in a manner that keeps at least some of her students guessing.

We offer one more instance of the pattern before stepping back to ask what it might mean from a moral perspective.

> One afternoon in November, Ms. Morton started a science class by telling the children that the hamster cage hadn't been cleaned and that they needed to do that later on. Then she said, "All right, I see that most of you are ready to start. Some are not." What she wanted was for all the desks to be cleared, and almost everyone got the message. One girl, however, still had a notebook out a couple of minutes later, and Ms. Morton complained, "Why are you still working on that? Look around at everybody else's desk."

Once again we witness a situation in which a student is not listening carefully or perhaps does not understand what the teacher wants. (It is possible, of course, that this is an act of open defiance but that possibility does not seem to us very likely.) As the observer points out, what Ms. Morton wants is for all the desks to be cleared but that request is never explicitly made. All Ms. Morton says is that she sees that most of the students are ready to start. Presumably she is looking at the students' desks when she makes that observation but if a student does not notice this, her words alone would make it hard to guess what she wants.

Back to the question of what to make of all this. We can say that life in Ms. Morton's room is often trying, in both moral and intellectual terms, because often it is not clear what the teacher wants from her students. Moreover, this uncertainty extends from the questions on tests to the rules about how to prepare for instruction. Nor is it limited to intellectual behavioral matters; consider the following episode, which has nothing to do with them.

> While her students worked at their seats, Ms. Morton was at the bulletin board, putting up some of their artwork. Most of the pieces she was hanging were "invented creatures" made from a standard set of materials — a paper plate for a body and variously cut and folded bits of construction paper for limbs and a head. Before pinning each creature to the board, Ms. Morton would hold it at various angles, stepping back and scrutinizing it after each change in position. Several times she asked students how they would like their creature posed — Should the legs be bent or straight? Where should the arms be? Would the creature look better at this angle or at that angle?

What strikes us in this episode, as it did in the others, is that the students are again faced with questions that either have no answers or are frankly ambiguous. How do they know whether an invented creature made out of a paper plate and construction paper looks better turned this way or that? Should the legs be bent or straight? Should the arms be up or down? How can they tell? What does it matter? We are reminded of the questions to the science test that almost everyone failed. Will there be a second chance on this little quiz as well?

Perhaps that last question is too cynical. Yet it does seem rather unusual, or at least inappropriate, for a teacher to request a group of ten-year-olds to make refined aesthetic judgments about the proper angles of a row of anthropomorphized paper plates. Maybe Ms. Morton is only taking her students' work seriously, as any good teacher would be expected to do. But she appears torn between treating the students as the children they are and treating them as adults capable of guessing the meaning of elliptical questions and phrases such as "She sat like Patience on a monument."

Assuming our detection of a pattern within the reported episodes to be both accurate and fair (and we readily acknowledge that it may be neither), what are we to say of its moral significance? We have already suggested that by not making herself as clear as she might, Ms. Morton sometimes keeps her students guessing about what is expected of them. Imagine living under that condition for an entire year. Again we ask: what must it be like, what might it teach a student about teachers and about going to school?

When an authority figure like a teacher makes unclear demands, the most likely reaction on the part of those toward whom the demands are directed is to become unsettled and perhaps even a bit fearful. After all, authority figures have the power to wield sanctions of various kinds (grades being the most obvious ones for teachers), which makes it especially important to understand what they want. So the first thing we might guess about life in Ms. Morton's room is that the room's inhabitants may feel a bit edgy at times. This is not to say that her students sit around biting their nails, wondering what to do or worrying about when the ax of disapproval will fall. But we do recognize that the best way to get along in such an environment is to stay on one's toes, keeping an eye and an ear out for what the teacher wants and, perhaps even more important, for what she may want but doesn't bother to say. The necessity of maintaining that kind of vigilance probably has different consequences for different students, because it stands to reason that some cannot manage to remain alert and second-guess their teacher as well as others can. For those who can, life in Ms. Morton's classroom may be a bit less edgy than it is for those who cannot.

So being correct—having correct answers, being properly equipped, doing things when told, arranging things at just the right angle—all these matters are important in Ms. Morton's room. But isn't that so in classrooms everywhere? Aren't we always expected to do things correctly in school? Indeed, isn't that what school is all about? In a sense, yes. But the press for correctness (the moral pressure, one might say) is obviously more severe and unrelenting in some school settings than in others. From the observational excerpts we have read, we gain the impression that the pressure to be correct is somewhat greater in Ms. Morton's classroom than it might be elsewhere — in a room like Mrs. Johnson's, for example. What we began to worry about while reading the observational record from Mrs. Johnson's room was whether the teacher was being sufficiently demanding in both intellectual and moral terms. We were even led to use the concept of being shortchanged to express that worry. Now we find our worries moving in the opposite direction. Instead of wondering whether Ms. Morton's students are being shortchanged, what begins to concern us as we ponder the significance of the observations from her room is whether her students are being *overcharged* — that is, whether they are being asked to pay too dearly for whatever educational and moral benefits they may receive.

We also may begin to wonder, as we did about Mrs. Johnson's room, whether the direction of excess, if that's the way to put it, may not be an expression of the teacher's own makeup as an individual. In other words, could the pressure to be correct emanate from Ms. Morton's current or prior worries about her own proclivities toward inexactitude and error? In raising this possibility we are not trying to pry into Ms. Morton's private life as a clinical psychologist or a biographer might. Our goal is simply to suggest that the moral climate a teacher helps to create is usually one that he or she feels comfortable with and believes in, one that is an outward expression of a way of life to which the individual passionately subscribes. Teachers who place a heavy stress on honesty, for example, are more than likely those who strive to be honest themselves, or at least wish to be so when dealing with others. This does not mean that these people necessarily succeed in being what they want to be, but it does imply that those admired qualities rank high in their moral vision and very probably in their self-image as well.

But what about the idea of excess or deficiency? Why do we believe that Mrs. Johnson doesn't demand enough of her students or Ms. Morton demands too much? Those are judgments that almost jump out at us from the observations. "Common sense," we called them at one point. But those observations come to us from the eyes and ears of a human observer, which means they had to pass through the filter of *his* moral sensibilities, *his* sense of what is important, before reaching us. Moreover, we ourselves have gone far beyond those observations in our interpretation of what was seen and heard or, more accurately, of what the observer chose to report upon. Our interpretation adds yet another moral filter through which a portrayal of the teachers' actions has to pass. And the process does not end there, of course, for now our readers are called upon to respond to what we have told them. They too can only do so from within a framework of expectations conditioned by their own moral upbringing and understanding.

Does what we have just said imply that we can't believe anything about the moral worth of the teachers' actions? On the contrary, it means just the opposite. It means that we can't help taking a position and believing what we believe. Doing so does not prove us right, of course, nor does it close the door to a change of mind. But it does commit us to a position we must call our own, no matter how tentatively we may hold it and no matter how much we may wish to hedge our bets by saying things like: "It looks to me as though . . ." or "I may be wrong, but . . ." Does this reduce all our beliefs to the status of one person's opinion? Not at all, except in the trivial sense that every opinion does, indeed, belong to a single individual, or else it has no existence at all. However, we still must defend what we believe as individuals and, in so doing, seek to convince others of its correctness. The most persuasive of those opinions we rashly call the truth.

But what about the possibility of forestalling judgment, holding it in abeyance? Isn't that what we should be doing in cases like this? Shouldn't we avoid jumping to conclusions? Shouldn't we wait until all the data are in? Isn't that what we say teachers ought to do — not judge their students too quickly but, rather, remain open to new insights into their needs, capacities, and interests?

We have several answers to that spate of questions, some

addressing the topic in general, others specifically related to class-room situations. In broadest terms we certainly endorse the tenor of the questions themselves and the course of action they tacitly recommend. Of course we should avoid making premature judgments, especially in situations where doing so could possibly be damaging to those involved. A cautious attitude in such matters is always appropriate. At the same time, it is also true that we can't wait forever. The data are seldom "all in." There is always the possibility of error, yet we must proceed to make up our mind in the face of that uncertainty. (Teachers must do this all the time.) The general rule, then, boils down to rather bland advice: be cautious but not too cautious; circumspect, but still decisive.

When it comes to classroom situations, however, and particularly when it involves watching what teachers say and do as they go about their work, the temptation to judge impulsively and at times prematurely seems to us to be markedly greater than in many of life's other situations. Why might that be so? In our case, part of it is clearly personal. All three of us are teachers and have been for some time. Moreover, we have each spent an appreciable amount of time studying teachers and teaching from a variety of perspectives. Given that background and the work we are engaged in here, we can hardly avoid making evaluative judgments as we go along. Had we been carpenters or lawyers or something else entirely we might have been less inclined to be so judgmental.

However, though there is a piece of the truth in that explanation, it doesn't go very far in accounting for the impulse to judge that we acknowledge in ourselves and that we suspect persons who have never taught also feel when they are sitting in the back of a classroom or reading an observational record. What else might be involved? Part of it may be that teaching is a performance of sorts and to look upon a performance of any kind is to adopt a judgmental stance. When we watch a stand-up comic or an Olympic gymnast go through a routine we are keyed to exclaim, "That was funny!" or "That was good!" the instant they have finished, even if we have never ourselves told a joke in public or worked out on a balance beam. To perform is to be judged.

But teaching is a very special kind of performance, one that inclines us to be morally judgmental in a unique way. Unlike telling jokes in a nightclub or swinging from a high bar, teaching calls for our being involved with others the way parents are with their children or physicians with their patients. As with participants in both of those relationships, the bond between teacher and pupil is, or can be, intimate. And like doctoring, teaching is also a form of *treatment,* a way of trying to make people better than they are, which means that it is always legitimate to ask questions about how well or how poorly the teacher's students are being treated. And to raise questions about how one person treats another, no matter what the relationship, is to enter the domain of moral judgment.

To add to all of this, the kind of treatment teachers give is even riper than most for the intrusion of our moral sensibilities, because of its semipublic enactment (there are plenty of witnesses to what goes on) and because of the differences in power and status that mark the teacher-pupil relationship, differences that become most acute in classrooms serving the very young. In those classrooms, and in most others as well, though on a diminished scale, teachers are all-powerful, in the sense of having control over resources and over the basic structure of what goes on, whereas students are relatively powerless. This means that teachers are in a position to be kind or cruel, fair or unfair, considerate or inconsiderate, domineering or cooperative, as their fancy or their moral temperament suits them. (There are, of course, legal constraints to the way teachers can act. We are speaking here of their freedom to perform within those constraints.) They are also in a position to embarrass publicly or shield from embarrassment those students who exhibit weaknesses. Not even parents are positioned so strategically to perform as moral agents within a quasi-public arena.

Classrooms, then, are *morally charged* environments, fairly bursting with combustible particles in the form of incidents and objects that might readily spark an onlooker's sense of moral outrage or approbation. Indeed, this heavily charged atmosphere is ripe for these judgments from the moment class begins, and sometimes before it, as we have seen, so that it is nearly impossible to avoid them. Furthermore — and this is a point we take to

be crucial—the more we become accustomed to looking at classrooms in these terms, the more readily we do so until finally,
over time, almost everything we witness while there (or read
about later) begins to take on a decidedly moral cast.

But something else happens as well. With time, our judgments become less sharp-edged and more equivocal, and where
they are initially negative, they also become more charitable.
The reasons for these changes are many and some of them are
fairly obvious. We quickly learn, for example, if we did not know
it already, that classrooms are complex, as are the people within
them, teachers and students alike. This means that the more
we observe, the more we begin to see good *and* bad, and sometimes good *within* the bad or vice versa. We become aware of
extenuating circumstances and compensatory virtues, counter-
balances and tradeoffs, shadings and nuances. This does not
mean that everything turns from black and white to a bland
shade of gray. Just the opposite; it means that black and white
do not make a varied enough palette to capture what we witness. We are no longer concerned with assigning events a position on a scale that runs from black to white, or good to bad.
We move beyond approving or disapproving as we come to
recognize that although we feel uneasy about, say, Mrs. Johnson's uncritical acceptance or Ms. Morton's hypercritical standards, we would feel equally uneasy telling either of them to
act more like the other. We see the moral as being too complicated, too interwoven in the thousand particulars of a classroom,
to insist on erasing isolated behaviors from one setting or in-
serting them into another. What we see when we look in this
way is a more muted and subtle landscape than the one that
first greeted us—one more filled with questions than answers.

Nor do all those questions have to do exclusively with external sights and sounds. For as we grow more appreciative of
the complexity of classrooms, we also learn to listen more carefully than before to nuances of our own reactions to what is going on. We ask: What does that remind me of? Where have
I seen something like that before? Why do I feel slightly annoyed by that remark? How would I feel if that was happening
to me? Why do I find this incident compelling? What makes

this room such a comfortable (or uncomfortable) place to be? Questions such as these, whose forms are endless, grow more numerous and more insistent as time goes on.

The final observational segment about Ms. Morton is somewhat longer than the others. In keeping with what has just been said, it is also fittingly complex.

> One afternoon in January, Ms. Morton was working with her fourth-graders on the theme of relative position, a subject the class had been discussing for several weeks. She had the children move their desks to clear a space on the floor in the center of the room, and there on the floor she laid a poster on which was printed a circle with lines resembling the spokes of a wheel. The children gathered around the circle, and Ms. Morton began the lesson.
>
> First, she laid "Mr. O" down at the center of the circle. Mr. O is a wooden stick figure representing an observer. In many lessons, the location of objects had been described relative to Mr. O, and what Ms. Morton was doing with the circle on this afternoon was introducing a new degree of accuracy in the children's ability to specify a location.
>
> She put down a number of objects around Mr. O and asked the children to give the location of these objects relative to Mr. O. They were able to do this using "direction" words, such as left or right, front or back, and so forth. However, four objects were correctly located using exactly the same words, even though the objects were not in the same place.
>
> "What's wrong?" Ms. Morton asked the children.
>
> Several of them responded that a better method of locating was needed, some way of describing the object's location more specifically.
>
> "Now, what can we do to make it more specific?" she asked.

"Well," said a boy in the back, "we could number the lines."

This idea was discussed for some time, and eventually Ms. Morton brought up the idea of dividing the circle into 360 degrees. She marked one of the spokes of the wheel as zero degrees and then began asking students, one at a time, to mark what number of degrees other spokes of the wheel would equal.

They proceeded to do this without difficulty until Ms. Morton announced "I called on two boys the last two times, so I think I need to call on a girl." The girl she choose was Ella.

Ella was supposed to show where the 30-degree line was, but she put her "30" down on the 240-degree line.

A handful of children laughed at this obvious mistake, but Ms. Morton cut the laughter short, saying sternly, "The one thing that is unacceptable in here is to laugh at people who make a mistake." Then, while the other children waited, Ms. Morton discussed the problem with Ella. She explained that the spoke at the top of the circle was zero degrees and that, as one moved around the circle in a clockwise direction, the number of degrees increased, so that the zero-degree spoke was also the 360-degree spoke. She showed Ella where the 90-degree spoke was, and also the 180-degree spoke and the 270-degree spoke. Then she asked again where 30 degrees would be.

Ella still could not answer the question, and Ms. Morton went over everything again, spending several minutes in a one-on-one session with Ella. She stayed with it until Ella showed by her responses that she truly seemed to understand. Only then did Ms. Morton return to the rest of the class.

A short while later, Ms. Morton brought the lesson to a close, had the children move their desks back into the usual position, and announced that it was time to hand out report cards. "What I would like to do," she said, "is to advise you to take these very seriously." She explained how grades are figured and what they mean, she discussed the behavioral categories that are marked with a check instead of a grade, and she suggested that there is usually a correlation between the number of checks (indicating behavior that needs improvement) and the grades: fewer checks go along, she said, with better grades.

After this introduction, she had the children get their coats and bookbags and make themselves ready to go. When they were all dressed, packed, and ready to go, she stood before them with the report cards in her hand and said, "I don't think that this is something to talk about. I don't think your report card is anybody's business but yours and mine and your parents'." Then she moved from her desk to the door and said, "Before I pass this out, I think it's better that nobody ask anybody else what they got. Why is that?"

The children answered that the grades were private and just for themselves and maybe someone got a bad grade.

"How do you think that's going to make your next-door neighbor feel, that is, if your next-door neighbor got a bad grade and you got a good one?"

The children agreed that the next-door neighbor would indeed feel bad. Ms. Morton then began to call the children, one by one, and hand each his or her report card.

When Ella's name was called, she approached Ms. Morton and took the envelope with hands that were trembling slightly. She held it for a moment before sliding out the card. Then she paused again, holding the unopened card in her hand. Finally, she took a breath and slowly bent back a corner so that she could just peek inside. At the first look, her eyes grew wide, and she opened the card fully. Her smile filled the room; she even seemed to grow a little taller.

While this was going on, Ms. Morton had been approached by one of the boys in the class, one of the better students. He pointed to his card as if something was wrong with it, then showed it to Ms. Morton, who nodded.

She turned to the group and called out, "Ella! Ella, I think I've made a mistake. I think I may have given you the wrong report card. In fact, I know I have."

The switch of cards was made, and the boy looked satisfied. Ella approached the new card with less coyness than she showed before. She simply opened it. Her smile disappeared, and her shoulders sagged a bit. She pushed the card into its envelope and got in line.

Although the above observation reports on a single classroom visit, it covers two distinct, though interrelated, activities: the science lesson and the giving out of report cards. Each of those activities features a noticeable mistake, the first by Ella, the second by Ms. Morton. Let us examine each episode in turn.

Perhaps one of the reasons why the observer chooses to report on this particular lesson in the first place is his sense of irony contained in the contrast between the lesson's content and its enactment. He could not know at the start how deep that irony is to become before the session ends and the students file from the room. Here is a science class whose topic, relative position, also becomes its subtopic. While Ella struggles to understand where 30 degrees falls within a circle of 360 degrees, her classmates evidently have no trouble figuring out where Ella stands in relation to most of them. It is true that the poor girl finally appears to understand how to locate the assigned number, but only after a steadfast effort on the part of her teacher, during which the rest of the class waits quietly, fully alert to what is going on. The lesson of the day deals with relative position in a double sense.

Of course it is quite possible, even likely, perhaps, that most of her classmates already know where Ella stands in relation to the remainder of the class. This is probably not the first time that she gives an incorrect response and has to be publicly coached by her teacher. The laughter that greets her first attempt at an answer is a sign that something similar has probably happened before, possibly often.

Ms. Morton's sharp rebuke in response to the students' laughter is also noteworthy, because of the explanation that goes along with it. "The one thing that is unacceptable in here," Ms. Morton says, "is to laugh at people who make a mistake." Of course, having read the prior portions of the observational record, we know that it is not so. There are many things that are unacceptable in Ms. Morton's classroom; laughing at people who make a mistake is only one of them. It may be one of the most important ones, we grant, and perhaps that is what Ms. Morton meant to say. It certainly sounds like a form of misconduct a lot more serious than beginning a test before being signaled to do so or not bringing a pencil to class. Errors, Ms. Morton wants her students to understand, are no laughing matter. But it is not just that errors are to be taken seriously. What the rebuke seeks to avoid is the hurt caused by laughing at someone for something that person cannot help.

The laughter stops abruptly, we are told, but what of the attitude of derision that lies behind it? Is Ms. Morton's rebuke sufficient to squelch that as well? Probably not. It's hard to imagine a single rebuke having that effect. Yet doesn't her sharp retort have at least some effectiveness as an instrument of moral education? Do remarks such as that operate cumulatively? Do they erase a trace of whatever offensive tendency they are directed at each time they are heard? Are they like drops of water wearing away at stone?

The image of weathering is appealing for it combines the inevitability of long-term effects with the near invisibility of immediate consequences. It allows persons who administer such rebukes or warnings to remain hopeful of having helped to bring about permanent change in the absense of any evidence. Yet there is something troubling as well about the metaphor of erosion. It encourages a mechanistic view of a process that is probably better conceived in organic terms as opposed to mechanical ones. Perhaps such actions operate more like morsels of food that are slowly digested and finally assimilated into the body itself than like the forces of wind and rain that eat away at mountaintops. The image of digestion has the advantage of being better suited to our biological makeup as humans, though it does sacrifice the guarantee of both effectiveness and permanence.

Whichever conception we choose, the fact remains that the students who break into laughter at Ella's expense probably continue to feel derisive toward her even after the overt expression of their feelings has been suppressed by Ms. Morton's rebuke. Moreover, it is more than likely that Ella remains aware of her classmates' reactions long after their laughter stops. That being so, we begin to wonder about the moral climate in which Ms. Morton's instructions to Ella are enacted. The observer reports that for "several minutes" Ms. Morton concentrated solely on correcting Ella's misunderstanding about the degrees of a circle. Pedagogically, her actions make a lot of sense. What better time to correct a misunderstanding than when it first occurs?

But what of Ella's feelings as she undergoes remediation in the presence of those who laughed at her error? Isn't she likely to be discomfited, possibly embarrassed, by the attention she receives? Shouldn't Ms. Morton take that likelihood into account? Maybe she does so and then decides to go ahead with her tutorial anyway. Either way, the situation leaves us wondering how teachers customarily reconcile their sensitivity to the possibility of causing discomfort with their diagnosis of an obvious need for remedial instruction. Is this a moral issue? It is only if the teacher in question recognizes it to be. And we don't know about Ms. Morton's sensibilities on that score. But whether she sees it in moral terms or not, we can be fairly certain that the situation is a morally charged one for Ella and possibly for the class as a whole.

We turn next to the situation that surrounds the handing out of report cards. Once again, the teacher, through her

preamble to the distribution of the cards, seems to heighten tensions for the class as a whole. She advises the students to take
the cards "very seriously," explains the details of how grades are
reckoned and what they mean, and then cloaks the cards themselves in secrecy, warning that comparison of grades may lead
to hurt feelings. The buildup of excitement is almost theatrical.
Small wonder, given that introduction, that Ella's hand trembles
slightly as she accepts the envelope from her teacher. (Incidentally, we might wonder if the observer actually saw Ella's hand
tremble or only surmised that it did. A "slight" tremble is not
that easy to observe. However, the detail feels right, so we will
let it pass.)

The ensuing drama forms a minuscule tragedy of the kind
that used to delight audiences in the days of silent movies. From
the smile of pride on Ella's face we sense immediately that something is wrong. After all, this is the same pupil who just a few
minutes earlier was struggling to understand a concept that most
of her classmates seem to have grasped with ease. The boy who
approaches his teacher, pointing to his report card with a quizzical look ("one of the better students," we are told) solves the
mystery for us even before Ms. Morton's public admission of
error. The exchange of cards and Ella's downcast look provide
a classic anticlimax to the chain of events, bringing to mind the
pathetic figure of Charlie Chaplin trudging disconsolately down
an empty road that leads to the horizon as the screen image nar-
rows to a pinpoint and "The End" flashes on the screen.

What shall we make of Ms. Morton's error? What is
its moral significance? One answer might be poetic justice. A
teacher who dwells on the importance of being exact at the expense of being alert to her students' feelings and circumstances
almost deserves to be caught in an error of her own. But the
consequences of this error are so unfortunate that no one would
wish it to happen, not even in the interest of poetic justice. We
would all much rather that Ella be given the bad news at the
start, instead of having her spirits soar and then be dashed within
seconds.

The error is obviously an innocent one on Ms. Morton's
part, as such errors commonly are. She surely didn't try to be

hurtful to Ella; of that we can be certain. But at the same time she exhibits no signs of remorse, or at least none we are told of. Does she even realize the significance of what happened? We don't know that either. Perhaps she doesn't even think about it. After all, she has handed out some thirty report cards that day, surely a large enough number to almost invite an error or two.

And what about Ella? Does *she* think about the incident on the way home or are her thoughts preoccupied with the grades on her report card and how her parents will react to them? We know nothing about that either. She may shrug the whole thing off as casually as Ms. Morton seems to do and forget the incident entirely within minutes.

Given all these uncertainties, why should *we* continue to ruminate on such a trifling episode? What can we hope to gain by doing so? Surely our goal is not entertainment, no matter how much the reported vignette may resemble a scene from a silent movie. Nor are we out to malign Ms. Morton, who, for all we might say about her handling of this or that situation, we know personally to be a well-intentioned person who takes her work seriously and tries to do as well as she knows how for her students. Our goal of illuminating the moral dimensions of everyday teaching has compelled us to criticize certain of the things she is reported to have done, but nothing in the report leads us to doubt her sincerity and her dedication to teaching.

The chief reason for pondering the significance of such an event is very much like the reason for pausing to consider the effectiveness of Ms. Morton's rebuke to the class as a whole when some of the students laugh at Ella's error. Both situations cause us to wonder whether events like these have long-term consequences, even though their immediate impact may soon be forgotten. Might they add up, in other words, like the slow deposit of silt in a riverbed, until their cumulative effect finally becomes too massive and too enduring to ignore?

That possibility has intrigued any number of philosophers and psychologists who over the generations have sought to understand how people acquire their individual traits and characteristics. Emerson, for example, in his famous essay "Experience," toyed with how such things could happen. Reflecting on the ordinariness of much of our experience, he was led to speculate on the origin of some of our more admirable human qualities. Here are his words: "All our days are so unprofitable while they pass, that 'tis wonderful where or when we ever got anything of this which we call wisdom, poetry, virtue. We never got it on any dated calendar day. Some heavenly days must have been intercalated somewhere. . . . 'Tis the trick of nature thus to degrade today; a good deal of buzz, and somewhere a result slipped magically in."[8]

"Heavenly days," magical results—the language is quintessentially Emersonian, even though the idea is not exactly new. As others have done before him, Emerson, at least in the passage we have quoted, throws up his hands at the question: Where do our virtues, our poetry, and our wisdom come from? We acquire them as if by magic or by divine dispensation, he says. "Reasonable enough," we might say, in the light of how ordinary most of our days turn out to be. But Emerson's answer, though venerable, is not much help to educators who are called upon to behave in ways that might increase the likelihood of such "magical" or "heavenly" results. As a matter of fact, Emerson did not truly believe that answer himself. For on numerous other occasions, even in the same essay, he spoke with eloquence on behalf of savoring each moment of life, dull and ordinary though it may appear. Only by so doing, he claimed, can we possibly reap life's rewards. Here he is, for example, several pages past his conjecture about the intercalation of "heavenly days": "To finish the moment, to find the journey's end in every step of the road, to live the greatest number of good hours, is wisdom. . . . Since our office is with moments, let us husband them."[9] Or a few lines further on: "Without any shadow of doubt, . . . I settle myself ever the firmer in the creed that we should not postpone and refer and wish, but do broad justice where we are, by whomsoever we deal with, accepting our actual companions and circumstances, however humble or odious, as the mystic officials to whom the universe has delegated its whole pleasure for us."[10]

What Emerson knew, and we educators would do well

to ponder, was that his inability to trace the origins of his most cherished characteristics — wisdom, poetry, virtue — did not relieve him of the obligation to "husband" each moment and to "do broad justice where we are," no matter how "humble or odious" our "companions and circumstances." He felt called upon to behave, in other words, as though each of those moments was both independent of all others (a world unto itself) and causally potent (a small link in a chain whose terminus was a fully developed person). For Emerson, that way of behaving constituted a *creed,* a code of conduct that he vowed to follow in the absence of vouchable knowledge.

Let us now see what Emerson's position might mean with respect to what we have witnessed happening in Ms. Morton's room. The preceding phase of our speculation began by our wondering whether Ms. Morton or Ella or any of the other students present would remember for long what are, according to the report, the three most singular events of the afternoon: (1) the laughter at Ella's error, followed by Ms. Morton's rebuke to the class as a whole; (2) the tedium of Ella's remediation under Ms. Morton's patient tutelage with all her classmates looking on; and (3) the mix-up involving Ella's report card. If all three of these events passed quickly from everyone's memory (a distinct possibility, we acknowledged, though rather unlikely), why should we now focus our attention on them? Aren't they better forgotten by us as well?

The broad answer to those two questions, one that applies both to what went on in Ms. Morton's room and to all the other minuscule happenings that we have been chronicling throughout the last two parts, is that such events are far more important than they look, even more important in many instances than they are perceived to be by those who undergo them. They are so, in part, because they do not happen in isolation. They tend to recur, or ones very much like them do. This means that, formatively, they have the potential of adding up, over time, to a crescive force whose power far exceeds what any one of them might effect on its own. To dramatize that potential we drew upon metaphors from nature — the weathering effects of wind and rain on the earth's surface, the digesting of food, the slow depositing of silt on a riverbed. Something like the same thing could be happening to us as humans, we argued, for we all stand exposed to the "drizzle" of passing events. Like water on stone, these "droplets," too, have a weathering effect if they are continued for a long period of time, an effect far greater than we might imagine if we think only of the single event.

We find the metaphors from meteorology compelling, but at the same time we are forced to admit that we are making an analogy and nothing more. In the final analysis we must join Emerson and others in confessing that we really don't know what the long-term effects of all those passing and largely forgotten events might be. We can only *surmise* that they may have significant and enduring outcomes. Moreover, not only will the answer to the question of whether they do or don't never be known to us; it would not help us to know that answer even if it were attainable. For by the time we could find it out, the opportunity to change or to counter those conditions would have been long past. We would be in the midst of new circumstances and conditions.

Therefore, we who are educators, parents, or anyone else whose actions bear heavily on the lives of others have no choice, it would seem, but to act as though what we did in the way of modeling or setting explicit moral examples made a difference in the long run, even though we may never live to witness the fruits of our effort. That position is a *creedal* one in the Emersonian sense, in that it rests on a kind of faith in the efficacy of good works, bolstered perhaps by a set of personal recollections involving such actions by others. Such a policy is absolutely essential for teachers, even though they may never speak of it as comprising a kind of pedagogical creed. We witnessed it in operation in Ms. Morton's sharp rebuke to the class for laughing at Ella's error. We observed it in the conduct of Mrs. Johnson and that of the four teachers we met in Part Two. This moral posture lies behind all of the schools' efforts to convey explicit moral messages to students. Do such efforts work? Again, we will never know for sure, but there is a sense in which the question is deeply misleading, if not pernicious, in that it demands a kind of hard evidence that is simply not available. Our creed, which is to say our trust that those messages are being listened to and will pay off in the long run, forces us to behave as we do, as it seems to have done for Ms. Morton.

There is an additional creedal element that the events in Ms. Morton's room also bring to the fore, even though they do so in ways that we fear are not entirely flattering to Ms. Morton. This element is even more integral to Emerson's position — and to the conduct of teaching — than was the one concerning long-term effects. It rests on an appreciation of the sanctity of human life and on a corresponding wish to alleviate as much human suffering as possible, particularly those forms of suffering occasioned by the way we treat others. In crudest terms it entails doing what we can to avoid hurting our fellow beings. This doctrine often creates difficulties for educators, as it does for parents, physicians, and others whose job it is to care for others. For such remedies are often painful or discomfiting in their own right, even more, sometimes, than the condition that needs correcting. That seems to have been the situation involving the tutelage Ms. Morton gives Ella in the science class. We do not know for sure that Ella feels embarrassed by the experience, but it is hard to imagine that she is not. Might that embarrassment have been avoided without sacrificing the remediation of her misunderstanding? Our reading of the record makes us think it might have been, but we cannot say for sure, much less specify how the remediation ought to have been handled.

What of the mixup over the report cards? Does that too evince an insensitivity to what Ella might be feeling at the moment? Again, we can't say for sure, for it is possible that Ms. Morton is keenly aware of Ella's reaction but for one reason or another is unable at the moment to respond to it. At the same time, her apparent indifference leaves us wondering whether another course of action might have been taken. More importantly, the event as a whole heightens our sensitivity to the moral nuances of what goes on in classrooms and to the importance of thinking about the immediate quality of what is experienced there, quite independent of its future consequences. We trust this account will have a similar effect on our readers as well.

III

We next visit an English class in an independent high school. The teacher is Mr. Turner, a casually dressed man (pullover sweater, tieless shirt, and jeans) in his early fifties. The observational record begins with a rather full description of the physical setting.

Most of the seventeen juniors and seniors enrolled in this elective course in English are in their seats before the start of the period. Some talk with neighbors in subdued tones. I overhear comments about how tired some of them feel and about their biology projects that are due soon, as well as comments about some upcoming regional elections. A few are looking together at a section of the *New York Times* one of them pulled out of a bookbag. Other students look through books and other materials; a few sit with arms crossed and legs stretched out, staring at nothing in particular. An occasional laugh, or a stressed word or phrase, breaks the general calm.

The classroom itself is furnished with twenty-five Formica-topped desks arranged to form a square. There are a few stray desks and chairs in the corners of the room. The east wall, opposite the door, is composed of floor-to-ceiling windows, with the blinds usually pulled at least halfway down. Fluorescent light illuminates the room, shining off the desktops. The floor is covered with faded red carpeting, stained here and there and littered with small scraps of paper. To the left of the door, the wall is covered with a long bulletin board that is completely bare save for a yellowed clipping from a

German newspaper, with a photograph of a town and accompanying text. The other two walls, on the north and south sides of the room, are movable but have been pulled tight to convert the area into a self-contained classroom. The movable panels are made of a dull gray plastic material and look stiff, as if they have not been slid open for some time. On the middle sections of each are small blackboards.

There are a couple of shelves near the windows, empty save for a few pieces of blank paper and a dozen or so fat Webster's dictionaries (each with the room number written on its sides). There is no desk specifically intended for the teacher's use. There are no cupboards, bureaus, or closets.

The social atmosphere of the room is one of anticipation, as of a group of people waiting for something to happen, which indeed they are. Yet they are clearly not in a state of agitation, like the crowd before a football game. They seem more like a matinee audience at a theater before the lights go down — sophisticated, undemonstrative, subdued, close to being bored, perhaps, prepared for what is about to happen but not exactly sitting on the edge of their seats, waiting for it to begin.

The room itself echoes the aura of "general calm," as the observer calls it, although the description also brings to mind words like *lassitude* or *ennui*. The window blinds are halfway down, like a pair of sleepy eyes; the carpeting is faded and somewhat stained, strewn with bits of litter; the bulletin board shows signs of neglect; the shelves are nearly empty; the dictionaries are "fat," rather than merely "thick"; even the plastic room dividers are stiff with age and disuse. The picture we draw from the description is of a room that once was fresh and bright but now looks a bit seedy and shopworn.

What is interesting about this description from a moral point of view is how our reading of it is conditioned by our knowledge that the setting is a private school rather than a public one, a fact reinforced by the students' informal chitchat about regional elections and by the copy of the *New York Times* pulled from a bookbag. Knowing it to be a private school that serves advantaged and perhaps even well-to-do students allows us to look upon the signs of wear and tear within the room and even the indications of neglect with a rather different eye than we might adopt if the same features were found within a school serving the underprivileged. If this were a classroom in an inner-city school we might have felt indignation about the signs of neglect, and sadness about the rundown conditions in general. As things are, the room's features strike us as only a trifle curious and perhaps even mildly amusing. They call to mind the sense of security enjoyed by established wealth, such as the dowager who refuses to part with a favorite item of clothing that is now close to threadbare. They contribute to the feeling of comfort and ease that the students exhibit in their manner and their talk.

The observational record continues:

> The students continue to chat quietly as Mr. Turner enters the room. He arrives seconds before the official start of the class (there are no bells in the school). Mr. Turner carries a well-worn briefcase that looks full to bursting. His reading glasses are shoved to the top of his head. He looks around the class quickly while talking with a student who trailed in after him. As he takes a seat along the south side of the square of tables, he tells the student he should go ahead and make up the missed quiz during the boy's next free period. The student takes his own seat while Mr. Turner again looks around the room, while also pulling out his roll book. Looking down, he begins reciting last names, rather loudly. Meanwhile, students continue their low-key conversations, although they quickly interrupt themselves to call out "here" when they hear their names. A few stragglers rush into class and settle themselves.

The description of Mr. Turner matches the room's appearance in important ways. His last-minute arrival and the glasses worn atop his head signal a casualness and insouciance much like that of the students. "Laid back" would be the modern term for it. His "well-worn" briefcase fits the faded and worn look of the room. The fact that the case is "full to bursting" suggests that it may contain more material than is necessary for that day's teaching, which could mean that Mr. Turner has not bothered to remove the excess, perhaps a sign of neglect, though certainly not a troubling one. Mr. Turner's quick inspection of the room and his procedure for taking roll—calling out last names only while the students continue to file in and to chat among themselves—reinforce the feeling of comfort and relaxation that the room as a whole gives off.

The record continues:

> Mr. Turner looks over some notes written on an 8" × 14" yellow pad he pulls from his briefcase. (It looks like there are four or five such pads in his case; Mr. Turner teaches four sections of this course.) Most of the pad's pages are dog-eared. Meanwhile, students begin to finger their books (Melville's *Moby Dick*) or they pull them out of their bookbags for the first time. Then Mr. Turner gets up and walks over to close the door, an act that seems to cause the students' voices to drop suddenly and the general stir to cease.
>
> Retaking his seat, Mr. Turner looks around the class. He lowers his reading glasses, opens the text, then says matter-of-factly while checking his notes, "I'm not sure where exactly we left off."
>
> Six or seven students remind him: "We were talking about changes in the narrative." The class begins to buzz with conversation over what they had talked about last time.
>
> Mr. Turner asks, "Did we look at page 140 where Starbuck 'breathes in Ahab'?"
>
> "Yeah!" several call out together.
>
> "Okay, well, let's talk more, then, about Starbuck and his thoughts on Ahab. You wanna—"
>
> "—I have a question about this part on page 139," a student interrupts.

"Yeah, okay," says Mr. Turner, lowering his glasses and opening his book. The class suddenly fills with the sound of shuffling pages.

The student's query begins a thirty-minute discussion of Starbuck.

These opening moments of the class serve to reinforce the impression that has been building from the start. Mr. Turner's manner is casual and matter-of-fact. His easy confession of uncertainty about where the class left off last time reveals no sign of discomfort or embarrassment. The students also take the situation in stride and are quick to offer reminders of what went on before. The student who interrupts Mr. Turner with a question does so abruptly, without bothering to say "Excuse me" or to wait for him to finish his sentence. Mr. Turner's ready acceptance of the interruption with his casual "Yeah, okay" only reinforces the spirit of informality and relaxation that has already been established.

A question that we can't yet answer from the record (and may never be able to) is what the room's casual and informal atmosphere portends from a moral point of view. The students' readiness to help their teacher remember where to begin ("six or seven" responding at once) suggests that many if not most of them have a distinct memory of what went on before and seem quite ready, perhaps even impatient, to get on with the discussion. The collective "Yeah!" in response to Mr. Turner's query about page 140 expresses a similar sentiment. Those qualities might be taken as signs of student involvement, which could also mean a readiness to come to grips with the moral dimensions of the text they are studying. Mr. Turner's nearly used-up, dog-eared pad also hints of a teacher who either has taken a lot of notes in class or has done a fair amount of preparatory writing, either of which would indicate dedication to the task at hand. At the same time, the atmosphere as described generates the nagging suspicion that no one in the room, including Mr. Turner himself, is emotionally capable of getting very excited about anything. Everyone seems so cool and sophisticated that we begin to wonder whether such attitudes might actually be barriers to engagement in the kind of discussion that would touch responsive chords among the moral sentiments of those present. About all we can say at present is that the evidence we have seen so far leaves us uncertain as to how engaged the teacher and his students actually are.

The observational record continues:

> During the discussion twelve of the seventeen students offer comments and read from the book. Mr. Turner repeatedly queries, "What are we told about Starbuck?" and also repeatedly asks students to read passages aloud whenever they turn to the text. I count at least thirteen instances when a passage is read aloud and then discussed.

This brief paragraph is worthy of comment for the light it sheds on the question we have been pondering — that is, how engaged are the members of the class? — and for other reasons as well. What it says about the class's engagement in the discussion is basically positive. Twelve of the seventeen students present, we are told, participate in the half hour's discussion — a commendable percentage within that period of time. Mr. Turner's insistent query about Starbuck, together with his repeated request for the text to be read aloud, reflects his task-orientation and also his determination to keep the students' attention focused on the text itself, both signs of his own involvement in the task at hand, as well as indirect evidence that the students are correspondingly engaged.

Here a moral consideration intrudes. The fact that the students repeatedly read from the text (thirteen times in a half hour, we are told) speaks not only to their involvement in the class as a whole; it also says something about the amount of attention being paid to the author's exact words, which is, we believe, very much a moral matter. A close textual analysis is by its very nature a *respectful* reading, even if its goal is to disagree with or discredit what is being read. To take a book seriously is, at least in part, to attend to its details, to reexamine what is really said, as opposed to relying upon what we remember from a prior reading. That process is moral. It is akin to the respect we pay to others in a face-to-face conversation when we listen carefully to what they have to say and fashion our own responses accordingly. Its opposite, disrespect, is what happens when we ignore the precision of what others say to us, whether orally or in writing. In these terms then, by requiring the students to read passages aloud in order to support their own arguments or make their questions precise, Mr. Turner is forcing them to adopt a respectful attitude toward the text they are studying. That practice, we would insist, is a form of moral education.

The observation continues:

> The class stumbles over some of Melville's language. At one point Mr. Turner goes to one of the shelves near the window, takes down a dictionary, brings it to his desk, and looks up the root of *blasphemous,* which was Starbuck's description of Ahab's intentions. At another point, a girl reads a passage after which Mr. Turner promptly asks, "What does 'outward portense [sic], inward presentiment' mean?" The girl shrugs and looks back at her text. Other students do the same, although a number are taking notes and seem to be marking the passage as an important one. A few look expectantly at Mr. Turner.
>
> After a long moment of silence, he asks, "Well, what does Starbuck see when he looks out on the world? What is his view of life?"
>
> Hands go up immediately. Four students in turn offer new glosses on what the class has already said, emphasizing how careful and troubled Starbuck is, how strongly he is against the pursuit of the white whale. Mr. Turner returns to the difficult passage: "So what does portense mean? or presentiment?"
>
> "Portense maybe means ominous," says one boy, "like Ishmael's view."
>
> "Yeah," Mr. Turner confirms, "it's like the world is always full of signs to him, it's not just a physical world. And this is important for Starbuck, too, when he says it's blasphemous to go after the

white whale." Mr. Turner embellishes this point at
some length. As he does so, several students raise
their hands. They hold them up patiently for a time,
then begin to support them with their other arms.
Then they lower them in their laps as Mr. Turner
continues to talk.

This segment of the report contains a curious anomaly,
one that is at once ironic, mildly humorous, and instructive.
The segment begins with the announcement that Mr. Turner's
students are having some difficulty with Melville's language and
it soon reveals that they are not alone. The observer, too, stum-
bles over one of the key words in the text, the word *portents,* which
he misspells three times as "portense." In the light of his opening announcement, the observer's error becomes both ironic and
humorous. What makes it instructive are the questions it raises
about the limits of observational insight into the moral subtleties of the classroom experience.

The observer obviously could not have been following the
discussion with an open copy of *Moby Dick* before him. If he
had, he would have seen the word *portents* spelled correctly, in
which case it is unlikely that he would later have misspelled it
in his report. But if the observer was *not* following the discussion with book in hand, what does that say about his ability
to make sense of what was going on? Can he be in a position
to judge the moral significance of the students' experience if he
himself remains outside of it in this way? Is his experience so
different from that of the students that it no longer sheds light
on the ways in which they are likely to be affected? In this connection, we might also recall the statistics having to do with the
students' participation in the discussion. Clearly the observer
was making those tallies while the discussion was under way.
Could he have been doing that and listening intently to what
was being said at the same time? Possibly, but the fact that he
reports on only a small fragment of all that must have gone on
within the space of a half hour makes us suspect that he was
only half-listening at least some of the time.

These remarks call attention to the "outsider" status of

the classroom observer, whether he or she is a researcher, a teacher educator, a supervisor, or a parent. This status is inevitable, given the closed and private nature of classroom affairs, and it is both advantageous and disadvantageous with respect to thinking about moral matters as we are doing in this book. What makes it advantageous is the observer's freedom to remain disengaged from the topic under discussion or the lesson being taught and, thus, to attend instead to aspects of the interaction that might go unnoticed by the participants. Teachers themselves are often surprised by what observers report having seen in their classrooms. Of course, there is nothing unusual about this. It isn't that the observers possess keener insights than teachers, but as visitors, their attention is not tied to the task at hand the way the teacher's is.

The outsider status of the observer becomes especially disadvantageous, however, in a classroom as casual and laid-back as Mr. Turner's, because an observer has less to see there than in, say, Mrs. Johnson's or Ms. Morton's rooms, where the structure of class life and the emotions of the participants are so blatantly on display. The disadvantage becomes especially acute when the primary activity in this restrained environment is a close reading of a text — an activity that the observer cannot take part in unless he or she ceases to be a "reader" of the classroom. Are Mr. Turner's students deeply engaged in what they are reading and discussing? Are they taking to heart any of the moral messages implicit in *Moby Dick*? That's hard to say. The signs of their involvement are so mixed. Moreover, the text-specific and low-key nature of the exchange between teacher and students is not only difficult to read in moral terms; it is even hard to concentrate upon as an observer. This may explain why so little of what goes on during the half hour's discussion shows up in the report.

The observation continues:

> Mr. Turner finishes his talk by drawing attention once more to the meaning of words. "It's a difficult chapter," he interjects in the middle of his remarks. He gets up and draws a large circle

on the blackboard. "Think of this as the world of
the novel," he says, turning to face the class. Everyone is watching him. He looks back at the circle,
then grins and shakes his head. He puts the chalk
on the sill and retakes his seat while remarking,
"Well, you know what's going to happen if I try to
draw something here!" His students laugh for a moment, then Mr. Turner proceeds to articulate the
point he originally meant to illustrate.

As he finishes, two students (without being
asked or told) check the dictionaries in the back,
and, after waiting until an appropriate moment,
read the definitions.

The noteworthy element in this segment is an inside joke
that the students obviously get but that we readers, and probably the observer as well, do not. This also calls attention to
the differences in perspective between "insiders" and "outsiders."
What would have happened if Mr. Turner had continued with
his chalk diagram? We obviously can't say for certain but apparently it would have been funny. Perhaps Mr. Turner would
have gotten himself all mixed up if he had proceeded with his
drawing. Maybe that had happened before. Whatever it was,
Mr. Turner's memory of one or more such happenings gives
him pause. He grins, shakes his head, and returns to his seat.

What is interesting about this segment is Mr. Turner's
relaxed and lighthearted manner. He seems to be poking fun
at himself in a wry sort of way and the students respond in much
the same fashion. The joke is on the teacher, yet there seems
to be nothing derisive or scornful in the students' laughter. They
recognize that their teacher has humbled himself, and they find
that amusing, as does Mr. Turner. No one seems to take the
incident seriously and the class quickly settles down and gets
back to work; in fact, the incident sounds more like banter
among friends than talk between teacher and students.

Is there anything moral in this playfulness? There is if
we consider the lessons the students might learn. One lesson,
if we tried to spell it out more fully, would be something like:

"Accept your limitations gracefully, learn from past errors, and don't be afraid to acknowledge to others that you are aware of your own shortcomings." This could be an important lesson for Mr. Turner's students because, in their class discussions, they are frequently on the spot and in a position to make an error in front of their classmates. When Mr. Turner asks, "What are we told about Starbuck?" or "What does 'outward portents, inward presentiment' mean?" the student who attempts a reply may be shown up as a poor reader, if not simply wrong. Mr. Turner's way of handling his own shortcomings says to his students, "Don't be afraid to be wrong. Learn a little humility."

We need to modify this lesson, however, by recalling that Mr. Turner does not complete the picture he begins to draw. He does not wish to make too big a fool of himself. With this in mind, we may wonder whether his students might be learning not only to be humble but also to be restrained, to choose carefully which questions they will answer. There is, in short, an ambiguity: from one point of view, Mr. Turner is encouraging his students to talk about their ideas freely, without holding back; from another, he is warning them that their contributions should be well-thought-out answers, rather than impromptu speculations.

A separate moral lesson for Mr. Turner's students that is also contained in this segment has to do with teacher-student relations. Mr. Turner's comfort in joking about himself in front of his students is a sign of trust. He doesn't seem to worry about whether he can maintain his authority if he admits a weakness; he trusts his students enough to be open with them. Without relinquishing his role as the teacher, the one who asks most of the questions and judges most of the answers, he invites the students to be his friends.

The record continues:

> The class in general is almost always calm. Students follow each other's remarks, turn to passages together, watch their teacher. Some students take notes as the discussion proceeds. (At the end of the term Mr. Turner collects all their class notes and assigns them a grade.) Some students slouch

further and further into their chairs as time passes,
although they typically straighten up quickly whenever they contribute something to the conversation.
From time to time some students glance at the clock
or at their hands or at their feet. Occasionally a few
doodle or otherwise drift into daydreaming. Eyes
droop now and again. Mr. Turner seems unaffected
by these signs of passivity. He rarely calls on students, preferring instead to take comments from
volunteers.

The observer returns to a description of the class in general. His use of "slouch," "doodle," "drift," "day-dreaming," and
"droop" calls attention once again to the apparent state of near
inattentiveness that seems to pervade the room. He also speaks
of the class as being "calm" and as exhibiting "signs of passivity,"
which, incidentally, seem not to bother Mr. Turner (a point
to which we shall return). At the same time, he says that the
slouching students "straighten up quickly" when they have something to say. He also points out that they listen to each other,
"turn to passages together," and "watch their teacher." The mixed
signals continue to be baffling and they are not limited to the
conduct of the class alone. What shall we make, for example,
of Mr. Turner's practice of grading his students' notes? Such
a formal assessment of the students' participation is at odds with
the casual, friendly style of the classroom. If Mr. Turner intends to evaluate what his students have gotten out of the discussions in class, he must have in mind some minimum standards of participation, which means that his students aren't as
free to go their own way as the easygoing atmosphere suggests.
The record goes on:

> The discussion turns to Ahab. A student re-
> marks on Ahab's refusal to permit a creature of na-
> ture to be "over him," while looking into his book.
> "What page is that?" asks Mr. Turner. When
> the boy tells him, the class turns to it as one, at
> which point Mr. Turner asks the boy to read the
> whole passage aloud.

Mr. Turner then opens a Bible he has pulled out earlier from his briefcase and reads about mankind having dominion over all the other creatures. "Although it's not clear what 'dominion' means here," he explains, "it's clear Ahab has a strong view on this."

The same boy who had raised the issue interjects another remark about Ahab's objection to the idea of the whale having dominion over him. The boy argues that Ahab wants to be more than a mortal man. Mr. Turner acknowledges the point and adds an embellishment of his own, to the effect that in Genesis it indicates that before being "given dominion" man was a vegetarian and did not kill animals. The student responds by turning to a passage in the novel and explaining that the whale is described as having godlike qualities.

"Good!" responds Mr. Turner, immediately taking up the text and reading more of the same passage. A girl interrupts him to ask the page number, at which point again the class turns to it together.

This brief pas de deux between Mr. Turner and one of his students constitutes the kind of exchange that teachers dream about. The student, with his opening remark, makes clear that he is on to something big in his search for a better understanding of Ahab's motivation. The teacher immediately senses the potential significance of the student's budding insight and is quick to build upon it by turning to the Bible, which he "just happens" to have at his elbow. The boy takes his argument a step further and the teacher "adds an embellishment of his own." The student comes back once again, evoking an enthusiastic "Good!" from Mr. Turner, and immediately the whole class turns to the relevant passage. The entire episode could not have taken more than a minute or so to play itself out, yet it forms a graceful whole, a tiny vignette of pedagogical give and take lodged within the larger framework of the day's lesson.

What shall we make of such an episode? There certainly is an excitement, even an electric quality, to the interchange between teacher and student. Mr. Turner's effusive "Good!" contrasts markedly with his generally cool demeanor and with all that has been said so far about the laid-back atmosphere of the class as a whole. For the moment at least, everyone seems attentive. Have conditions changed for good or is the change only temporary? Our guess is that it is only temporary. Neither Mr. Turner nor his students seem like people who could sustain a high level of overt enthusiasm and excitement for long periods of time, at least not while engaged in discussing a text like *Moby Dick*. (Readers might contrast the atmosphere of this classroom with that of Ms. Walsh's, as described in Part Two, where both teacher and students were excitedly involved in the lesson.) However, we caution against coming to a quick conclusion about the significance of such sudden outbursts of attentiveness or about the state of affairs with which they contrast. We still have to come to terms with both conditions but will delay doing so until we have come to the end of the record, which is not far off.

The observation continues:

> The class begins referring back to Starbuck. Mr. Turner asks questions about Ahab's claim that "Starbuck is mine." He alerts them to aspects of Starbuck's soliloquy on Ahab. He reads a brief passage from the Bible again, which he says shows the biblical idea that man was made from God's breath; "and here," he adds, "we saw that Starbuck inhales Ahab's breath."

The focus in this segment is on the teacher's activity. We have Mr. Turner asking, alerting, reading, saying, and adding. The subject of attention continues to be Starbuck throughout. Again Mr. Turner makes use of the Bible, this time drawing a parallel between Ahab and God. Do the biblical references add moral gravity to what is being read? They do not seem to, although they obviously enrich our understanding of both Starbuck's and Ahab's characters. They therefore serve to increase the moral complexity of both men. Do they do so in a way that is morally educative? Possibly, although it is hard to say what the students are learning about themselves or about human affairs in general as such insights into the characters within the text are being achieved.

The record concludes:

> A few minutes before the end of the period several students begin packing up their books and materials. Some have lunch the next period, some another class, some a free period. They pack up quietly as the discussion continues. Mr. Turner finishes a comment on the events they've discussed. He goes on beyond the "official" end of the period, explaining how important it is to really try to understand Ahab. Students wait patiently; about half are still holding their texts open, the other half are perched on the edge of their seats. After a pause, during which he looks around once more at the group, Mr. Turner says loudly, "Okay," and students leap out of their seats or stand up leisurely, a few stretching as they pack up their materials.

Even in its closing moments, Mr. Turner's class behaves characteristically. It dissolves slowly rather than abruptly. It unravels, one might say. Some students anticipate the end of the period and start readying for it, though quietly, well in advance. Others seem in no hurry at all. Mr. Turner maintains his cool demeanor to the end. He continues talking beyond the time of dismissal and even after he finishes what he has to say he pauses and takes a calm look around the room before he gives the loud "Okay" that triggers the students' departure. The ones who stand up and stretch before leaving seem much more expressive of the tone of the class as a whole than do their classmates who leap from their seats and bolt for the door, though even the latter had enough self-control to wait patiently for Mr. Turner's signal.

What about those of us who only read the report? Are we eager to leave as well or do we more closely resemble the dawdlers? Do we wish the report had been longer or were we pleased to see it conclude? And how do we imagine the observer feels when the class ends?

Speaking as commentators, we must confess that we had a more difficult time reacting to this set of observations than to the two previous ones. Throughout the process we found our thoughts drifting off to matters that were related only tangentially to what was being described. For example, in the midst of the description of Mr. Turner's trip to the dictionary to look up the word *blasphemous,* we found ourselves beginning to think more broadly about a teacher's ability to know for sure what his or her students are getting from their experience beyond a deeper and possibly more satisfying understanding of the text they are studying. That question led to extended thoughts about how literature contributes to the moral well-being of its readers. From there we were drawn to the question of how educators as a group have responded, and might yet respond, to public skepticism about the value of literary studies in our nation's schools. We began to write about such matters in an initial draft of this section, in the belief that almost any thoughts that were triggered by our reading of the observer's report were legitimate as "reflections" on what had been read. But our writing led us so far afield from our point of departure that we soon found ourselves worrying about how to get back to where we had left off.

The difficulty we experienced in staying focused on the report of what went on in Mr. Turner's room was due, we believe, to a combination of the quiescent nature of the room itself, the textual focus of the discussion, and the nonchalant demeanor of both students and teacher. All contributed to a sense of our having little to say—given our purpose in this book—about the details of what was going on. It wasn't that the observational report didn't stir us to think about moral matters. Quite the contrary. But, as we have just explained, our thoughts along those lines moved us further and further from the details of the classroom itself. Moreover, we suspect that the observer may have been having similar difficulty himself, though he obviously succeeded in remaining at least partially alert until the session ended. What do those difficulties say about the process of trying to discern the moral significance of what goes on in classrooms?

The most obvious thing they say is that we must be very careful about calling a class dull or devoid of moral significance simply because we felt somewhat distracted or bored while reading about it or viewing it from the back of the room. There is plenty of indirect evidence in the observer's report that a lot was going on in Mr. Turner's room from an intellectual and even a moral point of view, even though most of the action was not very exciting to watch. What those same difficulties also suggest, however (and what we can see hints of in the record if we look closely enough), is that within the classroom itself the observer may not have been alone in feeling somewhat "out of it." Others who were present, including perhaps some of the students who later bolted for the door, may have felt the same way.

Let's assume that the thoughts of some students in Mr. Turner's room were miles from where they should have been throughout most of the period. (The observer as much as tells us that was the case. He observes eyes that "droop now and again" and he speaks of "a few" who "doodle or otherwise drift into daydreaming.") What would such a condition tell us about the moral significance of what was going on?

In and of itself it would tell us nothing of great import, for it is hard to imagine a class in which there are *not* a few daydreaming students from time to time. But it might make us begin to ask about Mr. Turner's attitude toward the possibility of there being such students in his class. Does he know they are there? Does he even suspect they might be? Does he care? Does he do anything to identify those students and try to bring them back into the fold? Questions such as these *do* take on a moral cast: they deal with issues of equity and justice as those ancient and honorable ideals work themselves out within a classroom context. If, for example, Mr. Turner totally ignores the students who seldom or never speak up and who can be seen to be visibly distracted or nearly asleep during class, if he concentrates solely on those who are alert and who voluntarily contribute to the discussion, some educational critics would surely want to accuse him of failing to fulfill his responsibility as a teacher.

We certainly have no wish to make such an accusation ourselves. Moreover, it would be sheer folly to do so on the basis of a single observation. Anyone wanting to answer the questions we have raised would have to visit Mr. Turner's classroom many times and would need to talk with him at some length about his teaching goals and methods. At the same time we can't help noticing within the record a couple of details that point in the direction of such a judgment.

We note, for example, that Mr. Turner "rarely calls on students, preferring instead to take comments from volunteers." The word *rarely* implies that the observer *has* seen Mr. Turner call on a student before, though perhaps not during this particular class session. In any case, the event, we are told, is a rarity. We also might note the total absence within the record of any sign that Mr. Turner was at all alarmed or worried by the students who looked as though they might be daydreaming or falling asleep. Short of calling on them, he might easily have frowned or tapped on his desk for attention or done something else to indicate his displeasure or concern. However, we are given no sign that he did anything at all in response to those conditions, at least on that particular day. We should remember that, as the observer noted, most of the students did participate in the discussion (and sometimes impressively so). We suspect that many readers, particularly high school English teachers, would regard that level of participation with approval.

But there is something else noteworthy in the record that we failed to catch in our first reading. The report contains no names of individual students. Mr. Turner is not quoted as addressing anyone by name other than during the roll call at the start of class, and the observer does not use proper names either. The observer refers to everyone who speaks or is spoken to, except Mr. Turner, simply as "a student." Contrast that situation with the one in Mrs. Johnson's room (observed by the same person, incidentally), where the teacher addresses everyone by his first name. Why the difference? Might it reflect an attitude of greater detachment on Mr. Turner's part? Could it be that he cares less about individual students than Mrs. Johnson does? That seems to us to be far too hasty a judgment—and the wrong question to ask as well.

It is the wrong question because the purpose of our commentary is not to judge the teachers in comparative terms. Nor do we wish to determine whether any one of them, considered singly, is morally lacking or morally admirable. Mr. Turner obviously cares a great deal for the literature he reads with the classes. He may also care for his students as persons far more than the observational record discloses. In fact, based on our three-year acquaintanceship with him, we believe Mr. Turner to be a very caring person indeed.

On the basis of the report alone, however, we remain puzzled by Mr. Turner's apparent habit of not addressing his students by their first names, or by any names at all so far as we can tell. Might that characteristic be another manifestation of his cool manner, an attribute that we remarked upon at the start? Possibly. But that leaves us still guessing as to what that cool manner might mean from a moral perspective, particularly when it seems to be shared by the class as a whole or at least by a fair number of those present. Are the students merely mimicking Mr. Turner's attitude or does the demeanor of both teacher and students derive from something beyond them all — a school-wide ethos, perhaps, or possibly a watered-down version of the world-weariness stereotypically associated with certain segments of the privileged class? Either way, we depart from our encounter with Mr. Turner's English class still wondering what to make of what we have seen.

IV

Our final set of observational segments describes a third-grade classroom in a Catholic school. The teacher is Sister Grace, a good-natured woman of Irish descent, short in stature and in her mid- to late forties in appearance. Though she belongs to a religious order, Sister Grace dresses in street clothes when teaching.

> One afternoon, late in September, the children were assigned to make posters as part of their religion lesson. They had, the week before, clipped out pictures of "people helping people," and now they were to work in groups of three or four to mount their pictures on a poster. Explaining the project to the class, Sister Grace held up a piece of poster paper and against it she held two pictures at oblique angles to one another.
>
> "Would you put your pictures on like this?" she asked.
>
> The children sang out in chorus, "No!"
>
> Sister Grace twisted the pictures so that they overlapped. "Like this?" she asked.
>
> "No!"
>
> She held the pictures parallel to the edges of the paper. "Neatly?"
>
> "Yes!"
>
> "Would you put a lot of glue on the back of the picture or a thin line around the edge?"
>
> "Thin line!"

There is something both very familiar and rather peculiar about the form of Sister Grace's questions in this opening segment. They resemble a certain way of questioning that adults often adopt when conversing with young children, which accounts for their familiarity. What makes them a bit peculiar is not as easy to say. Part of it is their rhetorical nature. The teacher obviously knows the answer to each of the questions and so do the children. The way they shout the answers in unison makes that abundantly clear. Moreover, to add yet another layer to the business of who-knows-what, the teacher clearly knows in advance that the children know the answers. She frames the questions in such a way that they could hardly be answered otherwise. Why, then, does she bother to ask? Presumably because she wants to remind the children that they should put their pictures on the poster neatly (i.e., parallel to the edges and not overlapping) and that they should apply the glue sparingly. If she failed to remind them of such matters it is quite possible that at least some of the students would have produced crooked pictures and would have used an excessive amount of glue in doing so.

Fair enough, we might say, but why use questions at all for that purpose? Why not just *tell* the children what to do, with perhaps a demonstration thrown in for good measure? We are not exactly sure how Sister Grace would answer that question, but we can easily imagine her saying that it's simply a little more fun to do it her way. And it probably is. But the mere mention of fun helps to pinpoint what we initially found to be peculiar about the questions.

From a pedagogical point of view, which is to say, from the standpoint of their function as instructional devices, Sister Grace's queries are not real questions at all. They are *mock* questions, part of a little game being played between teacher and students. She isn't trying to find out what the children know or understand. She knows perfectly well what they will say to the two examples she offers. The same is true of the questions about the glue. Moreover, it is equally clear that the children know that she knows they know. They know, in other words, that this is all part of an elaborate game, which is why they shout out the answers with such evident glee. Their teacher is simply teasing them and they are delighted to join in the fun.

We have already said that this is a familiar form of "questioning" between adults and young children. One setting in which it has become an almost classic mode of interaction is the circus. There we find clowns using it all the time to "work" the crowd (which typically contains its share of youngsters, needless to say). They do so by miming "questions" that prompt the audience to shout back answers that in turn lead to the clown's outlandish actions. Audiences usually love being called upon to participate in this way and we might well imagine the clowns having a good time as well.

When this form of clowning occurs in a classroom, however, considerations beyond the fun it entails inevitably come into play. Classrooms, after all, are not circuses, even though most of today's educators would probably — and properly — insist that laughter and fun have a rightful place in schools. But what is that place and what forms of fun fit in? Those are questions to keep in mind as we return to the observational record.

> That same afternoon Sister Grace was quizzing the children about maps. She read a statement and then wanted the children to tell her whether it was true or false. The first statement was: "A map is a picture of a place." The statement seemed ambiguous to me, but the children called out together "True!" which was obviously the answer wanted.
>
> Later in the quiz came this statement: "You can only show small places on a map." To this, there was a confident chorus of "False!"
>
> A look of disbelief came over Sister Grace's face, and she said, "False!?"
>
> Immediately, many of the children sang out, "True!"
>
> "True!?" said Sister Grace with wide, seemingly surprised eyes. She then let the children think about the statement before resolving the confusion and acknowledging that, yes, the statement was false.

In this segment too we find the teacher questioning her pupils, though not in the same mock style as before. This time her questions are much more instructional in character than in the first instance. However, a fuller comparison of the two situations reveals noteworthy similarities as well. As before, the children call out one-word answers in unison. They also seem to enjoy doing this, just as they did previously. Here too an element of playfulness and teasing enters the picture, although not the same kind as before. Let us look a little more closely at how it compares.

In this instance the teacher's playfulness consists of an attempt to convince the children that they have given an incorrect answer when in fact they have not. In response to this deception many of the youngsters immediately change their minds, only to be confronted with yet another look of disbelief from their teacher. The children are confused by this turn of events, since it clearly implies that both answers were wrong. Their comportment brings to mind Mr. Gradgrind's rattled students in Dickens's *Hard Times,* who promptly changed their answers each time their teacher frowned. In the episode reported here, Sister Grace dispels her students' confusion by assuring them that the first answer was correct after all, just as they had originally thought.

The chief difference between this situation and the previous one is that in this one the teacher adds an element of deception that was not present before. Strictly speaking, we might want to call the teacher deceptive in the first instance as well, for she acts as though she is posing genuine questions rather than rhetorical ones. But in that situation the children readily saw through the deception, whereas here it works. They are thrown into momentary confusion because what appears to be going on turns out not to be the point at all. The lesson is supposed to be about maps, but as a result of Sister Grace's teasing, the children find themselves dealing with a lesson about classroom questions and how to answer them.

Again we feel prompted to ask why a teacher would behave this way. Our previous answer, which we imagined Sister Grace herself making, was "Just to inject a little fun into what would otherwise be a routine activity." That answer fits here as well, certainly, but somehow it doesn't sound as convincing as before. Certain kinds of deception (e.g., mild teasing) may be somewhat enjoyable under almost any circumstance but a form of it that generates genuine confusion in an instructional situation, even if it is only momentary, begins to test the limits of what is sensible and proper under such circumstances. Is Sister Grace in this instance putting play before work, or at least mixing the two up in an unhelpful and therefore unwise manner? Asking whether that is so raises a moral issue, for the question of how well a teacher fulfills her instructional obligations is surely a moral one.

The observational record continues:

> One afternoon at the end of November, Sister Grace drew the children to the prayer corner to talk about the Christmas season. "Do you know," she began, "what it's like to wait for a birthday or for your vacation or for a baby to be born?" The children nodded yes. "Is waiting hard or easy?"
>
> "Hard," they said.
>
> "Do you ever get grumpy when you're waiting?"
>
> "Yes," they said.
>
> "The whole world is getting ready for Christmas," she said. "What do we call the four weeks before Christmas?"
>
> About five children raised their hand, and Sister Grace looked mightily disappointed. She said, "I'm going to shut my eyes until there are more hands than that." She put her head down and lifted it in a moment, and nearly all the children's hands were raised. She called on one child, who said, "Advent."
>
> "Are good things worth waiting for?" asked Sister Grace.
>
> "Yes," said the children all together.

Here we have yet another question-and-answer format. As before, Sister Grace presents questions that call for one-word answers. This begins to look like a pattern with her. Assuming it is, what shall we make of it? If we consider only the format — the leading questions and the short answers — we find a striking resemblance between Sister Grace's method of interrogation and what is sometimes called the Socratic method. In many of the Platonic dialogues, Socrates leads his interlocutors through arguments, with them contributing little more than a periodic "Yes," or "No," or "Absolutely" — about as much as Sister Grace's students contribute to their class discussions. This similarity in form is, however, all the two have in common. Unlike those of Socrates, Sister Grace's questions are not part of any obvious strategy of argumentation. In fact, they hardly operate like questions at all. They are more like moves in a game whose chief purpose is to maximize the participation of the players.

With that possibility in mind, consider Sister Grace's reaction to the small number of children who raise their hands in response to the question of what to call the four-week period before Christmas. With a look of disappointment she announces that she is going to close her eyes until more hands are in the air, which she then proceeds to do. Her disappointment might be readily understandable if we assume that the children were told about Advent on some previous occasion. But why close her eyes? Why not just give the children additional time to think of the answer and wait, open-eyed, for more of them to do so?

One answer, which would be in keeping with the impressions we have gathered so far, would be that the act of closing her eyes makes the situation more gamelike, and therefore more fun. By closing her eyes, Sister Grace is saying, in effect, "Let's make believe that I can't see you for a few seconds. That will give you the opportunity to do something that I will later find to be surprising or puzzling or both." The children are doubtless very familiar with this maneuver. Its exact analogue occurs at birthday parties at which the guest of honor is asked to close his or her eyes while the cake is carried in. Moreover, in a variety of different forms, it plays a crucial role in countless games of childhood, and Sister Grace, as we have already begun to discover, seems to enjoy playing games with the children.

Another possibility, which doesn't really conflict with the

one just given, is that Sister Grace wants to turn her back on what might be considered "cheating." She suspects, let's say, that the only way for more hands to be raised is for some students to help others come up with the answer by whispering or silently mouthing it. However, the test of "knowing" the answer is being able to come up with it on one's own. So, to avoid witnessing such "illegal" exchanges, Sister Grace conveniently offers to close her eyes. She chooses not to see what she would otherwise have to condemn.

Either way we read them, Sister Grace's closed eyes introduce an element of magic or make-believe into a process whose overall structure is not itself magical or gamelike. That element fits oddly, we feel, within an otherwise straightforward discussion of the upcoming holiday, for her performance overshadows the alleged purpose of the class and raises questions in our minds about the proper mix between the playful and the serious in our dealings with very young children. What is that mix? How do we know when it has been achieved or lost? And what do we mean by calling it a "proper" mix? What could be proper about it? Instead of trying to answer those questions at this point, let us return to the record.

> One afternoon in early December, at the beginning of the handwriting lesson, Sister Grace asked what new letter the children were going to work on today. She was not inviting suggestions, however; rather, she was asking the children if they could predict what letter was next in the sequence by recalling the letter they had practiced in the previous handwriting lesson. One child was called on and said, "*N.*" Sister Grace said, "No." And then the hands began to wave excitedly, and a scene was played out that is repeated often enough in the classroom to attain the status of a running joke. The children were so enthusiastic, so eager to be called on, that they could not settle for merely holding their arms in the air. Even waving them vigorously was not enough for many. They wiggled or bounced

in their chairs. Some began to vent their enthusiasm vocally with cries of, "Oh! Oh! Oh!"

Sister Grace responded to the scene as she usually does—by pretending to take the children's chant of enthusiasm as a proffered answer. "No," she said, "not *o*." As always, the children laughed, and then some of them changed their "Oh! Oh! Oh!" to "Ay! Ay! Ay!" And to this, Sister Grace pretended to be confused and said, "I hear a strange sound—*ay*."

The earlier pattern repeats itself with some variations. We once more witness a question-and-answer format in which the children's responses (not their answers to the question, but their cries of excitement) occasion mock replies from the teacher that are greeted with laughter. This time the teacher appears to misread what the children are saying. She treats the cries of excitement as though they were genuine answers to her question. Moreover, according to the observer, Sister Grace has pulled the same trick often enough to have it become a standing joke. Possibly some of the children even cry "Oh!" on purpose, just to see their teacher react in her standard way. Their quick switch to the expression "Ay!" would seem to confirm their eagerness to participate in the humor and keep the joke alive.

The humor of this recurrent situation is worth looking at a little more closely. It arises, as we have seen, from an apparent misunderstanding. A spontaneous cry of excitement is taken to be an answer to a question. But of course the teacher is not really making that mistake and the children know it. If she were, the joke would be on her and it would be unlikely to repeat itself. What is really happening is that the teacher is making fun of the children's inability to refrain from crying out in their eagerness to answer the question. She is teasing them, in a good-natured way. And they love it.

Again, we raise the question, which by now has become standard: Why tease the children in this way? The straightforward answer—just for fun—is still available. More than that, it begins to sound once again like a perfectly reasonable explanation.

For in this instance, unlike the one involving the question about the maps, nothing untoward seems to happen and, as we have said, the children appear to love it. It looks like they're having fun. But is that a good enough reason for Sister Grace to behave in this way? Might there be other things going on that a "just for fun" answer does not take into account? For example, what lesson might children draw from a teacher who constantly shifts attention away from the subject matter? Will they begin to doubt the importance of the declared purpose of schooling? If the subject matter seems somewhat disconnected, will they begin to doubt their competence to understand such things? We acknowledge that a teacher who plays and jokes with her students shows that she understands their needs, but so does one who is more serious and sobersided. It may be that the teacher who regularly jokes around in class, contributing to an atmosphere of playfulness and high spirits, does so at the risk of overshadowing and eventually undermining the alleged purpose of the total enterprise. Might that be so in the case of Sister Grace? Is hers just harmless fun, or might there be more to it than that?

The observation continues:

> A week or so before Christmas vacation, on an afternoon when her third graders were in gym, Sister Grace put a surprise in each child's desk — a candy-cane-striped pencil with a Santa Claus figure at one end. The children were thrilled when they returned from gym and found the pencils — all were, that is, except Reginald, who didn't have one in his desk. Once Sister Grace assured herself that Reginald really hadn't received one of the pencils, it occurred to her that she might have mistakenly put the missing pencil into the desk of one of the three children who were absent that day. She asked Emily to check the three desks.
>
> This was just one of many instances in which Emily worked as Sister Grace's aide. Emily's special status appeared in other ways as well. Later that

same afternoon, Sister Grace announced that it was time to get ready for social studies. "Clear your desks," she said. "I wonder which row will be most ready to start."

Emily was at the computer, and although all the other children returned to their seats and cleared their desktops, she remained at the computer. Sister Grace began a review of a chapter the children had read about the Hopi. She asked questions about Hopi homes — how they were built, what they were called, how they were heated. She asked what kachinas are, and she asked how the Hopi pray.

"Do you think, " she asked, "there would be lots of fighting among the Hopi people?"

Hands went up, and she called on a student, who said, "No."

"No," said Sister Grace. "Why not?"

Again hands went up, and Sister Grace called on a second student. "Because they're peaceful," said the student.

"Because they're peaceful," said Sister Grace. "I'm thinking of a word. The word I'm thinking of means 'table.'"

Hands waved in the air, some of the students bouncing up and down, eager to be called on. Sister Grace called on a third student, who said, "Mesa."

"Mesa," said Sister Grace.

Throughout the first part of this review, Emily remained at the computer (a privilege I never saw any other child allowed), and neither Sister Grace nor the other children acted as if there were anything surprising in Emily's delay in rejoining the group.

This observational segment is peculiar in that it offers details about two different activities — the distribution of the gift pencils and, later, the discussion about the Hopi — but its real subject is Emily and the privileges she seems to enjoy in Sister

Grace's room. The account of the discussion about the Hopi reads as though the observer is trying to stay engaged with what is going on but is unable to because his mind is also on Emily and the special treatment she seems to be given. The observer can't figure that out. He also can't figure out why the other children do not seem to object to the way Emily is treated. "Is Emily the teacher's pet?" is the question he all but puts into words.

Let's suppose she is. What would that tell us about the moral climate of Sister Grace's room? It would say, first of all, that Sister Grace plays favorites, which most people would probably condemn a teacher for doing. Of all the moral qualities a teacher might possess, a habit of being fair is surely one of the most highly praised. The rules of fairness call for treating all students alike, at least insofar as granting favors and privileges is concerned, although they usually also allow special awards to be given to acknowledge outstanding performance of some kind. Even the youngest student understands those rules and is mindful of their violation, which is why the apparent acceptance of Emily's privileged status by her classmates is especially puzzling. It seems unlikely that they would remain silent in the face of such unequal treatment. Perhaps they know something that is unknown to the observer. On the strength of the supposition that there is a sensible explanation for Emily's special treatment, let us move on, though, once having been aroused, our suspicion that Sister Grace may be guilty of unfairness is bound to stay with us at least until it is resolved in some way, as do so many of the hunches and guesses aroused by visits to classrooms and the reflections that accompany them.

Is there anything more to say about the gift of the pencils and the discussion of the Hopi? The gift of the pencils certainly has to be read as a thoughtful gesture on Sister Grace's part. We assume it is an action she took on her own and probably paid for out of her own pocket. Although the cost likely was not very great, it is, as they say, the thought that counts. The children's evident delight upon receipt of the gift leaves no doubt that it is appreciated.

The discussion of the Hopi is too briefly reported to reveal much of anything, but it does suggest that the material being studied portrays the Hopi and their culture in a positive light. We wonder, however, from the kinds of questions being asked, how deeply the children are being asked to reflect upon what they have read. Most of Sister Grace's questions call for one-word answers and there does not seem to be any follow-through or further probing once the correct answer has been given. Also, the total set of questions comprises a strange jumble, from the topic of homes to that of prayer, although that may only be because this is a review session. However, when these questions are added to the ones we considered earlier, our growing impression is that Sister Grace has not given much thought to the way children think or, better put, to the ways they are capable of thinking. In her style of questioning she *behaves as though* the goal of schooling was the acquisition of "bits" of knowledge, capable of being displayed on demand.

We emphasize "behaves as though" because we think it likely, given all that we know about Sister Grace, that she could articulate a much more sophisticated conception of teaching and of children's thinking than the observational record so far reveals. However, at the risk of being unfair to her by taking only an observer's- or student's-eye-view, we press our somewhat negative judgment in order to make the point that the idea that a student's job is to store up bits of knowledge is not simply a psychological outlook or even an educational one. It is also a moral position in that it constitutes a conception of human worth and human capability, which in turn dicates the way we go about treating others. Thus, a teacher who consistently acts as if education consists primarily of accumulating tiny bits of knowledge is not just someone who happens to adhere to an out-of-date psychology. Being out of date has moral ramifications as well.

The observational record continues:

> One afternoon in January, Sister Grace was giving a language arts lesson that dealt with phonics. She presented groups of words with similar sounds and asked the children to pick out the one word from the group that possessed a given sound,

such as the sound of the word *all* in *drawl*. Sheila
had trouble with *drawl* (presumably because she
wasn't familiar with the word) so Sister Grace tried
to help her by asking what the word would be without the *l* on the end. Sheila could recognize *draw*
and managed to figure out *drawl*. Then Sister Grace
asked Sheila to read the rest of the words in the list,
one of which was *hell*. With difficulty, Sheila got
all of the words except *hell*. That word she couldn't
seem to get.

Sister Grace turned off the overhead projector
she'd been using to present the word lists, and while
the rest of the language arts group waited, she went
to the board and wrote a new list of words — *fell,
well, sell,* and *hell*. Sheila read off the first three with
no problem, but insisted that she didn't know the
fourth. Sister Grace wrote *hello* on the board and
Sheila read it immediately.

"Then how about this one?" asked Sister
Grace, pointing to *hell*.

Again Sheila acted as if the word was an
impossible mystery.

Finally, Sister Grace said angrily, "We're not
going to put up with that kind of nonsense. We're
not going to hold up the whole class while you're
not cooperating. Do you know what I'm talking
about?" Without waiting for an answer, she went
back to the phonics review with the rest of the group.

What a strange occurrence! All of the signs point to Sheila's
being unwilling to say the word *hell* because she understands
it to be a curse word and possibly has even been forbidden to
say it by her parents or some other adult. Yet Sister Grace seems
not to consider either possibility. Surely a member of a religious
order ought to be more sensitive than most others to the emotional significance of a word like *hell* and to the power of admonitions against swearing. Why does she seem so insensitive to
such matters in this instance? Why doesn't she ask Sheila if there

is some reason she refuses to say that word? Presumably, Sister Grace doesn't care why Sheila doesn't want to say the word.

From a moral point of view, this indifference is disturbing. Sister Grace cannot want her students to be insensitive to one another's concerns. In fact, she categorically rejects insensitivity in one of the "class rules" posted on the wall above the blackboard—"Respect one another." Yet she is not showing respect for Sheila—despite all the time she devotes to tutoring the girl—if she is indifferent to the girl's feelings.

What if Sheila had said, "I'm sorry, but I'm not supposed to say that word"? Would Sister Grace have reacted with anger and insisted that she would not "put up with that kind of nonsense"? Probably not, because if what she means by *nonsense* is Sheila's pretense of ignorance, then it is the student's feigning that angers her, not her refusal to say the word. This is ironic, because Sheila is doing in a less sophisticated way what Sister Grace so often does—that is, engaging in a display of mock ignorance. But unlike Sister Grace's habit of teasing, Sheila's pretending not to know the word *hell* is not at all playful. She is obviously not trying to tease her teacher. Her refusal to pronounce the word is evidently done in earnest. Why can't Sister Grace see that and deal with the situation in a less heavy-handed way? The information we have available does not allow us to answer that question.

The observational record continues:

> One morning in January Sister Grace asked her students if they would like to make sympathy cards for Mrs. Lamp, the third-grade teacher in the adjoining classroom, whose father had recently died. They were eager to do so. Some of them were in one of Mrs. Lamp's reading groups, and all of them knew her.
>
> Before having the children begin, Sister Grace asked them how they planned to decorate their cards and what they planned to say. When a number of children suggested a picture of a coffin, Sister Grace said, "I'd like you not to have a whole lot of coffins

on there. You can still do what you want, but I'm
giving you my advice." Other than this, she did not
tell the children how to make their cards. She only
listened to their ideas. Then she passed out sup-
plies and put on a record.

The children became absorbed in making the
cards and for the next twenty-five minutes were unusually quiet. So intent were they on their work
that they seemed oblivious to their surroundings,
except that many of them silently mouthed the
words of the songs on the record.

As the children finished, Sister Grace looked
at and commented upon each card. When she had
seen them all, she asked the children if "the observer" might examine the cards, too. No one ob-
jected, so I did look at them. Most of the children
wrote of understanding how Mrs. Lamp felt, many
telling how one of their family members had died.
Others tried to comfort Mrs. Lamp with assurances
that she and her father would be reunited in heaven.
One boy tried to make Mrs. Lamp feel better by
telling her that things were going well at school.
He wrote: "I did all my seatwork."

This brief episode typifies the spontaneous intrusion of
moral matters into the ongoing school day, a relatively frequent
occurrence in the classrooms we visited, as several of the prior
observational records have made clear. In this instance the students are being asked to offer solace, in the form of a sympathy
card, to a grieving teacher. The experience as a whole constitutes
a lesson in manners even though it contains little in the way
of formal instruction. From another point of view we might look
upon it as an impromptu art lesson with, again, very little intervention on the part of the teacher.

In trying to think of what such an experience might mean
to those involved we are led to consider the routine nature of
sending messages of condolence. One question that arises immediately has to do with the relationship between *feeling* sympathy

and *expressing* it. The children are invited to send *expressions* of sympathy to Mrs. Lamp. Are we to imagine that they also *feel* sorrow over her loss? Is this experience conducive to such feelings or are the students merely being schooled in one of our culture's social proprieties? The fact that most of the children write of "understanding how Mrs. Lamp felt" and that some of the cards mention deaths that the children have directly experienced suggests that the exercise may have aroused or rekindled genuine feelings of sorrow. However, the conventional nature of some of the other responses, such as assurances of a reunion in heaven, makes us doubt the genuineness of the sentiments expressed in the messages. This is not to say that the encouragement of such a social convention among school-age children, even when their feelings do not match the sentiments expressed, is necessarily a bad thing. But it does raise the question of whether Sister Grace might have used the occasion to probe some of the moral issues connected with the prescribed expression of social sentiment.

What shall we say of Sister Grace's behavior in this episode? She seems to be accepting and relatively nondirective in her approach to the task the children are about to undertake. Her mild discouragement of "a whole lot of coffins" sounds quite reasonable. Asking the children whether they would be willing to have the observer view their cards, rather than simply assuming that they wouldn't mind, reveals a degree of sensitivity and respect that contrasts rather markedly with what we have witnessed in some of the other excerpts. This contrast is itself instructive for it helps to reveal the often contradictory nature of much that we see in classrooms — a point amply illustrated in our commentaries throughout Parts Two and Three. We often found that the longer we observed, the more mixed were the moral messages emitted by the classrooms and teachers we observed. We will return to this unexpected discovery after completing our visit to Sister Grace's classroom.

The observational record continues:

One afternoon in January, Sister Grace read aloud *"I Can't" Said the Ant,* a children's story with

short rhyming lines. She stopped before each end
rhyme and called on someone to guess what the
word was. At one point, the word was *sling*, and
Sister Grace called on Jerome, who could not guess
the word. After another child was called on and said
the word, Sister Grace turned back to Jerome.

"Why did I call on you?" she asked him.

"'Cause I was playing around," he answered.

Sister Grace seemed taken aback, but quickly
recovered. "You were," she agreed, "but I called on
you before that, because before Christmas your arm
was in a sling."

What is interesting about this brief exchange is not so
much Jerome's misunderstanding about why he was called on
as it is his clear awareness that teachers do indeed call on pupils
when they are "playing around" as a way of curbing their misbehavior and causing them to focus once again on the subject
of the lesson. Sister Grace apparently did not call on Jerome
for that reason on this occasion but we can easily imagine her
having done so in the past. Few teachers of young children could
possibly have failed to use that strategy on numerous occasions.

What does the strategy reveal about the way instructional
and managerial or disciplinary matters are combined in classrooms? It suggests that teachers sometimes have ulterior motives in the way they direct their questions and comments. They
call upon students not just to find out what they know but also
to warn or admonish them for not paying sufficient attention
to what is going on. They do not necessarily conceal this practice and, in fact, may even bring it to the attention of the offend-
ing student, as Jerome obviously believes Sister Grace is doing
when she asks him why he was called upon. Sister Grace's surprise and quick recovery carries with it the suggestion that
though she is genuinely caught off guard by Jerome's reply she
is by no means shocked by the suggestion that she would behave in that manner.

The record continues:

One afternoon in February, Sister Grace reviewed with the whole class a chapter from the "family life" book dealing with reproduction in plants. When they finished the review, she had the children turn to the next section, which dealt with reproduction in mammals. The book pictured different kinds of mammals, showing where in each mother's body the offspring develops, and Sister Grace talked about how the sperm from the male enters the female's body to fertilize the egg. She said that the sperm enters through an opening and asked, "What is the name of the opening?"

One girl raised her hand, and Sister Grace called on her. "Vagina," said the girl. As soon as the word *vagina* was spoken, several of the other girls began to giggle. Sister Grace ignored the giggles and continued to talk about how the baby grows inside the female mammal. Then she asked, "Is the female the only parent?" She followed the question by saying, "Hands," indicating that she wanted the children to raise their hands to answer. Only a couple of children had their hands up, so she asked, "What does the male have to do with it?" Still, no one else raised a hand, and Sister Grace announced, "Well, you must agree that the female is the only parent. Only two people have their hands up." She continued, however, to wait for more children to raise a hand and after a bit encouraged them again, saying, "I'm still looking for new hands."

This episode parallels the situation involving Sheila that we have already discussed. Once again we witness a reluctance to participate, this time involving all but two of the students. Again, the motivating circumstance that prevents fuller participation seems to be the wish to avoid speaking out in a way that could cause embarrassment or teasing from others, as already happened to the girl who answered "Vagina" when asked to identify where sperm enters the female body. As before, the teacher does not directly acknowledge the students' discomfort but, instead, continues to press for greater participation as she waits expectantly for hands to be raised.

Again, we find ourselves somewhat puzzled by Sister Grace's actions. Why does she insist that there be more than two hands in the air before she calls on someone when she did not do so with the prior question? Why does she switch the form of the question from "Is the female the only parent?" to "What does the male have to do with it?" thus giving away the answer to the first query? Why, once more, addressing those whose hands are still not up, does she insist that they "must agree that the female is the only parent," having just made it clear that the male has something to do with it? Our own reading of those inconsistencies leads us to suspect that Sister Grace may be as uncomfortable discussing the anatomy and physiology of sex as are some of her students. We wonder, in fact, whether those students may not sense this and whether Sister Grace's discomfort might be contributing to their own uneasiness.

But what about the parallels between this situation and the one involving Sheila? Are they just coincidental or do they imply that there, too, Sister Grace may have been uncomfortable and was somehow communicating her discomfort to Sheila, thereby strengthening the child's resolve to remain silent? We have no way to answer such questions, of course, but something about Sister Grace's behavior in the two situations makes us think that such a hypothesis may not be far from the mark.

What is it about Sister Grace's behavior that makes us feel as we do? In both contexts she fails to acknowledge the emotionally charged nature of the subject matter. It's as if by being nonchalant and casual about the mention of such highly charged words and subjects she is trying to prove (to the students? to the observer? to herself?) how liberal and open-minded she is. Might that be why she tries to cajole Sheila and later the class as a whole into participating when it seems obvious that they do not want to? Is she acting from a sense of duty that tells her that, personal or religious feelings aside, she ought to be able

to discuss such issues coolly and frankly? Again, we cannot answer such questions but must simply file them away for later
consideration as we have done with several of our previous
queries.

The record continues:

> At the end of an afternoon in March, Sister
> Grace was releasing the children to pack their book-
> bags and line up at the door. The desks were ar-
> ranged as tables, and she called each table in turn.
> Mark was not sitting at any of the tables, however.
> His desk had been by itself all that day, a fact that
> Sister Grace apparently forgot, because when she
> finished calling all the tables, she went to the door
> and stood there, overseeing the children who were
> lining up.
>
> There was a lot of bustling around in the
> room — children packing bags and getting on coats —
> and I realized that in the confusion Sister Grace was
> unlikely to notice Mark still sitting patiently at his
> desk. I was only a few feet from him, so I leaned
> over and said, "Maybe you'd better get your coat."
>
> "We're not supposed to go until our table's
> called," he explained.
>
> "I think your teacher just forgot that you
> weren't at any of the tables," I said. "I'm sure it
> will be all right."
>
> Mark shook his head. "We're supposed to get
> permission."
>
> "Everyone else is going to be ready to go,"
> I warned. "You don't want to miss your bus."
>
> Mark nodded and seemed for a moment to
> be thinking over his situation. When Vicky, the girl
> sitting closest to him, agreed with me that he really
> ought to get ready to leave, he finally relented. But
> he got up cautiously, and all the way to the
> coatroom he kept his eye on Sister Grace.

Sister Grace hardly appears in this episode but we feel her presence all the same. She holds the key to Mark's release and continues to do so even after he has been almost literally sprung from confinement by the joint effort of the observer and Mark's classmate, Vicky. "Poor Mark," we want to say, "doesn't he understand that Sister Grace has simply overlooked him this time and that she would release him immediately if she suddenly became aware of her oversight?" "Apparently not," is the readiest answer to that question. But, then again, maybe Mark does understand. For even after the likelihood of Sister Grace's forgetfulness is explained to him, Mark holds fast in his determination to wait for permission. Indeed, all the way to the cloakroom he continues to behave like someone who is still waiting for a final nod of approval from his teacher.

Consider what such an attitude means from a moral perspective. It implies that rules are to be obeyed unthinkingly, their authority untempered by considerations that take into account the possibility of human error or oversight. Of course Mark finally does give in to the reasoning of others, so it seems he is not entirely committed to blind obedience after all. But the task of convincing him takes some doing. The impression abides that Mark would not have reached the conclusion to leave the room on his own. The urging for him to do so has to come from the outside.

Would all of the other students have behaved like Mark if they found themselves in his position? Probably not. Vicky, for one, probably wouldn't. Nor, perhaps, would most of the others. So it may be that all we are witnessing in this episode is the idiosyncratic response of one of the more weak-willed and obedient youngsters in the room. But even if that is so, we still need to ask what Mark's reluctance to break the rule might tell us about the climate of authority that he lives under and what Sister Grace, either wittingly or unwittingly, might be contributing to that climate. Our job here, however, is not to answer those questions. We raise them only to illustrate the kinds of moral concerns that begin to emerge once we start to look closely at the minutiae of classroom life.

The observation continues:

One afternoon in May, Sister Grace divided her class into groups and was asking each group to report on its ideas about "safety rules." When the children began to talk instead of listening to the group that was reporting, Sister Grace walked to her desk, sat down, and lowered her head. After a moment, she looked up at the children as if surprised to see them. "Oh! Did you want me to teach you?" she asked.

Here Sister Grace engages in yet another act of pretense, similar to the one in which she closed her eyes, waiting for more hands to be raised. We are not told how her pupils respond to her feigned withdrawal and sudden awakening but we might well imagine that her ploy works — in other words, that the children are chastened by her actions and that they subsequently quiet down and begin to listen to the group that is giving its report. What makes her behavior of interest to us, however, is less its effectiveness than its typicality. In moving to her desk, lowering her head, and then pretending to be surprised by the watchful eyes of her pupils, Sister Grace is acting in character. She is behaving the way we have seen her behave before — playful, humorous, childlike, clowning around, engaging in make-believe — but never just for the fun of it, always in the interest of establishing or maintaining control of the instructional setting. "That's just Sister Grace's way of doing things," we want to say by now. "That's part of her teaching style. She kids around a lot."

We usually contrast "kidding around" with "being serious." But the two are not opposites, the way play might be said to be the opposite of work. They are more closely related than that. Kidding is a form of play offered as nonplay, which moves it into the realm of deception. It is playfulness in disguise. Kidding works best when it is momentarily successful, when there is a brief lull, a moment of puzzlement or confusion, between its presentation and the audience's catching on. During that lull the people being kidded mistakenly believe what is not true. If the lull becomes too prolonged, kidding becomes something else. Its victims then begin to feel that they have been lied to or patently deceived.

But even within the limits of acceptability we sometimes have difficulty knowing how to take people who reputedly are always kidding around. The question is not how to tell when they are kidding, for that is usually obvious enough. Rather, it is what to make of their style of relating to others. Why do they find it necessary to relate in that way? The standard answer — that they do it because it's fun — simply begs the question, for it only prompts us to ask why fun is so necessary or, at least, why this kind of fun is.

When we stop to think of the kind of fun we have been witnessing in these observational excerpts from Sister Grace's room our worries about its appropriateness within an educational setting begin to mount. A person who kids someone else presumes to have a position of authority with respect to the other person. Momentarily, at least, the kidder seeks control of the other's sense of reality. The goal, as has been said, is to deceive. But education, as a process, has quite the opposite objective. Its goal is to dispel confusion, to enlighten. What then of the teacher who, like Sister Grace, kids around a lot in class? Is such playfulness totally out of place when working with young children? Certainly not. Indeed, there is a sense in which it is perfectly natural. Children seem almost to invite such reactions by the adults with whom they interact. They also seem to enjoy being teased and kidded, as we have seen. Indeed, Sister Grace's third graders are typically enthusiastic participants in their teacher's gags. But enthusiasm is a poor indicator of the educational worth of the activity.

What we find worrisome about Sister Grace's playfulness is the way it fits with other things that we have witnessed in our reading of the observational record: for example, the superficiality of her questions during question-and-answer periods and her inability or seeming refusal to consider how her students might feel when discussing sensitive subjects. Such observations create the impression that Sister Grace may not be particularly sensitive to her students' feelings and also may have a rather low opinion of what they are capable of accomplishing in intellectual terms. Might she be shortchanging them, as we suspected Mrs. Johnson of doing?

Have we gone overboard in these speculations? Might we be taking Sister Grace's playfulness, and some of the other things we have seen her do, entirely too seriously? Possibly. And that possibility, with its built-in irony, worries us fully as much as anything we might think about Sister Grace. For it is not just Sister Grace who comes off looking less pedagogically attractive than many who know her might have guessed. The same is also true of each of the other three teachers whose descriptions we have examined in this section. We know that to be so because we ourselves, well acquainted with all four teachers and on very friendly terms with each of them, were quite unprepared for what a close scrutiny of the observational record would disclose. Though we anticipated that such a process would reveal aspects of each classroom's operations that we had heretofore overlooked, we did not anticipate that the four observations-cum-commentary would raise the many doubts and questions that they ultimately did. What caused that to happen? And what does this say about the usefulness, the validity, and even the fairness of much that we have been trying to do in this part?

Unfathomable Complexity

To answer the questions we have just raised requires us to back away from the details of what we observed in the four classrooms. We need to see these details from a broader perspective. A return to one of our primary purposes in writing this book offers the best vantage point. Our goal throughout has been to show how the moral complexity of classrooms becomes evident when we look carefully at what goes on there and then proceed to reflect upon what was seen and heard. Our focus on the emerging appreciation of moral significance has narrowed our way of looking and reflecting, as any choice of subject is bound to do. It has led us to overlook, for example, much that would interest the instructional technologist and others concerned with extending the so-called knowledge base of teaching.

It has also diverted our attention from matters that a sociolinguist or a conventional ethnographer might reasonably wish to study. At the same time, however, our concern with the moral has broadened and deepened our vision beyond our original expectations. It has caused us to pause and to think about fleeting events and commonplace objects that we ordinarily would have ignored. That is what we mean by saying that it has broadened our vision. It has also prompted us to probe beneath the surface of much that we have seen and heard, which is why we speak of our vision as having deepened as well as broadened.

When applied to what teachers say and do, our probing for moral significance has yielded a mixed bag. It has revealed many practices and personal predilections worthy of applause and others — more than we had anticipated — that are of dubious worth from a moral perspective. And all these from teachers who have been performing successfully for years and who are highly honored and admired by all who know them. How do we explain that outcome? What significance might it have for the prospect of encouraging others — whether as observers in other teachers' classrooms or in their own — to adopt a perspective similar to the one enacted here?

The explanation that comes most readily to mind is one that calls attention to the universality of moral imperfection. Look closely at any person, it says, and we are bound to discover flaws of one kind or another. That being so, it should come as no surprise that our observations of teachers in action and our later reflections on those observations have revealed a number of questionable practices. According to this view, the surprise would have been if we had *not* found such imperfections. Moreover, in line with this reasoning, we are quite prepared to acknowledge that we observers and commentators likely would have fared no better had it been our own teaching that was so minutely scrutinized.

But it is one thing to acknowledge that everyone has imperfections and quite another to observe them pile up as they seem to have done in Part Three. Either we have been working with an unusually flawed set of teachers, or our procedures of observation and commentary have so biased the picture that those teachers come out looking more flawed than they are. We incline toward the latter explanation, though with important qualifications, as will soon be evident.

To the question of whether the teachers with whom we worked were more flawed than is common among teachers in general, we would emphatically say no. On the contrary, based on everything we have come to know through nearly three years of close association with them, we would assert that, as a group, they were considerably above average in their dedication to teaching and in their eagerness to explore its moral ramifications. They showed themselves to be intent on improving their own practice. Moreover, these judgments apply as much to the teachers we have concentrated upon in this chapter as to the remainder of the group. To us, the possibility of our having inadvertently chosen to work with a group of teachers who are more morally deficient than average is not only implausible but entirely out of the question.

What of the possibility of what researchers call sampling error? Might we, as observers, simply have been looking for the problematic, keeping our eyes out for the slightest hint of morally questionable practices? And might we later, as commentators, have been equally keen to ferret out flaws of one kind or another, simply to have something interesting to say? In retrospect, we believe that those two forms of bias did operate, though not as blatantly as suggested here and certainly without any intention of casting the teachers in a poor light. The bias, as we now look upon it, seems built into our way of working, placed there, in effect, by the goals of our inquiry.

To enter a classroom and look upon it as a moral environment is to see it in an unfamiliar way. One of the things that makes it unfamiliar is that the moral significance of what we see and hear is seldom obvious. Consequently, the observer who is on the lookout for the morally interesting is constantly having to ask, "Is this event morally significant? Does that object or activity have a moral side to it that is worth considering?" The trouble with those questions is that they usually can't be answered on the spot. The moral significance of what is witnessed does not usually reside on the surface of events and activities.

Thus, the observer is forced to decide what is important and what is worth writing about without pausing to give it much thought, doing this well before its moral depths (assuming it turns out to have some) have been even partially fathomed. How is that selection made? Usually it begins with a feeling of puzzlement. The observer sees and hears things that cause him or her to wonder why they occurred as they did. It is here, we believe, that the bias in the direction of writing about morally problematic practices begins to creep in. For what often puzzles the observer, quite naturally, are things that the teachers and students do together that don't make sense, at least not immediately. These, it turns out, include a fair amount of morally suspect actions, which is one of the reasons they jar the observer's sensibility or appear so odd in the first place. Here, then, is at least a partial explanation for why the observational record makes the teachers look rather more morally dubious than we know them to be.

But the explanation does not stop there. In addition to the observer's natural proclivity to record morally questionable events and actions, there was also the effect of our policy of not questioning the teachers about what we observed. We instituted that policy, our readers will recall, because we did not want to put the teachers in the uncomfortable position of having to constantly defend their actions. We also wanted to restrict our own reflections to what was actually seen and heard, believing that by doing so we would be coming closer to the perspective that the students themselves might have. The students in each room, we reasoned, were equally limited in their perceptions in that they were not usually in a position to ask the teacher for an explanation of his or her behavior. We recognize, however, that some of what the observers saw and heard might have become more understandable, and hence less questionable in moral terms, if the teachers were routinely given the opportunity to explain and justify their actions. Thus our policy of not asking for such explanations may have brought the morally problematic aspects of the teachers' actions into greater focus than might otherwise have been the case.

Among other possible explanations for the somewhat critical tone of our descriptions and reflections, one deserves special mention. More accurately, it deserves special emphasis, since we have already touched upon it here in Part Three. This is the possibility that there is something about classrooms and perhaps about teaching itself that triggers a judgmental and evaluative attitude in visitors almost against their will, particularly if they have been teachers themselves. This proclivity comes as no surprise to the teachers who are being observed. They usually anticipate that visitors to the classrooms will automatically be judging them, or so we have found, which probably explains the unwillingness of many teachers to tolerate visitors.

What is there about teaching that brings on this critical stance? We are not sure but we think it may have to do with teaching's many moral demands. Teachers are expected to be knowledgeable, yet respectful of those who are ignorant. They are expected to be kind and considerate, yet demanding and stern as the situation requires. They should be entirely free of prejudice and absolutely fair in their dealings with others. They must be responsive to the needs of the individual student, without neglecting the class as a whole. They are expected to maintain discipline and order, while allowing for spontaneity and caprice. They should be optimistic and enthusiastic, even when harboring private doubts and misgivings. They must deal with the unexpected and sometimes even with surly and abusive students without losing their composure and control. And they must smile and appear cheerful on days when they are not quite up to par and would rather be somewhere else.

Those are impossible demands for anyone to meet on a regular basis, no matter how hard he or she tries. Consequently, it is inevitable that all teachers, at all levels of education, sooner or later will fall short of what is expected of them. Perhaps they could be seen to do so every day if we were to look closely enough. In our own observational work we did not find each of our teachers failing to live up to moral expectations every time we paid a visit. But that may only be because we were not looking for such shortcomings. The scope of our concern was much broader than the teacher alone, although we quite naturally paid a lot of attention to what each teacher said and did.

In the final analysis, what our observations have revealed from a moral perspective is exactly what we might expect to discover if we look closely at anyone. No one is perfect, plainly enough, and teachers, even good teachers, are no exception to that rule. Did we witness more imperfections among our teachers than the average classroom visitor might find? We believe so, in part because of the nature of what we were looking for. Other influences, some of which we have conjectured upon, no doubt contributed to the selective nature of what we saw and reported.

What about those who take our suggestions seriously and try to adopt the perspective exemplified in this book in their own schools and classrooms or as part of an exercise within a teacher education program? What will such a perspective enable them to see? Will they become hypercritical of the teachers they observe? Will the process increase their own pedagogical self-consciousness to a point that is disabling? Will it bring on cynicism and despair with respect to what teaching can and should accomplish in moral terms? These questions make us think of all the current talk about teacher burnout and other morale problems said to beset today's schools. The last thing teachers need, it seems clear, is to adopt a point of view that promises to make them less content with teaching than they would otherwise be.

We not only believe that none of those negative effects need to occur; even more, we confidently assert that the practiced application of the way of looking we have been advocating is one means of *preventing* their occurrence. We believe that the adoption of this perspective will actually bolster teachers' morale. That assertion, which may seem to run counter to much that has been said so far, will receive its fullest explication and defense in Part Four. But first we will describe briefly what happened to some of our own perceptions of the teachers with whom we worked as we became increasingly immersed in trying to make sense in moral terms of what went on within each of their classrooms.

The single most dramatic change in our outlook involved a deepened appreciation of the complexity of forces at work within even the simplest of classroom settings, together with a corresponding increase in our respect for the way each teacher managed, as a rule, to cope with that complexity. As our acquaintance with them grew, each room and each teacher became increasingly unique and therefore increasingly special to us. This is not to say that we equally enjoyed all of our visits or even that we wound up liking each teacher and each classroom equally. We certainly had our favorites among both, though we tried not to reveal those preferences, just as most teachers try not to reveal their unequal likings for the students with whom they work.

Our growing familiarity with the teachers and settings also does not mean that we ultimately came to know them so well that we exhausted their novelty and capacity to surprise. On the contrary, the more we got to know each classroom and each teacher, or perhaps it would be better to say the more we *reflected* on what we had come to know about each one, the more mysterious and unfathomable each became—something like what happens with thoughts of our friends: the more we think about the individuality of each one, the more multifaceted he or she becomes. This was perhaps the second most dramatic shift in our perception during the course of our work. We attribute it directly to our coming to understand the importance of probing the expressive significance of what we saw and heard. We will have more to say about this in Part Four.

About the time we were becoming aware of the point we have just made, we recalled some of the methodological advice we had learned in statistics courses and elsewhere over the years. One piece of that advice suddenly struck us as humorously ironic in the light of what we were learning from our experience. This had to do with the concept of reliability. In classes and textbooks we had been taught that one of the chief ways to increase the reliability of our findings as researchers was to increase the number of our observations. "When in doubt, look again" would be the simplest way of putting that advice.

But what we were discovering as classroom observers was that often, the more we looked, the more puzzling the situation became and, consequently, the more *unreliable* were our conclusions about the situation in general. Contrary to what we had previously learned, repeated observations seemed to breed doubt, rather than certainty. We were so amused by this seeming contradiction that we jokingly toyed with the idea of submitting to one of the educational research journals an article entitled, "On the Unreliability of Repeated Observations," which would contain an account of our experience. We realized, of course, that the seeming contradiction was more semantic than real and that, all humor aside, there do remain circumstances under which repeated observations directly contribute to the reliability of conclusions. In fact, that is precisely what ours were doing for us, only not quite as the textbooks said they should. For the longer and more repeatedly we looked, the more convinced we became that further looking would almost always reveal something new. There was no way, or at least none that we were able to discover, of exhausting the complexity of what we saw and heard. So, in a sense, the reliability of *that* judgment did indeed increase in line with the frequency of our observations.

Putting together these shifts in our perception amounts to this: the longer we looked and the more we thought about what we saw and heard, (1) the more mindful we became of the unfathomable complexity of classroom life, (2) the more respectful we became of the teachers we were visiting, and, (3) of chief importance within the present context, the more convinced we became that our procedure of looking and later reflecting on the expressivity of what we had seen and heard was doing its job of helping us tease out the moral dimensions of much that was going on in the classrooms we visited. In short, our procedure worked for us without engendering cynicism or despair or any of the other negative outcomes that a confrontation with the limits of every teacher's moral perfectibility might be thought to provoke. Our approach also worked, as we trust is apparent, to keep us from becoming sentimentalists or Pollyannas about teachers and teaching — the flip side of the cynical and despairing attitude that we have mentioned and one no less disabling to teachers than to researchers. We believe the same will happen to others who are willing to give it a try.

❧ PART FOUR ❧

Cultivating Expressive Awareness in Schools and Classrooms

*T*he essence of all we have presented thus far reduces to two main points. The first is that the five schools we have visited (and, by inference, other schools like them) explicitly seek to have a moral influence on their students in a variety of ways, some more obvious than others, to be sure, but all readily discernible to the attentive observer. The second point is that the moral influence schools and teachers actually have is far from limited to those explicit efforts. It extends to what teachers say and do without consciously intending to act as moral agents. It further applies to aspects of the classroom environment and the school as a whole that also are not specifically designed to achieve moral ends. In preparation for our discussion of this final topic, which deals with the question of how to cultivate the outlook we have been describing, let us briefly review the highlights of what has been said about each of these two main points.

In Part One we presented a set of eight categories. The first five refer to the schools' *explicit* efforts to influence students morally. These include (1) specific curricular offerings of the kind we might formally call "moral education" (and of which we saw practically none, except in the two Catholic schools, where there was formal instruction in Christian ethics); (2) the introduction of moral topics into the regular curriculum (for example, talking about the character of a historical figure or someone in a story); (3) various rituals and ceremonies of a celebratory and affirmative nature (for example, a graduation or an awards assembly); (4) signs and bulletin boards conveying moral messages of a variety of kinds (everything from a hand-drawn sign urging students not to be litterbugs to commercially produced posters extolling the virtue of staying in school); and (5) the spontaneous and often disruptive interjection of moral talk and discussion into the flow of ongoing classroom activities (for example, a teacher suddenly saying, "Richard, please give others the respect you would like to have!"). There may be other major types of deliberate intervention that schools and teachers undertake in order to exert moral influence on their students but these five suffice to encompass all that we ran across.

We further identified three additional forms of moral influence that schools and teachers actively exert. These tend to be unintentional for the most part or at least take place with little if any formal acknowledgment of their moral significance. These too we introduced in Part One. They include (1) classroom rules and regulations that govern interactions between and among teachers and students, (2) commonly held assumptions that undergird and facilitate instructional and curricular arrangements of various kinds (we referred to these broadly shared understandings as "curricular substructures"), and (3) the expressive content of actions, objects, and events whose moral meanings are not immediately apparent unless one has become accustomed to looking for them. Within our own developing framework of understanding, these three categories of potential influence grew in importance as our work progressed. By the time we had finished, they had become central. We came to see them as crucial to a full appreciation of the schools' potential contribution to the moral makeup of everyone within the institution — principally students, of course, but teachers as well, and perhaps even administrators, office workers, and other employees, though we did not specifically look at the role all such nonteaching personnel might actually play in the moral life of the schools. We devoted Parts Two and Three almost exclusively to demonstrating what can be seen and learned when we begin to attend to the phenomena classified in our final three categories.

The fact that we only gradually came to understand and appreciate these three less evident forms of potential moral influence sets the stage for what comes next. For it suggests that those of our readers who try to replicate that portion of our work may have a similar experience. They too may have difficulty discerning some of the less visible and more expressive aspects of classroom life. That being so, it seems fitting that we say as much as we can about the outlook we finally adopted and about some of the difficulties we encountered along the way. This will be our task in this part. We must point out, however, that our own view is still undergoing change and therefore what we have to say about it must be understood to be tentative and unfinished. Furthermore, as we approach this task we are keenly aware of differences among our intended audiences of practicing teachers and school administrators, teachers in training, teacher educators, and classroom researchers. Though the interests of these four groups will surely overlap, each will have its own concerns and questions about the cultivation of expressive awareness. To the extent that we can foretell these interests, we will do our best to address them.

Our goal in this part of the book is not to present a how-to manual. Instead, we want to examine circumspectly the process by which expressive awareness might be cultivated, drawing heavily on our own experience and referring back to a lot that was said in Parts Two and Three. Although we do not offer anything like a step-by-step procedure, we hope that our remarks will make it easier for others to adopt our way of looking at classrooms.

Beyond Looking and Listening

Throughout the preceding chapters and within this one as well, as far as we've gone, we have made use of a lot of visually oriented terms and expressions to talk about our way of working. We have described ourselves as having adopted an outlook, a point of view, a perspective. We have repeatedly referred to our visits to classrooms as observations and have spoken of our reports on these visits as the observational record. We have talked much about looking and seeing and only somewhat less about listening and hearing.

This emphasis upon the organs of sight and sound is perfectly understandable, given the amount of time we spent actually looking at and listening to what was going on in classrooms. However, it tends to give the wrong impression of what the total process entails, by making it sound as though all we need to do to perceive the morally relevant aspects of classroom life is to take a seat in the back of any classroom and keep our eyes and ears open. There is a sense in which that is true, of course, but only superficially so. It takes a lot more than passively sitting and looking or sitting and listening to bring the moral aspects of classroom life into focus, as we trust most of our readers by now understand. At the very least it requires *thinking* about what we see and hear. But thought is only one of the additional ingredients required and not necessarily the first to be called upon, at least not in any sustained and systematic way.

Even before we begin to think about what is going on within a classroom, we must settle upon something to look at or listen to. This is as true for the casual visitor as it is for the teacher who resides there daily, although the latter may seldom have the luxury of sitting in an obscure corner and letting his or her gaze wander lazily about the room. That initial choice of what to focus on is not always easy. Classrooms are busy places, some more than others, of course, but even in the most quiescent room there is invariably much more to see and to listen to than can be taken in at once. As a result, the newcomer's attention usually flits from one object to the next or from one student to another before fixing itself on a target of more enduring concern. This preattentional phase of looking and listening can hardly be called looking and listening at all. It is more like being somewhere that we have never visited before, surrounded by many new sights and sounds that vie for our attention. In our experience, this preattentional phase can go on for several minutes and there are even times when it never seems to stop. On such days (which occurred infrequently for us, we are pleased to say) one often begins to feel distracted and even bored. What is interesting about that experience, however, is how quickly it can change. The room that was boring today can become absolutely fascinating tomorrow. Indeed, if we are patient enough, the activity that we have been watching for some time through heavy-lidded eyes can suddenly spring to life most unexpectedly. When that occurs it often is not because the activity itself has undergone a change but, rather, because something has happened to our perceptual apparatus or whatever we might wish to call the means by which the scene before us suddenly takes on new meaning. We now "see" for the first time what we presumably could have seen much earlier, if we only had the "eye" to do so.

Such moments of belated insight are characteristic of what happens when one adopts the point of view we are trying to explicate here. There are good reasons for that and we shall want to explore them before long. But we defer doing so for the present in order to return to the plight of the casual visitor who we presume has entered a new classroom and is trying to decide where to focus his or her attention. Our essential point is that right from the start there is more going on in the interaction between observer and observed than can be conveyed by the simple descriptions of looking and listening as they are conventionally defined. Moreover, the surplus, whatever else it may include, is far from being purely rational. This initial period of settling in is guided not so much by careful thought as by an intuitive feel for what is important or by the irresistible pull of one object of attention over another. Those internal and external tugs and pushes are not always reliable guides to what is ultimately important, naturally enough, but usually they are all we have to go on. They differ, incidentally, in elementary and high school classrooms, or so we have found. The typical elementary classroom contains so many visual stimuli — bulletin boards, posters, displays of students' work, science tables, areas set aside for special activities (such as computers or "listening corners" containing record players with headsets), and more — that the newcomer can hardly avoid spending a considerable amount of time just looking around at all there is to see. High school classrooms, in contrast, are usually much drabber environments that contain much less on display. Also, high schools are less likely to

have several things going on at once than elementary schools,
where a combination of seatwork, small-group activity, and
teacher-led instruction is practically the norm. Consequently,
the observer in a high school usually faces fewer decisions about
what to look at or listen to than does the observer sitting in the
back of an elementary classroom. In both kinds of settings, however, the activity in which the teacher is personally engaged typically wins out as the most natural place to look unless something very special is going on elsewhere.

After the observer does settle down and begins to concentrate on a particular object or activity — a teacher at work
with a reading group, let's say — there remains the question of
what to make of what he or she sees and hears. For many observers this is inseparable from the question of what notes to
take, which, in turn, is equivalent to asking which aspects of
all that is seen and heard should be preserved for future reference. Those questions are readily answered if the observer knows
in advance what he or she is looking for, but another crucial point
about the outlook being discussed here is that such a condition
rarely holds. The observer who is out to become attuned to the
moral dimensions of school life, as we were, seldom knows in
advance precisely what he or she is looking for and, moreover,
that state of affairs is to be desired. It is an asset rather than a liabil-
ity, because it allows the observer to remain as open and alert
as possible to all that is going on within the narrowed scope of
his or her attention rather than lying in wait for the emergence
of some prespecified occurrence, as observers do whose vision
is constrained by checklists and observation schedules.

What all of this means is that the process of choosing and
selecting is by no means over once we have settled on something to look at. Choices must be made continually, throughout every observational session. These choices, like those made
during the initial settling in, call, on one hand, for something
more than passively looking and listening and, on the other,
for something less than a fully rationalized process of decision
making. Once again, the term *intuition* springs to mind as a kind
of catch-all label for the vague sense of impulsion that guides
our selection of the memorable or notable aspects of what we

see and hear. But calling it intuition does not help very much. Moreover, our own experience allows us to be slightly more precise than that.

In place of *intuition* we would substitute a term like *wonder* or *puzzlement* or even *strangeness*. For what we repeatedly discovered when gathering observational material was that what often arrested our attention and got us to reach for our notepads in the midst of watching an ongoing activity was something about it that felt odd or strange, something that wasn't quite right — perhaps it was the way a teacher answered a question or possibly the way the question was framed in the first place, or it could have been the way an instance of misbehavior was handled or something about the conditions that led up to it. Sometimes the sense of strangeness emerged even before the observer had settled in on something definite to look at. In Mrs. Johnson's room, for example, the observer was first struck by the many posters and pictures that covered almost every available surface. What made these decorations noteworthy (and therefore strange in a sense) was that they seemed out of place in a high school classroom. They looked more like something that would be found in an elementary school. Was that why the observer took note of them? He does not himself say but it seems reasonable to assume that something about them struck him as being out of the ordinary.

As evinced by the observational material that we have discussed, this reliance upon a sense of the strange and unusual as a guide for what to take note of turned out to have both advantages and disadvantages. On one hand, it almost always yielded material that was rich in layered meaning and therefore worthy of continued reflection. The preceding two parts have shown that to be so. On the other hand, as Part Three in particular reveals, a proclivity toward noting the problematic and questionable in what one sees contains a built-in bias toward singling out the morally questionable as opposed to the morally laudable aspects of human action. This is so because violations of moral expectations are often more noticeable and also more puzzling than are instances of conformity to what is expected. Sister Grace's habitual teasing of her students, Mrs.

Johnson's prominently displayed folder of accolades, Mr. Turner's languid manner—these were the peculiarities that aroused our curiosity.

If it were relied upon exclusively, this orientation toward the problematic would cause us to overlook or at most pay only cursory attention to common expressions of many of the more homely virtues of patience, attentiveness, enthusiasm, and the like, evidence of which is so abundantly present in most classrooms. To achieve balance it is important that these commonplaces register upon the observer. However, that more balanced view, we discovered, does not require a conscious decision to take note of every small act of kindness a teacher performs or every smile of encouragement he or she gives. Indeed, to do so would be quite impossible. Instead, the balanced view is built up over time as the cumulative impact of those countless small acts and fleeting smiles or frowns begins to register within consciousness as an acknowledged liking or disliking for the teacher in charge or even for the whole classroom (for it is possible to like or dislike the feel of an entire room, as every observer soon learns). Once such judgment emerges, we then see the teacher as a kind or considerate or enthusiastic person, not because of any *particular* thing he or she does but because *that's the way he or she appears to be.* It is only long after such a judgment has been made that we can begin to pinpoint, either concurrently or retrospectively, instances of those qualities that characterize the person we have come to know.

The dynamics of this process are well known and are by no means restricted to what we think about teachers and classrooms. They apply with equal force to human affairs in general. What makes them of special significance within the present context is what they add to what has already been said about the importance for the conduct of classroom observation of the hunches, intuitions, and kindred vague promptings that the observer may feel. These properly include not just the feelings of puzzlement and wonder with which we began, but also those of liking or disliking, of attraction and aversion, of delight and annoyance. Moreover, and here is the important point, *all of these feelings, if they are to be used as effective guides, must be continually monitored,* for it is while they are still embryonic that they are most helpful. By the time the observer is confident in feeling this way or that about whatever is being observed, the opportunity to take note of the details of what is going on may well have passed. This means that the observer is as much an observer of his or her own reactions as of the scene being viewed.

One reason for underscoring this fairly obvious point is that the advice it contains runs counter to the standard conception of how to be objective and scientific. Normally the person who aspires to those laudable conditions is enjoined to lay his or her own subjectivity aside and try to see things "as they are." That may be sound advice for certain kinds of looking, but it is exactly the wrong way to behave when we are trying to come to grips with the expressive significance of what lies before our eyes. For it is precisely at the level of vague feeling and dim awareness that the expressive becomes manifest. Subjectivity, insofar as it refers to those as-yet-unverbalized stirrings of affect, whether positive or negative, provides a source of information that we must learn to draw upon, rather than ignore.

There is, incidentally, a special message in what has just been said about the dynamics of expressiveness, one that teachers, parents, and others who deal with young children might well heed. When children of school age are asked the standard adult queries of how they like their teacher or how they feel about a particular school subject or the overall experience of going to school, they often answer with certainty: "She's great," "He's awful," "Math is okay," "Social studies is boring," "School stinks." But they are often hard-pressed when it comes to saying why they feel as they do. "I dunno, she (or he or it) just *is,* that's all," they reply. Sometimes they even look surprised when reasons are called for, so obvious do their own judgments seem to them. To many of their adult questioners, however, children's lack of reasons undermines the validity of the views they express. Without reasons to back them up, such judgments are seen as being premature at best, if not downright irrational. (Older children and the more precocious among the very young soon catch on to what is expected. They quickly find reasons when called upon to give them, even if it means making them up on the spot.)

But if our own experience as classroom observers is any guide, the testimony of children reveals the normal order of events for people of all ages and is not simply a childlike way of responding to the world. Throughout life, it seems, we typically identify reasons for feeling as we do *after* rather than *before* those feelings have begun to register. We may defer making up our minds about how we feel until all the evidence is in, as we sometimes aver to be our goal, but that way of speaking usually refers solely to final judgments rather than preliminary ones. There is no way to prevent such preliminary reactions, though we may certainly choose to ignore or suppress them — and it may be that this is the way most of us go through life. It is exactly the wrong way to behave, however, if we are to take in the expressive dimensions of what we witness — to perceive the kinds of meanings we identified in Parts Two and Three. For our initial reactions to what we see and hear, dim and inchoate though they might be, are often clues that can lead us to perceive qualities that lie embedded in the surface of appearances, qualities that might otherwise go undetected. And even if those initial reactions later turn out to have been misjudgments, as they sometimes do, they are no less helpful in *attuning* us to the expressive qualities of what is going on. We would go so far as to claim that only by attending to those initial and preliminary hunches and reactions can we place ourselves in a position to arrive at a richer and truer judgment of what we have seen.

This talk of the difference between preliminary judgments and those that come later readies us to move on to the next of our subtopics, which will deal with the temporal aspects of the process of sensitizing ourselves to the moral dimensions of schooling. Before doing so, however, we need to underscore the three pieces of advice to classroom observers, whether teachers or outside visitors, that have emerged in this section. These are (1) that the observer not specify in advance what he or she is looking for but, instead, remain as open as possible to the subtleties of what is going on within the events or situations that capture his or her attention; (2) that the observer cultivate an eye and an ear for the problematic, for those aspects of what is seen and heard that are off-key in some way or jarring to the sensibilities, even if ever so slightly; and (3) that the observer always include himself or herself among the objects being observed and learn to audit his or her own reactions, which include likings and dislikings of what is seen and heard, however faint and seemingly premature such reactions might be. In these ways the observer's task extends far beyond passively staring at the kaleidoscope of classroom events.

The Process as Temporal and Phasic

Having just acknowledged a possible difference between the observer's early and later judgments of what he or she sees and hears in classrooms and having further insisted that there is a lot more to the business of bringing the expressive dimensions of classroom life into focus than simply sitting in the back of the room and passively taking note of what is going on, we are now in a position to begin exploring how the process changes over time. As was true with respect to the last set of comments, we have little in the way of precise knowledge about this matter and we certainly have no recipes to offer those who might want them. What we offer instead is a set of reflections based on our own experience, trusting, as we did before, that each of our different categories of readers will find something of personal worth within the sum total of our remarks.

To say that our views of a teacher or of a classroom change over time is not to say very much. The reason is that the same observation applies elsewhere. In fact, it's universal. Everything changes over time if we take a long enough view, so how could it be different for our perceptions of teachers and classrooms? The really interesting point has to do not with the fact that perceptions change, but with the nature of the changes and with how they come about.

To arrive at an understanding of the expressive dimensions of classroom life commonly takes time, often a lot of time, such as weeks or months. The process itself is divided into two recurrent modes or phases, one that takes place within the classroom itself and another that usually occurs elsewhere. These two phases of first observing and then later reflecting on what we have observed—or having someone else reflect on what we have reported, the strategy we employed in Parts Two and Three—are of course reciprocally related. We reflect on what has been seen and heard and, as a result, we not only come to perceive those past events differently but we also return to the task of observing with eyes and ears attuned to nuances that were initially overlooked. In short, what we think partially determines what we see and hear and vice versa.

The reflective phase of this process, at least as we have experienced it, resembles the observational phase in at least three important ways. The first resemblance is that both phases require us to be selective, which is to say that both require interpretation on the part of the observer. The second resemblance is an attitude of openness crucial to both, a willingness to have our thoughts move in unexpected directions. And third, equally essential to both observation and reflection, is the close monitoring of how the situation or event (or our memory of it or notes about it) makes us feel. The common goal of both phases is to be led or directed to questions and ultimately to insights that were unavailable at the start.

The chief difference between the two phases is obviously the absence, in the reflective phase, of the many competing stimuli that clamor for attention when we are actually sitting in the back of a classroom. By the time we reflect back on what we have seen or heard, or share our report with someone else, the complexity of the initial situation has been greatly reduced, leaving only a paltry residue in quantitative terms, a mere sketch of what was previously a much richer and more varied experience. But that residue, meager though it may be in comparative terms, is also highly selective; it has been shaped through language into a narrative or expository form that calls attention to itself and thus becomes a legitimate object of scrutiny and sometimes a source of puzzlement in its own right. "Why do I remember those few seconds in the classroom when Ms. Hamilton asked Felicia and Richard if they were visiting or helping?" the observer muses. "Why did the observer bother to report on the hallway display outside Mrs. Johnson's room, and why did he describe one student's map as 'crudely drawn'?" the reader of the observational report wants to know. Such questions remind us that the search for expressive qualities in schools and classrooms is by no means restricted to what the observer can see and hear. It extends to the fruits of that labor. They too are expressive objects that must be read or collected with the same interpretive patience and zeal that prompted their collection in the first place.

Is there a rule covering the optimal ratio of observing and reflecting, a formula that would determine how much time to spend at each activity? We know of none, although we can report on how such matters worked out for us. Though we spent a lot of time at both activities, we clearly spent more time cogitating than observing and we suspect that most others, whether classroom teachers or outside visitors, would do the same. Moreover, if we shift from a ratio of total hours spent in each activity to one that compares the time spent thinking about a particular event to the actual time it took that event to occur, the difference becomes enormous. What lasted only a few minutes or even a few seconds in the classroom often consumes many minutes or even hours of reflective thought. Consider, as an instance, the episode in Ms. Walsh's room, reported in Part Two, in which she initially reacted in a startled manner to the principal's announcement over the intercom and then, quickly regaining her composure, turned and bowed in a stately fashion in the direction of the speaker on the wall. That entire sequence of actions, including the principal's message, could not have consumed more than fifteen or twenty seconds of class time. Yet the total time spent writing about it and pondering its significance was probably close to an hour. The same is true of most of the other observational fragments that have found their way into this book. Each took far longer to write about and reflect upon than it did to occur.

What goes on during this process of reflection and why does it take so long? To call what happens "thinking" is both true and false. Thought is certainly entailed but it's not the kind of thought that moves deductively from point A to point B. It doesn't do so inductively, either. It is a kind of meandering thought that dawdles and backtracks and sometimes goes off on its own, venturing far from its starting place. It is experimental thought, in that it tries out and subsequently discards numerous reactions to the situation or episode before hitting upon one or more that satisfy two criteria: they make sense and they feel right. Perhaps it is wrong to think of it as thought at all, which is why we say that calling it thinking is both true and false. It is more like what some would label an exercise of the imagination. And yet it is not imaginative in any make-believe or fanciful sense, for the goal remains one of discovery rather than creative invention. What it comes to in the final analysis is a search for meaning, a wish to make sense of something whose significance we dimly feel but cannot quite articulate. The difficulty we encounter in doing this accounts for the process taking time.

There is something else about both phases of this process — the observational and the reflective — that the notions of dawdling and meandering bring to the fore. The business of coming to grips with the symbolic significance of what goes on in classrooms constitutes, at least for the practitioner, an interlude of sorts, a break in the ongoing activity of coping with the press of everyday affairs. This is so even for those who explore such matters as part of a research undertaking, as we have done, although here the interlude comes close to coinciding with the limits of the working day. In either case there is something escapist about the process, something that makes it seem like a kind of luxury, an indulgence perhaps, all of which may help to explain why it is not regularly undertaken, especially by those who feel tossed from pillar to post by the demands of the here and now. We must *find time* for the kind of detached observation we have been discussing and for the reflection that follows in its wake. We must even *make time* to do so — "take time out," as we say, or "set time aside" — in order to accomplish both, and that is not always an easy thing to do.

The necessity of having to set time aside to go looking for the expressive dimensions of classroom life may be enough to discourage the busy teacher and may have a dampening effect on others as well, including the casual observer who is often in too much of a hurry to see anything anyway. Moreover, there is an additional source of discouragement that we all may face, which is the possibility of looking in vain. For there is certainly no guarantee that the expressive will come into focus simply because we will it to appear. We know that to be so from experience. Not infrequently we ended a morning or an afternoon of observation with little or nothing to show for our labor. And try as we might, we sometimes failed to enrich, by further reflection, what we had seen earlier.

We cannot account for these dry or fallow sessions, other than to guess that they were caused by variations in our own receptivity on particular days. For, again, it isn't enough to declare that we will now "tune in" to the expressive meaning of our surroundings. We must also be in the mood to do so, which means, among other things, being sufficiently relaxed to look and listen carefully and also sufficiently alert to our own reactions to what is going on to have them serve as guides to continued observation and further reflection. That kind of readiness cannot be forced. There are times when it is absent and when no amount of coaxing can bring it on. On those days, we discovered, it is better to throw in the towel and turn to something else.

On the positive side, we can report that the process does seem to grow easier and also more richly rewarding over time. This is not to say that fallow periods disappear entirely but they do diminish in frequency and, more importantly, we increasingly come to trust our intuitions as an observer, a welcome modification, we must say, and one that serves to magnify the volume of those faint inner voices, or at least it often did so for us. In short, we have found that we became better observers of the expressive the longer we worked at it.

Does that mean that there comes a time when such an outlook has become so habitual that it no longer gets turned on and off during isolated interludes but remains on, so to speak, all the time? We doubt that such a complete transformation of perspective ever takes place, if for no other reason than that the press of reality does not allow it. The world of everyday affairs seldom affords us the luxury of musing for long about the expressive significance of anything. We are constantly being bombarded by demands and pushed into action. Consequently, we are often forced to respond in purely instrumental terms to much that we see and hear, which often means paying little or no attention to expressive meanings. The necessity of responding to life's demands never disappears, as we all know, not even for the most expressively oriented person we could imagine.

At the same time, habits do get formed through repetition. And we see no reason why that should not happen within the domain of perception as well as elsewhere. Thus, we believe that, over the long haul, the continued practice of looking at classrooms expressively will leave its mark and will contribute to a generalized way of looking and listening that stays with us and continues to operate, at least sporadically and semiconsciously, even when reality presses down hard and makes calm observation and prolonged reflection a luxury to be desired.

The Embeddedness of Expressive Qualities

Where does the expressive make its home? Where do we find it when we go looking? Consider a simple virtue, like patience, which is one that educators are frequently called upon to exhibit. Teachers often *show* patience, as we know, but the attribute itself is not like a sign carried about for all to see; it is more like a glow whose source lies within. It surfaces in the way the teacher behaves and is revealed by her actions. Moreover, those actions do not simply signal an internal state of affairs, the way a placard announcing "I have a headache!" might do. Rather, a teacher's mode of behaving *instantiates* the condition. Patience resides in the way she looks while waiting for a student's answer to a question or the way she stands about as the class comes to order. We see it in her eyes, her facial expression, the tilt of her head, the way her arms hang slack at her sides. And that's just the beginning. It also shows up in her response to interruptions, the way she regulates the pace of instruction, and in countless other ways as well. In a word, the patient teacher *acts* patiently throughout the day and does so especially in the face of conditions that would make others *im*patient. Her looks, her posture, her way of working embody patience. If she truly exemplifies that particular virtue, we might prefer to say, with emphasis, "She is patience personified."

In like manner we might describe the enactment of any other vice or virtue. All are somehow embedded in human actions, in what people say and do and, most importantly, in the *way* they do things. The same is true of other expressive qualities as well, including those having nothing directly to do with human actions. They too come embedded — suspended — in the object or event that serves as the medium of their conveyance. Consider, as an instance, the aura of tension in Ms. Morton's classroom that builds up during her dealings with Ella (Part Three). Where does that aura reside? Where is it located? It is everywhere at once! It pervades the room, as might an odor, or the light that enters the window, or the air itself.

Given this pervasiveness, it is small wonder that educators have employed meteorological terms, like *climate* or *atmosphere,* to refer to such an aura. We have done so ourselves throughout this book, because those metaphors come so close to capturing what it feels like to be in such places, where the aura appears to surround or envelop us. Classrooms do indeed develop climates of their own, which is to say that the many expressive features of the environment combine to form an amalgam of influences that work in concert upon those present. As environments, they are not unique in this respect, of course, for the same could certainly be said of churches, marketplaces, living rooms, and, in fact, any other setting that we might mention. The ambiance of each location conveys a distinctive set of qualities to the discerning perceiver. What concerns us here, however, is less the generality of that phenomenon than its connection to what has already been said about the embeddedness of the expressive features of classroom life. To that end let us move on to the consequences of our argument. Let's accept that all classrooms do indeed have climates that envelop everyone present. Let's also allow that the expressive qualities of everything we might gaze upon within classrooms is likewise embedded in those very objects or persons or events. What does that state of affairs augur for those of us who seek to observe the expressive and describe it to others?

Turning first to the task of description, it suggests that our efforts to convey the expressive dimensions of our experiences in classrooms are unlikely to be totally successful. Try as we might, we rarely are able to catch the precise quality that we sensed in the presence of a particular person or object, or when we witnessed a specific event or situation. Yet this is not a failure of language. It comes about because those qualities are in some way bound up in or possessed by — that is, embedded within — the person, object, or event being described. Because the quality is inherent in the thing itself, we inevitably seem to leave some of it behind whenever we try to describe it to others. We introduced this point in Part One, where we said that it is not so much that expressive meaning is *on* the surface of things — as if it could be peeled off like a label — but, rather, that it resides *in* what is perceived and therefore cannot be communicated to anyone in its fullness if they have not experienced it firsthand. "You had to be there," we say apologetically to those who do not appear to grasp what we are trying to get across about what we have seen or heard.

At the same time, to the extent that we are successful at such efforts (and we almost always are partially so), our description invariably comes closer to capturing the essence of whatever it is we are describing than does any account of comparable length and detail that focuses solely on the readily observable. This too has to do with the attribute of embeddedness, for those qualities that we have been calling expressive are not only inextricably a part of the object or situation they describe; they are also more meaningful in the literal sense — that is, they are more full of meaning. They tell us more about what something is *really* like than do reports restricted to so-called surface features. It is easy enough, for example, to describe the gross physical characteristics of a classroom, count the number of desks and chairs, give the room's size, and even say something about the general characteristics of its inhabitants (such as how many are boys and how many girls) without conveying any information at all about what the room is like as a moral environment. It is only when we turn to matters such as the room's climate (e.g., the relaxed mood in Mr. Turner's class) or try to say something about its teacher's style of working (e.g., Ms. Walsh's enthusiasm) that we begin to convey what it might be like to live in that room for hours, days, and weeks and to undergo its moral influence.

So even though we inevitably will fail to convey the expressive richness of all we see and hear as classroom observers, we can at least rest assured that what we do manage to describe will come closer to capturing the humanly significant attributes of classroom life than do the bare facts alone, which is another way of saying that it will come closer to capturing what counts in moral terms. That assurance makes the effort extremely worthwhile.

Looking for the Expressive

What does the attribute of embeddedness imply about the way we look and about what we look at in classrooms? It suggests, first of all, that we look closely. For it is in the details of what we see and hear that the expressive most often surfaces concretely. Moreover, it is through the depiction of details that we are most likely to convince others of the expressive significance of what we have seen or heard. Details function as symbols. They come to stand for things. Of course not every detail works that way. A goodly portion of the minutiae that the attentive observer dutifully notes turns out to be of no significance at all. Moreover, it is not always easy to know at the start which details to attend to and which to ignore.

The crooked window shades, the unwatered plants, the dustballs under the teacher's desk — all hint of someone's indifference to his or her physical surroundings, an indifference that may appear to extend to living things as well. Whose indifference is it? the observer starts to wonder. The teacher's? The janitor's? The students', perhaps? And is it really indifference or might there be some other explanation? The frayed and curled corners of the pull-down wall map, the tiny clusters of thumbtack pictures in the bulletin board display, and the scored desktops with their carved initials and penciled graffiti tell a story of objects that have weathered years of use. Yet the story's moral significance, if it has any, remains obscure. What are we to make of those details? Do they contribute to an aura of sadness the way the stained rug and the dusty room dividers in Mr. Turner's room seemed initially to do? Perhaps so but, then again, perhaps not. The reason we can't say for sure is because as isolated observations they lack a broader context that allows them to function symbolically. In other words, we do not know how those details fit within the larger picture that constitutes the classroom as a whole. Possibly all those signs of use and neglect will be counterbalanced or drowned out by the spanking freshness of the room's wall paint or by the effervescent cheerfulness of the room's young teacher, in which case the sheen of the paint or the sparkle of the teacher's eyes when addressing the class will be the detail that we want to isolate and describe.

What all this adds up to is the dual recognition that, on one hand, details are crucial in conveying the expressive features of classroom life but, on the other, this is only true when they are treated as symbols. It is their power to stand for conditions that are otherwise difficult if not impossible to communicate that affords them their descriptive worth. Sharing well-chosen details allows a reader to re-create through the vicarious encounter with the classroom the sense of puzzlement that motivates the writer. Only in this way can a reader view the classroom scene as an "open work," as a situation of unfathomable complexity. Expressive details invite the reader to begin the potentially unending search for the moral significance of the events that are described.

We spoke earlier of the importance of the hunches, intuitions, and kindred vague promptings that the observer typically feels. We talked about how important it was to monitor those so-called subjective states rather than trying to overlook them or, worse yet, trying to suppress them completely. Often, we claimed, they are the sole guides available when the observer is faced with the question of where to turn his or her attention. Now we have reached a point in our discussion where more needs to be said about those dimly felt aspects of the observer's experience. To do so, however, requires a switch of metaphor. Instead of looking upon them as vague promptings, as guides that point the way, we now must see them as constituting the shadowy boundaries of consciousness. Seen in these terms, our hunches, intuitions, and the rest form the outermost edges of our knowledge. They lie on the horizon of our vision. They are as far away as we can see.

What the metaphor of a horizon captures that the prior one of a guide does not is the unending nature of the search for the significance of classroom affairs. The expressive meaning of all that we see and hear in classrooms expands and deepens as we go along, and it continues to do so for as long as we are willing to invest time and energy in probing its depths and stretching its boundaries. Like the horizon, it can never be reached. There are always limits, of course, to how far we are willing to pursue our search. Some are set by contingencies such as cost and the vagaries of our capacity to remain alert and interested, others by more intellectual criteria, such as our sense of satisfaction with the level of meaning that has been reached. But hypothetically, at least, there is no end to such probings. In the search for new meaning and deeper significance there are no limits save those we set ourselves. We can always go further than we have gone.

What makes this infinitude of meaning significant in a practical sense is what it implies about the time spent in actually observing as well as in postobservational reflection. It suggests that we give expressive meaning a chance to reveal itself as fully as circumstances allow, which means a lot of observing, plus ample time for reflection. It also means that throughout that time we stay prepared to change our mind about what we earlier saw and heard or at least that we remain open to an increasingly nuanced interpretation of our prior observations. It is often the case that first impressions turn out to be lasting ones, as we all know, but they seldom endure without any change at all, at least not as long as we continue to look and reflect. We trust that the discussion in Parts Two and Three has amply illustrated these points. Unfortunately, as we have said before, we know of no formula that will establish how much time should be spent at either task. "As much time as one can afford" would be our counsel.

The Value of a Sympathetic Bias

If we hope to recognize the positive qualities or virtues that a teacher, a student, or a classroom expressively exhibits, it pays to follow a course of action that maximizes the likelihood of finding them. The best way to do that, in our opinion, is by adopting and maintaining a sympathetic outlook, by going about the task biased in the direction of making positive errors, of seeing virtues where they are not, rather than the other way around. This may be easier said than done for some people, for it really isn't as simple as choosing one thing over another, Brand X over Brand Y, let us say. As much as we might wish otherwise, not everyone has a deeply felt sympathy, perhaps not even a fundamental liking, for today's teachers and for what goes on in today's schools. But those without such an orientation are almost sure to miss much that happens before their very eyes. For many of the positive qualities of teachers, students, and classrooms are subtly expressed and are only visible to those who look closely and who do so with a sympathetic eye. The way a teacher exhibits trust, for example, may at times be evinced by nothing more noticeable than how long he remains with his back to the class while writing at the board or the way he keeps his head down while working at his desk or, better yet, the expression on his face when he looks up from his work and scans the classroom. Friendliness, patience, care, respect, and other social virtues find expression in the way students and teachers react to one another, the glances and gestures they exchange, the way they stand and move in each other's presence. Many such evanescent happenings come and go in a twinkling and we must be on the alert to catch them. A sympathetic eye takes note of such ephemera far more readily than one that is coldly clinical.

There are, as we might suspect, potential dangers in this way of looking. Chief among them is that it may lead us to construct too cheery a picture of what goes on in schools and classrooms. "Pollyannaish," "goody-goody," and "looking at the world through rose-colored glasses" are but a few of the epithets that unfriendly critics rightfully hurl at those who adopt too positive a view of their subject. But our accounts in Parts Two and

Three should by now have made clear that the adoption of a sympathetic point of view does not entail being blind to imperfections. On the contrary, nothing prevents the sympathetic observer from seeing a good portion of the not-so-savory side of whatever he or she might be looking at. In the light of our own experience, we would say that it is nearly impossible *not* to do so. No matter how positively biased we may be, we cannot visit any classroom for an extended period of time without witnessing events and actions that occasion negative judgments. There is simply no way of overlooking such matters completely, other than by resolutely closing our eyes to them. It is one thing not to overlook the questionable, however, and quite another to focus upon it exclusively (an orientation that we would call "bitter" or "cynical"), which is what we have tried to avoid. Our way of doing this has been to maintain a sympathetic bias toward all that we have witnessed in the schools we have visited.

We here encounter a curious and powerful affinity between the point of view that we have been advocating and teachers' own views. Teachers, too, or at least most of the ones we have encountered over the years, gaze upon their classroom environments with sympathetic eyes and strive to see their students and their students' work in the best light possible. They look for strengths rather than weaknesses. They take what students say in class — their contributions to a discussion, for example — and turn those remarks around until they make better sense, asking questions about them or rephrasing them in a way that makes them more substantial than they were when first stated. They applaud those who try, no matter how slight their success. They have the knack of discerning latent grace within the awkward gesture.

This widespread inclination of teachers to see the potential worth of their students' contributions to class and, more broadly, to detect within students themselves the early signs of incipient strengths that have yet to flower has its analogue in the process we have been describing as looking for the expressive within classrooms. The strengths that teachers see or think they see are, like virtues or character traits, embedded in what students say and do. They constitute a portion of the meaning of what is seen and heard. Metaphorically speaking, they lie beneath the surface of things. Indeed, all of the metaphors that we have employed in talking about the expressive dimensions of classroom life—notions like embeddedness, surface versus depth, and horizons of meaning—apply with equal force to what teachers perceive when they gaze with sympathetic eyes upon their assembled students.

Does this resemblance mean that teachers naturally adopt the perspective we have been advocating in this book? If they do, why did we include them in our audience? Why not direct our remarks solely to classroom observers who have never taught or whose teaching experience is so long past that they now forget what it was like to have been in charge of a classroom? If experienced teachers are already in the habit of looking upon students sympathetically—if they are already alert to the expressive aspects of what students do—and, moreover, if neophytes come to take the same posture almost instinctively, why not forget about both groups as potential readers and concentrate instead on those who might still benefit from what we have to say?

Our chief reason for wanting to include both teachers and teachers-to-be in our audience, and not just include them but make them central, rests in the obvious fact that teachers, by virtue of their direct contact with students, are in the best position of anyone to effect the kinds of improvements in the moral climate of classrooms that the adoption of an expressive outlook makes possible. However, on the basis of our own experience, plus what we have learned from the teachers with whom we worked, we conclude that most teachers, unless or until they have made a special effort to do so, probably do not adequately understand what the adoption of such a perspective actually entails, which means that they do not practice it fully or appreciate as much as they might what they and their students stand to gain from such an altered outlook.

It is true, as we have said, that teachers, as a group, tend to look for the best in what their students say and do. That tendency leads them in the direction of having what we are calling a sympathetic bias, which in turn positions them to be on the lookout for the expressive qualities of their students' actions.

However, adopting a sympathetic view toward students is only the beginning of what such a posture affords with respect to perceiving the moral life of classrooms. The expressive, as we have sought to make clear in this book, is by no means limited to qualities that students may be seen to exhibit in their words and actions. *Everything* within the classroom, including the teacher, is capable of being viewed as a conveyance of expressive meaning. The room's desks and chairs, its bulletin boards, blackboards, posters and pictures, books, boxes, lighting fixtures, closets, drawers—and every nook and cranny in which objects have been stuffed, stored, and perhaps forgotten—can be looked upon as artifacts whose physical properties do not begin to exhaust what might be said of them as expressive objects. So the first thing that such an outlook calls upon teachers to do is to enlarge the scope of their customary perspective, as we did, to include much more of their surroundings than students alone. This does not mean that every single object within the room must be examined closely and carefully scrutinized for its symbolic significance, but it does mean that every such object has the potential of serving as a repository of expressive meaning.

A second thing that expressive awareness entails and that many teachers may not come to appreciate on their own—their sympathetic bias notwithstanding—is the necessity of stepping back from the ongoing flow of day-to-day activity in order to look upon persons and objects as isolable entities worthy of contemplation in their own right. This means seeing students, for example, not simply as learners who at this moment are mastering or failing to master a particular school subject, but as objects of curiosity, enigmas whose outward appearance veils a complex inner life. Teachers must look at them at such moments in a questioning manner, the way they might gaze upon a person who was sitting for a portrait or a prisoner at the bar of justice. "What kind of person *is* this?" they ask. This also means looking at physical objects in a similar fashion, seeing them not simply as tools waiting to be picked up and used or as clutter that needs to be pushed aside or ignored, but, instead, as tools without an immediate job to do, as objects with a character of their own, worthy of intense scrutiny. The goal, in other words, is to look upon the room's bric-a-brac as though its individual items were housed in a museum showcase and ask, "What does this object stand for? What might it symbolize?"

This kind of leisurely, reflective looking takes time, of course, a commodity that today's busy teachers have little of. However, even brief glimpses of the kind that might be stolen during the recurrent lulls that punctuate the school day can often be illuminating and worthwhile. Moreover, when such a perspective has become more or less habitual, as tends to happen with practice, the time available for its exercise also seems to increase.

Part of the reason for this increase is that we learn to make better use of recollection. Even the busiest teacher can usually find time after the close of school or during the evening hours to reflect at least briefly on what took place earlier in the day. Scenes can be recalled, as can the actions of individual students. Time and again, the teachers we worked with recalled particular moments and events that called for further thought — a lesson that took an unexpected turn, the surprise of a student's suddenly showing insight into a topic that was discussed months earlier, a teacher's flash of anger over a bit of misbehavior, a student's proud smile over a job well done. The significance of what went on can often be seen more clearly from such a vantage point than it can from up close. "Emotions recollected in tranquillity," Wordsworth reminds us, often serve as the source of poems and other works of art. No less do we need to be reminded that recollections of a more ordinary sort can continually deepen the significance and meanings of our prior experience.

What about the extension of sympathetic awareness and its daily practice to the domain of self-understanding? Can teachers view themselves as they do their students? Can they step aside from their daily activity and cast a sympathetic glance at their own doings and undertakings? Can they, in short, look upon themselves as expressive objects? It is not clear that they can. The power to see ourselves as others see us, to borrow from another poet, turns out to be a gift at best and a rare one at that. Even a kindly and forgiving view of ourselves, of the sort that good teachers automatically take toward their students, may not be all that easy. Yet, having acknowledged the difficulty, we still insist that it is possible for teachers, as for all of us, to attain increased insight into their own character and into the kind of person they appear to be to others. This task calls for the same willingness to reflect that we have described as essential for gaining insight into the expressive qualities exhibited by students and by the classroom environment as a whole.

Beyond extending their naturally sympathetic view to take in everything they see and hear, which includes themselves, teachers who want to explore the expressive meaning of their environment to its fullest need to make a special effort to *say* what they see and think. They need to put into words their hunches and suspicions, their doubts and budding convictions, no matter how tentatively held or crudely phrased such premonitions and intuitions may turn out to be. This may involve keeping a diary or notebook. It may also be accomplished simply by talking to others—other teachers, for example, or their friends. The three of us found that talking to each other was absolutely essential in extending our individual perspectives. (We also found those conversations to be particularly sustaining when one or more of us began to worry about what critics might say about our work!) Talking with others, or at least doing some writing and thinking on their own, can help teachers to remain open to new meanings and may also help guard against their developing either a Pollyannaish or a bitterly cynical view of what takes place in school.

Our belief in the importance of trying to articulate thoughts and feelings about classroom matters springs from our conviction that the expressive significance of our surroundings is first experienced vaguely and is subsequently clarified by the process of trying to put those vague feelings into words. It is not simply that we find words for what we already think, but that the choice of words is itself a necessary and integral part of the discovery process. We formulate what we think in the process of trying to put into words that which is initially inchoate. This is hardly an original observation yet it remains one that teachers and all others who visit classrooms would do well to keep in mind.

The Value of Expressive Awareness

What does a reflective and sympathetic outlook on classrooms yield? Why adopt it? What is its payoff, its "cash value," as William James might say? That set of questions is hard to answer definitively. In fact, if we stick with definitiveness as the criterion, it is a lot easier to say what *not* to expect than its opposite. The practice of looking reflectively and sympathetically at what goes on within the classroom (and within ourselves as well) is very unlikely to yield a set of do's and don'ts about teaching. No recipes for action can be expected to flow from such an approach. Nor is it likely to yield a set of principles for the design of a program in moral education. Those in search of such a design had best look elsewhere. It also is not likely to deliver a set of novel and startling insights into the human condition. Its practitioners can hardly expect to unearth any ground-breaking new truths about human nature.

Techniques of teaching, principles of curriculum design, and bold new discoveries about humankind in general — all three of those desiderata, if our own experience serves as a reliable guide, are hardly to be hoped for by those who practice what we have been trying to preach in this book. "Why, then, bother to listen?" the critic shoots back. "Why follow these recommendations?"

The best answers that we can give to those questions are anecdotal and testimonial and by no means definitive. They describe what happened to us and to many of the teachers we worked with as we became increasingly conscious of the teacher's role as a moral agent in classrooms and as we talked together about that growing awareness over a period of three years. This section and the next will take up these emerging insights. They do not describe outcomes that happened to us all; nor do all of them apply to any single one of us. In fact, calling them "outcomes" turns out to be misleading, for they don't behave the way outcomes are supposed to behave. They don't stay put, for one thing. They keep shifting about in a most un-outcomelike manner. And they persist in doing so even now, well after the project has ended. "Changes" would be a better word for them, for their significance derives in large part from a comparison with what went before. But calling them that does not make them settle down. "Changes that keep changing" would be more like it.

They are of two kinds, or at least that is how we will speak of them. How distinguishable they are in real life is a question we leave to our readers. One category of change pertains to what we see and hear. It describes how we do so differently once we begin to view the world as being full of expressive meaning. The other category covers changes of a more interior and personal kind. Of particular relevance within that category are modifications in how teachers conceive of their jobs and their professional responsibilities. The distinction between these two categories is not a sharp one, as we have already pointed out, but it remains analytically useful all the same.

We have already said a lot about what happens to our view of the world once we begin looking at things from an expressive point of view. We have talked about the deepening of our perception and the broadening of it as well, and about how persons and objects become saturated with meaning, vehicles of expressive significance, media whose physical properties convey messages that seem to lie within the properties themselves or at least are inextricable from them. To all of that we have very little to add at this point. Here, with our focus on the benefits that might accrue to those who adopt the perspective we have been describing, we need to stress that the meaning that comes to us through this way of looking is typically felt to be either a genuine *addition* to what we currently believe or a *correction* of a prior belief. It is experienced, in other words, as either an extension or an improvement of our working knowledge — in either case, a move toward greater truth. Often its objects are the people around us, which for teachers means their pupils. Ms. Hamilton comes to see Gary as a hard worker now that he is paired with Amy. Ms. Morton begins to notice a longing in Ella that she never noticed before. And, as we have pointed out repeatedly, such changes overtake our perceptions of the physical world as well. Features of the environment that were overlooked can suddenly stand out with a vividness that is close to unnerving. The window curtains that looked so bright and cheerful at the beginning of the school year have suddenly gone limp and drab. When did that happen? Was it when our back was turned? The freshly washed blackboard, rid of yesterday's tired smudges, now glows in the morning light like a beacon of hope, an invitation to begin again.

Changes like these occur all the time for those who are receptive to them. But they are not always welcome changes, sad to say. We may regret having noticed some of the things we see when we look carefully and may wish to ignore them. Reality, as we all know, can often be as harsh as it is inviting. As we pointed out before, when we began our observations and later when we undertook their analysis, described in Parts Two and Three, we certainly did not anticipate that we would come upon as many morally questionable or ambiguous practices in the teachers' classrooms as we did. We knew the teachers well and we liked them, all of which makes our surprise that much stronger. However, we doubt that we are alone in making such discoveries. We suspect that anyone who looks at teachers and classrooms as we have tried to do will invariably come upon the ambiguous, the questionable, the troubling, just as we have done. That, to us, comes with the territory; it goes with taking seriously the expressiveness of human affairs. Perhaps it even signals a modest increment of moral wisdom, surely a welcome outcome to all who teach or who care about teaching.

There is more to be said about what happens when we try to look carefully yet sympathetically at what goes on around us, whether in schools or elsewhere. The first thought is that such a view entails a willingness to forgive the bad or at least a readiness to see it as issuing from the same source as the good—that is, enacted by a basically decent person or embedded within an environment such as a school or classroom that is intended to be beneficial. (If the wrongdoing turns out to be egregious or the environment excessively harsh, we may of course be forced to abandon our initial sympathies entirely and replace them with antipathies of corresponding bias that cause us to lean in the opposite direction. Fortunately, we never had to execute such an about-face during our work on the Moral Life Project.)

This willingness to forgive or at least tolerate the foibles of those whom we believe to be basically good, or to overlook the shortcomings of a generally pleasing and ostensibly beneficial environment, constitutes a loosening up or a relaxing of the tendency to rush to judgment, a tendency, as we have argued, that seems to be almost instinctive among classroom observers. A more relaxed view replaces the kind of petty, moralistic bookkeeping that tallies the good and the bad of everything we see and hear, as on a bill of lading, in the hope of toting up a sum at the end. A readiness to be more forgiving and more understanding than that is, in effect, a gesture of magnanimity: toward students; toward teachers; even, when our vision turns inward, toward ourselves.

An additional payoff of the outlook we have been advocating is the way it yields a more *encompassing* view of educational practice than we might have had at the start. In our own work we set out in the beginning to see if we could identify some of the ways in which schools and teachers might be having a beneficial effect on today's students. We never abandoned that original goal, as the preceding three parts of this book make clear. But we did add to it. For what we came to understand, as we got to know the teachers and began to struggle with the significance of some of the more questionable teaching practices that we encountered, was that the total process by which we generated our "findings" — the observations, the reflection afterward, the discussions among ourselves and with the teachers — was fully as intriguing and as worthy of reflection in its own right as were the findings themselves. This was so not only because our way of working differed radically from the usual conceptions of how research should be conducted but also because we felt it moving us away from the usual concerns that educators have about teaching practices that "work" or "don't work." What we felt ourselves moving toward instead was a more encompassing set of concerns that had to do with the *orienting attitudes* of both teachers and researchers. It was in this way that we became interested in expressiveness and related concepts and sought to understand how they bore upon the practice of teaching as a moral enterprise.

Readers accustomed to the language of research might call the questions in which we became interested *methodological,* and they would certainly be right in one sense, for our questions clearly dealt with how one does something. But they were worlds apart from the methodological issues with which empirical investigators typically struggle; in other words, they had little or nothing to do with the usual worries about interjudge reliability, construct validity, sampling strategies, and the like. Instead, our chief concerns dealt with issues such as how to come to grips with our personal reaction to what we were witnessing in classrooms, how to describe what we had seen, and what significance to attribute to the seemingly mundane matters of a teacher's personal style or the physical details of the room — issues that we have touched upon repeatedly throughout this book and have treated in some detail in this final part.

These research-oriented remarks give rise to a question that some readers may have already posed in their own minds while following our account: Is there any way of bringing together under a single term all of the different aspects of the way of looking discussed in this book? Is there a name we might give to the approach we have taken? We can think of none, though to tell the truth we have not really tried, because we doubt that our settling upon a label would be of much help to anyone. We have used terms like *expressive awareness* and *sympathetic bias* to refer to aspects of our work, but such expressions, though they do say a lot, do not manage to say it all.

The closest we have come to communicating what lies at the heart of our proposed way of looking at teachers and classrooms is by likening it to the outlook of artists, poets, and others who strive for a more imaginative, as opposed to a less imaginative, view of things (a view completely devoid of imagination would be a virtual impossibility, as we see it, because it would also be devoid of meaning). We have already hinted at this resemblance, for example, in Part Two when we made use of Eco's terms *open* and *closed* in setting the stage for our classroom observations-cum-commentary. Readers may recall that we employed his terms in order to emphasize the essentially open nature of interpretation, the fact that new insight can take place if we presume that the meaning in human affairs far exceeds what can be seen from any single perspective.

However, the danger with a comparison to what artists do is the ease with which it can be misunderstood. Some might take it as a move on our part to claim "artistic" status, in the honorific sense of the term, for our own work. We have no such intention. Others might see it as an ill-considered effort to distance ourselves from those who employ more conventional methods than ours in their studies of educational issues. They too would be wrong.

Our sole reason for wanting to situate our outlook in the same intellectual hemisphere as that of the arts (though still oceans apart, of course) is because we share with artists everywhere the underlying conviction that the world abounds in meaning. Turn where we might, there is more to be seen and heard than meets the eye or the ear, or any of the other senses, for that matter. Artists know that to be so, though they may seldom bother to say so explicitly. Their works speak for them. Poems, paintings, drama, dance — all make clear their creator's commitment to *showing* (as opposed to simply declaring) that the world of ordinary experience is far richer in meaning than we commonly allow. It isn't only artists who hold that view, needless to say. Others do as well; perhaps we all do at some level of our being. But artists, at least the good ones, constantly *act* on that belief. They put it to work daily, whereas most of the rest of us have hardly given the idea enough thought to call it our own, much less adopt it as a guiding light, a principle of action.

Works of art, properly studied, also have a lot to teach us about the process of extracting meaning from the world. The critic Robert Hughes describes that process rather succinctly in a set of remarks that turn on the distinction between signs and art objects. He is speaking principally of the visual arts but what he has to say has great generality: "A sign is a command. Its message comes all at once. It means one thing only — nuance and ambiguity are not important properties of signs — and is no better for being hand-made. Works of art speak in a more complicated way of relationships, hints, uncertainties, and contradictions. They do not force meanings on their audience; meaning emerges, adds up, unfolds from their imagined centres. A sign dictates meaning, a work of art takes one through the process of discovering meaning."[11]

A "process of discovering meaning" rather than dictating it; exploring nuanced and ambiguous "relationships, hints, uncertainties, and contradictions"; saying that meaning, unforced, "emerges, adds up, unfolds"—all of those words and phrases from Hughes's commentary about works of art certainly fit as a description of the work we did in the project leading up to this book. It was that emerging sense of similarity between our work and what artists typically do that led us by stages to the comparison we have just made.

However, having made that comparison, we must quickly temper its tone of exclusivity by emphasizing, as we have already begun to do, the similarities between artistic endeavors and more mundane forms of activity. For if we take a close look at human experience in general, what we find, as we have said, is that the artist's way of working, at least in the terms outlined above, is not all that different from what everyone does all the time. We all gradually discover the meaning of the world around us and we do so in a manner closely akin to the one Hughes describes. Our daily experience, examined with care, would be seen to contain countless instances of such artistic probings and explorations. The difference is that the customary degree of care taken by the artist as he or she probes and explores the world of experience, which includes the peculiarities of the artistic medium of the work itself, far exceeds that taken by most of us as we go about our daily lives. Therein lies one of art's chief lessons for us all.

What does the analogy with art have to do with teaching in particular? Earlier we discussed several ways in which a sympathetic bias may deepen our appreciation for what is involved in interpreting what teachers and students do. We spoke of this bias as inviting an attitude of forgiveness toward the "bad," in part through recognizing that bad and good are inextricably intertwined. We also said that a sympathetic viewpoint results in the loosening up or relaxing of the usual rush to judgment, a tendency to which all who enter classrooms, teachers and researchers alike, seem prone. Third, we argued that a sympathetic viewpoint takes us beyond the narrowness of worrying solely about the discovery of effective and ineffective practices. It extends our breadth of vision and thus leads to a more encompassing perspective on educational affairs. To all this we now add the claim that this rejuvenated and expanded perspective, which stems in the main from a sympathetic understanding and which points toward the continued exploration of meaning, resembles in fundamental ways a viewpoint prevalent among artists.

The comparison with the arts also triggers questions that we must face. Can teachers successfully maintain a sympathetic and accepting rather than judgmental attitude toward what they see, in the manner of most artists? Can they adopt such a way of looking and still remain teachers? How contemplative and morally neutral can they afford to be while operating within the confines of their professional role? Isn't there something fundamentally judgmental and, hence, moralistic built into the job that would prevent them from becoming too accepting of their surroundings, particularly those features of their surroundings that they as teachers are paid to correct: the imperfections, ideational and otherwise, of their own students?

Teachers do indeed have responsibilities that prohibit them from sitting idly by as their students commit errors, flaunt a lack of knowledge, or openly persist in behavior that is potentially harmful to themselves and to others. By definition, teachers are sworn foes of ignorance in all its forms. They are also guardians of our cultural heritage. Those dual obligations commit them to action. However—and here our analogy with art comes to the fore—within the framework of those agreed-upon duties, whatever actions teachers take, if they are to be both wise and prudent, commonly demand a degree of understanding, a full appreciation of the situation, that can only come from the kind of detached contemplation and reflection that artists typically employ.

This detachment must not be confused with indifference. On the contrary, when it is the kind of detachment we have been talking about, it expresses a degree of caring uncommon in its intensity. One thing that accounts for its uncommonness is the time it takes in its enactment. As we hope the contents of this book have by now amply demonstrated, there is no way of looking carefully at anything that goes on in schools, or anywhere else for that matter, without spending a considerable amount of time doing so. How much is "considerable"? That depends on what we are looking at and what else we have to do. During our own work we often found that "considerable" meant spending as much time as we had available, and then some. In any case, because time is such a precious commodity for most of us, its expenditure in looking and listening and later reflecting on what has been seen and heard bespeaks either an attitude of idle curiosity (in which case it usually doesn't last very long and the time it takes is therefore decidedly *in*considerable) or one of concern and caring. There is also this to be said about such an expenditure of time: the longer we look and the more we reflect upon what we have seen (both within broad limits), the more we come to care about whatever we were looking at and reflecting upon. Thus, the act of looking and listening carefully, together with subsequent periods of reflection, not only expresses to onlookers an attitude of interest on the part of the observer; it also serves to increase the observer's genuine interest in what he or she is observing. What this means for teachers and others who work in classrooms is that the time spent in stepping aside from their roles as immediate caregivers and in trying to view their students and their classrooms from a somewhat more detached point of view is actually time invested in *adding* to their own sense of involvement in what they are doing.

How real is what we come to see through a sympathetic and artistic way of looking? Do the objects of expressive awareness exist solely in the eye of the beholder, as beauty is alleged to do, or are they really "out there," the way we take physical objects to be? We have responded to this question several times already, beginning in Part Two where we rejected the usual distinction between the terms *objective* and *subjective,* calling it unhelpful. We now have a slightly different answer to give, one that takes advantage of the comparisons we have drawn with art. Accordingly, we introduce it with the words of a poet, Jean Garrique, written some thirty or forty years ago. What she has to say is rather effusive in its sentiment, her use of the male pronoun makes it sound a little out of date, and the statement as a whole is hardly a model of clarity. (In fairness we must point out that it was found among her papers after she died and it is quite certain that she did not intend it for publication.) However, it does state a fundamental truth in a form that, for all its imperfections, we find compelling. Garrique says, "It is the poet's faith that there is reality, if not realities upon realities back of, behind, beyond the enchanting surfaces and appearances of 'reality.' Perhaps his most strenuous occupation is to peel himself, to divest himself, to bare himself of the evil enchantments that 'surface reality' may cast upon him in order that he may strip himself down to that level of seeing and feeling whereby his reality may be able to meet the reality within and behind what is seen and known to the senses."[12]

Along with Garrique, we too believe that reality comes to us layered. Anyone who wants to make contact with the fullness of meaning that the world has in store must look "within and behind what is seen and known to the senses." However, our own explanation of how reality is constituted goes beyond Garrique's observation. To her talk about layers of reality we would want to add that the poet (or anyone else who bothers to look intently at his or her surroundings) actually brings those subsensible levels of reality into being in a functional sense — *realizes* them, we might say — making them real through the simple act of noting and, as appropriate, celebrating or deprecating or responding in some other way to their presence. Once a teacher, for example, perceives one of her students as being sullen and untrustworthy, once she describes him to herself in those terms, her reality (i.e., the field of forces to which she accommodates as she goes about the job of teaching) has undergone a significant change and so has the reality of the student who has been so judged (i.e., *his* reality now contains a teacher who perceives him in that way), although he may never recognize that to be so.

Does this mean that anything the teacher thinks about

the student, any attribute she might casually attribute to him, is thereby real? In one sense yes and in another no. Anything she might think is certainly real in the sense of being a part of her perceptual world. Whatever she thinks of the student is almost bound to affect how she reacts to him and it may color other aspects of her behavior as well. As a perception, therefore, it is indeed real, no matter how erroneous or unfair it might be. However, though perceptions may be real functionally, they still may be unwarranted or undeserved, which is where prolonged observation and reflection become helpful if not indispensable. There is no way of ensuring that what we perceive is absolutely accurate but there are ways of increasing our confidence in the meaning of what we see and hear. The manner of looking that we have been describing here is one of them.

There is, however, a drawback to this way of perceiving, especially for those who insist upon quick decisions and univocality of judgment. Our examples should have made that clear by now. In the normal course of events we look long and hard in order to be sure of what we see. But it often happens that the more we look and the longer we reflect on what we have seen, the more complicated the perceived object, scene, or person seems to become and the more we are led to reject simplistic interpretations of its meaning or significance. Recall, for example, how often we witnessed questionable practices among the teachers who participated in the Moral Life Project, teachers whom we had initially judged to be at least average or above, if not outstanding, in their respective domains of expertise. Faced with such apparent contradictions, we at first shrugged them off by telling ourselves that no one is perfect.

But that trite observation, true as it may be, obscures a deeper truth which is that *nothing is anything until judged to be so* and that all judgments are abstractions and hence leave out of consideration as much as, if not more than, they include. This is not to say that judgments need not be made. Of course they must. But we warn against making them sooner than necessary. And we acknowledge that the notion of coming to a *final* judgment refers only to the termination of a process and not to the attainment of perfect knowledge. Truth as an ideal, the *whole* truth, as we might say, refers to the potential fulfillment of human understanding, to everything that might be known and taken into account when judging a person or an object or a situation. By that standard, all judgments, even those unanimously agreed upon by an entire community of believers, as such consensual bodies are sometimes called, can never be more than partial truths. These facts may be unwelcome to those who prefer swift decisions but they require acknowledgment all the same.

The phrase "the whole truth" leads by a process of association, especially for an educator, to the phrase "the whole child," a term that has enjoyed considerable popularity in educational circles over the years. That term also remains popular today, particularly among teachers and administrators who work in elementary schools. Along with "progressive" and "child-centered," it has come to stand for a coherently distinctive ideology of teaching. The point of that ideology, as almost everyone knows, has been to insist upon treating students of all ages as whole persons, rather than as disembodied intellects whose brains alone, figuratively speaking, were the only organs to which teachers need properly attend. To teach the whole child or the whole student, according to advocates of this position, is to take into consideration the student's feelings, attitudes, interests, and more. It is to think of each learner, in the degree to which it is possible to do so, as an individual whose uniqueness calls for an individualized response from the teacher.

Like those who espouse a child-centered view, we too would urge that students be seen as individuals rather than as walking "brain boxes" or as statistical averages that exist only as abstractions. Moreover, the view we have taken makes clear what it means to look upon students (or anyone else) as individuals. It means stepping back from the rush of ongoing events, detaching ourselves from the immediacy of pedagogical demands at least long enough to begin to wonder what Ella or Lisa or Mr. Bailey or Richard is really like as a person. It also means taking into account our own feelings about that individual, and wondering why he or she makes us feel pleased or annoyed or simply puzzled and confused. It means, above all, being open to all that observation and reflection can reveal about that person while at the same time seeking to maintain a sympathetic frame of mind to encompass the growth of our understanding. In all such ways our view remains consonant with what most of the child-centered educators have been urging for years.

But our view also adds to what so many others have long advocated. First of all, it extends the coverage of such a way of perceiving. The child-centered educators are doubtless correct in calling for teachers to focus their attention on students as individuals. But in our view their plea does not go far enough. We urge that such a particularizing view be applied not only to individual students and their teachers but also to the total environment of classrooms. What does such an extension accomplish? It allows, among other things, for the consideration of questions that have nothing to do with individuals per se but that are no less important than those that do. These would include questions that have a direct bearing on the quality of life of everyone present in these highly specialized environments — questions about classroom climate and atmosphere, for example, or, following our own lead, questions that ask about the teacher's own moral contribution to the well-being of all.

Second, the view we are advocating restores the teacher to center stage or at least places him or her *on* stage if not exactly at its center. This placement is important, for advocates of a child-centered perspective usually ask teachers to choose between their own approach on the one hand and a subject-centered approach on the other. The latter, which is usually portrayed so unattractively that it turns out not to be a choice at all, depicts the teacher as someone for whom the transmission of subject matter is of paramount importance. Teachers, in this view, must consent to serve one master or the other: the child or the school subject.

We are not proposing the addition of a third option that might be called a teacher-centered approach. It sounds to us just as limited as the other two, at least if it is taken by itself, or if it is taken to mean that the teacher should put considerations of self above those of either students or subject matter. In fact, putting it that way makes it sound much *less* attractive than either of the other views. However, when we speak of our own view as placing the teacher at least on stage, if not at its center, all we mean is that the teacher must be acknowledged, and must come to acknowledge himself or herself, as being the single individual in every classroom whose decisions, opinions, and outlook on life in general count the most in giving shape to what goes on in that environment. We do not say that the opinions, decisions, and outlooks of others count for nothing, or deny that the teacher's freedom to act on what he or she believes and desires may be greatly constrained by both institutional and social forces, some of them emanating from outside the school itself. But we do insist that within such limits teachers must be seen and see themselves as occupying key roles in classrooms — not simply as technicians who know how to run good discussions or teach encoding skills to beginning readers but as persons whose view of life, which includes all that goes on in classrooms, promises to be as influential in the long run as any of their technical skills. It is this extended view of a teacher's responsibility that makes it appropriate to speak of teaching as a moral enterprise.

There is nothing new about such a view of teaching, we hasten to admit. In fact, it is quite old. Its origins doubtless go back to the Greeks or beyond. But it is a view that has gone out of favor of late in certain quarters. Many who train today's teachers, for example, no longer appear convinced of its importance. The same is true of a whole company of individuals who study teaching through research. Even teachers themselves, from the poorest to the best of them, may need reminding from time to time that there is more to teaching than meets the eye or than can be encompassed in a compendium of pedagogical do's and don'ts.

The fact that teachers too may temporarily lose sight of some of the more venerable truths about their trade — truths that even the ancients knew and whose prior grasp drew many of today's practitioners into teaching in the first place — is one of the several insights that emerged during our biweekly group discussions that were part of the Moral Life Project. Those insights, those rediscoveries, help tie together the benefits of the way of looking that we have been discussing with a range of additional benefits that accompany prolonged conversation among a group of professionals who share a common undertaking. They thus form a set of lessons that fittingly serves to bring our book to its close.

Talking Together

For the teachers who worked with us, by far the most rewarding part of the project was the continuing series of biweekly dinner meetings during which the group's conversation ranged widely from personal anecdotes and tidbits of local gossip to matters of considerable weight and moral significance. Oddly enough, however, as rich and rewarding as those discussions were for everyone present, they yielded very little in the way of quotable material that might fill out a volume such as this and have it end with the words of the teachers themselves. There are two reasons why this was so, one of them technical and fairly trivial, the other substantive and of far greater importance.

The technical reason is easy enough to explain. In the interest of trying to make everyone in the group feel as comfortable as possible, we decided at the start not to record any of the discussions electronically and we stayed with that decision throughout the life of the project. One or two of us did manage to take notes at each session while remaining an active participant in the discussion, but what got written was usually quite skimpy, seldom more than a page or two long — more like an outline than a running account of what transpired. Direct quotations seldom exceeded a line or two of telegraphic prose.

The substantive reason for the scantiness of our notes and for our staying with our original decision not to record each session, even long after the participants had become sufficiently comfortable for us to do so, was that there usually was little said at those meetings that was noteworthy, at least to anyone other than the participants. Most of the issues the teachers discussed, even most of the insights they ultimately attained, were of local interest only and even then not always of interest to everyone present. Here is the way one of us remarked upon that phenomenon in a note scribbled at the close of a fall meeting during the project's second year: "In describing this group to outsiders, we're in the position of someone who, having told a funny anecdote without getting a laugh, says to his listener, 'You had to be there.'" That feeling of not being able to explain to an outsider what was so special or interesting about our biweekly discussions was widespread within the group and even became a source of discomfort and near embarrassment when it came time at the close of the project to report on the group's accomplishments to funding officials and nonparticipating colleagues (i.e., fellow teachers and administrators) from the schools where the project's teachers taught.

Why was that so? Why did we initially feel that we had little to report that would be of interest to others? Part of the answer was that most of the "insights" we came to and most of the truths about teaching that we found ourselves voicing were neither novel nor freshly expressed. They were, instead, *familiar* truths and the language we used to speak of them often revealed their age — in other words, they consisted of aphorisms and clichés that everyone present had heard dozens of times before. In fact, not infrequently someone about to speak would feel compelled to apologize for the apparent triteness or banality of what he or she was about to say and would introduce it with something like, "Well, here comes another old bromide . . . " or "Excuse me for repeating the obvious, but . . . " and the rest of us would nod and smile indulgently, for we had all done the same thing from time to time.

Yet despite the familiarity and even the triteness of much that was said, there was nothing about the sessions themselves that was tiresomely repetitive or boring to those present. Quite the contrary. Although the conversation on many evenings began slowly and sometimes awkwardly, by the close of each session almost everyone had been an active participant, often a highly spirited one, and when it was time to stop there were almost always scattered groans of disappointment. It was not at all unusual for participants to continue to chat about the discussion as they traveled home together and perhaps even return to it a day or so later when they chanced to meet at school or elsewhere.

Here, then, is a seeming paradox. On one hand, the content of most of our discussions was so ordinary and our individual contributions to it were usually expressed in such conventional language that when it came time to address the public it seemed as though we had little to say that would be of interest to anyone outside the group. On the other hand, we participants were usually quite pleased with the meetings, even at times exhilarated by what had been said. In fact, participants so enjoyed the time spent together that the group as a whole voted to continue the discussions for a full year after the project had officially ended. Yet to understand that enthusiasm it apparently had to be experienced firsthand. Tales of what had taken place, even when they were told with enthusiasm, never seemed to do the trick.

What was it about being there that made the experience itself so memorable and exciting for us? Part of it was simply having the opportunity to talk about aspects of teaching that most teachers seldom discuss. "It feels good to talk about moral issues," one member of the group announced one evening when asked what she was getting from the meetings. "I'm able to raise questions of interest," another said. "It's important to pay attention to the unmeasurable," a third declared. "You can't put the growth of a kid on paper." Comments such as these echo the point made earlier that it is easy in the hurly-burly of classroom life to lose the conviction that teaching is a moral enterprise, because there is little time and little encouragement to reflect upon what happens.

But there was more to the group's sense of accomplishment than simply being able to talk about ideas that seldom get discussed. Another source of the excitement that many of us experienced was the feeling of having been reminded of something we once knew but had somehow forgotten. Here's the way one of the teachers put it: "In teaching we're mostly so caught up in measuring, we don't think about creating a more humane environment. We've lost sight of what's truly important, but the project has brought it back in view." Another added, "The group has been a reminder that you get pulled away from kids by the success of your career." The spirit of recovery or rediscovery of something that had been temporarily lost from view was dominant in many of the sessions. It accounts in part for the excessive reliance on formulaic ways of saying things — the hackneyed speech that we referred to above. For most of the insights that got recovered were indeed old ideas, not just autobiographically but historically as well.

In the last section we talked about the reality of perceptions, the way they function as genuine forces in shaping our behavior and in influencing the behavior of others. To emphasize that point, we used the verb *to realize* in its literal sense. To realize something, we observed, is to make it real, to give it life within the world of the perceiver, if not beyond. Now we want to extend that observation to what has just been said about the process of recalling old truths about teaching. For the act of remembering is also a form of realization. It is not the same as realizing something for the first time, of course, but it is a process by which something that was once forgotten is brought back to life. Unfortunately, this revivification does not ensure that the newly remembered notion will endure. For that to happen, other conditions also have to hold. We all know how easy it is to forget something we have only recently recalled. But it is certainly true that unless something is recalled — realized, as we are partial to saying — it can no longer play an active part in our conscious life and we can no longer employ it as an example that guides our behavior, a reason for doing something, or an excuse for not doing it. So the act of remembering is closely tied to what is or is not real to each of us.

These rudimentary observations about the nature of human perception and the workings of memory seem to us to be of crucial importance not only in understanding what occurred during the discussions that were part of the Moral Life Project but in coming to grips with what is happening on a much broader front within today's schools. For as we look upon the current state of those institutions from as broad a vantage point as our combined experience allows, what seems to us to be lacking in many quarters and at many levels of institutional authority is not so much *new* knowledge about how to do this or that (although additions to our store of educational know-how are surely always welcome) as it is *old* knowledge about what teachers and school administrators can and might accomplish with the tools at hand. If our guess is right, and we base it in large part on what we learned from the teachers in the Moral Life Project, at least some of that old knowledge no longer functions as it once did because, quite simply, those in a position to put it to work have forgotten it. They have done so not the way we might forget the words to a song or the combination to a safe but, rather, the way we sometimes forget to say goodnight to a spouse or fail to act in accord with our convictions. They have let that old knowledge slip from sight, like the reminder to return a call that gets buried in the stack of papers on our desk. It therefore has to be resuscitated, revivified, made the subject of discussion with our colleagues, reflected upon and jotted down, pinned to the bulletin board if necessary, and even, under certain circumstances, traced in huge, black letters and affixed atop the blackboard of the classroom, like a banner for all to see.

That last possibility is not as outlandish as it may appear. It was suggested by a conversation one of us had with Mr. Peters, a high school teacher of religion, who during the first year of the project had such a reminder atop one of the bulletin boards in his classroom. It said "KNOWLEDGE IS POWER" in big, black letters. But then, inexplicably, Mr. Peters took it down; he later was asked why. Here's the way the conversation went:

Interviewer: I noticed that a sign is missing from your bulletin board — "Knowledge is power."

Mr. P.:   Purposely.

Int.:   How come?

Mr. P.:   Is that what it said — "Knowledge is power"?

Int.:   As I remember.

Mr. P.:   "Knowledge is — "? Yeah, I think you're right. In any case, I remember taking it down because it — I found that it didn't express what I wanted to have in my class. . . . Upon reflection and upon just considering what I'm teaching and considering the symbols I want to convey—that wasn't one of them. And just the way it was up there, in big, black block letters, you know, conveyed power in a certain way. And the dryness of knowledge, you know, just knowledge. For some reason that meant something to me after my first year [in this school]. And I really wanted to convey how important knowledge was and that you needed knowledge. But after having it up there and going through another year, I felt that raw knowledge isn't what I'm about and neither is power, at least the type of power that seems to be expressed in that [display]. So for my classroom, it became a little too stark.

Mr. Peters's experience is not quite an example of revivifying old knowledge (in fact, it strikes us as an example of trying to forget a piece of knowledge that was revived earlier!), but it reveals something akin to that. It also shows what can happen when a teacher starts brooding on the expressive significance of a classroom artifact like this sign and tries to match what it says in expressive terms with his emerging sense of what is important.

And, as the conversation with Mr. Peters also suggests, it is not just knowledge in the epistemological sense that gets stirred into life as a result of reflection. Not just "knowing that" and "knowing how," which is all that some would include under the rubric of knowledge. There are also the associated states of conviction, allegiance, intentionality, and determination that accompany those forms of revivified knowledge and transform them into action. Those conditions too must be revived and rekindled no less than the knowledge itself or else the revival of that knowledge will have been for naught.

What are some examples of the kind of knowledge we are talking about? Instead of citing independent instances of the sort of intellectual reawakening that we have been discussing, we have decided to focus on a set of insights that relate to each other in a thematic way. In fact, the theme they form was one that recurred many times in our group discussions throughout the three-year duration of the project. It was more emphatically sounded on some occasions than on others but it was almost always present as a kind of basic motif. The theme is epitomized in a three-word phrase that could easily have served as the group's slogan, had it ever elected to choose one. The three words are "We teach ourselves."

We have no record of when that phrase was introduced into our discussions or who first said it. But those three simple words obviously struck a responsive chord in the sensibilities of many who were present, for it wasn't long before its echoes were heard again and again. Most often the phrase was used as a kind of tag ending, the way a moral gets tacked on to a fable. But it was not uncommon to hear it erupt spontaneously in affirmation of what someone else had said, like the solemn intonement of an "Amen" in the midst of a sermon.

What did the teachers mean by the phrase "We teach ourselves," and how did those simple words come to embody a revitalized insight? The phrase was initially used as a way of acknowledging the potency of the teacher's own character and personality traits, not only as *pedagogical instruments,* as means to attain standard educational goals (e.g., "They know that when I get angry they'd better get down to work"), but also as *curricular content,* as "lessons" to be learned. As Mr. Turner put it one evening, "I not only teach senior English, I also teach Turner 101." Moreover, the "lessons" embodied in the way each teacher can be observed dealing with the demands of classroom life, which we talked about in Parts Two and Three, are not only "lessons" about that particular teacher. They also have to do with life in general.

Here is Ms. Morton, explaining in an interview how she tried to get one such lesson across. She began by saying that she believed that "part of what fourth grade is about is . . . helping kids learn how to negotiate school, helping kids figure out what the teacher wants." She went on to tell about a class that recently had done poorly on a language arts test.

Ms. M.:   So I spent quite a bit of time the next day saying to them, "Look, I'll give you a chance to do this over. I'm going to tell you exactly what I expect. . . . You know in my class I'm going to ask the questions the way I want them answered, and that's something you have to learn in school. You have to learn not only what is being taught, but you have to learn what each teacher expects."

She then went on to explain to the interviewer:

Ms. M.: At fourth grade, even the smart kids don't know how to negotiate school. . . . They need to be told that's one of the things they're learning. And they need to have it made easier for them. There are lots of things in school they shouldn't have to guess about. They shouldn't have to guess about me.

Interviewer: So you are giving them a lesson about yourself.

Ms. M.: A lesson about myself and a lesson about how you get through life.

If such "lessons" were scattered throughout the school year, would Ms. Morton's students really end up not having to guess about her at all? Surely not. The aspects of her uniqueness that might keep them guessing are by no means limited to her expectations about how they should take tests and otherwise conduct themselves as students. Instead, they extend to questions whose answers lie *behind* her expressed intention to be explicit about what she wants in order to make it "easier" for her pupils. Those questions would have to do with how likable she is as a person, how fair, how kind, how mean, how tough, and so forth. Such questions are very hard for teachers to address directly. Moreover, those who try run the risk of not being believed. Instead, the answers to all of those "What is he or she really like?" kinds of questions have to be inferred by taking note of other things those individuals say and do.

None of the other teachers reported being quite as explicit as Ms. Morton was in bringing at least one aspect of the "we teach ourselves" lesson to the attention of their students. However, almost every one of them ultimately came to acknowledge in his or her own way that such "lessons" were being conducted all the time in classrooms, whether formally announced or not. Hence the nearly instant popularity of the saying: "We teach ourselves."

The phrase "role model" gets used a lot these days in discussions having to do with how teachers and other adults can and should influence young people. Teachers, we are told, often become important role models for their students. That being so, it behooves teachers, so the argument goes, to behave like role models, which essentially means that they should exhibit virtuous qualities when in the presence of their students.

As part of the "we teach ourselves" mind-set that ran through so many of our group discussions, there was a clear recognition that students do indeed look to their teachers for guidance in matters that go far beyond the confines of instruction in the school subjects. Teachers, the group agreed, were under a moral obligation to conduct themselves accordingly. On occasion, the modeling metaphor was explicitly brought into play. For example, Father Maran talked about how "a teacher can model a way of managing one's emotions, of managing oneself as a person." Mr. James, a special education teacher, when asked about how his participation in the project had influenced him, had this to say:

Mr. J.:   I feel I have a stronger awareness of how much a role model I am. [Our discussions have] made me think about the right way to act, for example, about when I should suppress my emotional responses to students, when I must express them.

For the most part, however, participants did not make extensive use of the phrase "role model." We are not exactly sure why that was so but we suspect it may have had something to do with the fact that the phrase, as commonly used, connotes a more heroic posture than some of the participants were willing to picture themselves as adopting. To speak of someone else as a role model is one thing; to describe oneself in those terms is quite another. Moreover, the attributes that a number of the teachers depicted themselves as modeling for their students (usually without using that term) were not among the standard virtues that we associate with public figures, our most publicized role models. It was not qualities like courage, wisdom, or generosity that the teachers saw themselves as modeling. They spoke of much humbler virtues, things like showing respect for others, demonstrating what it means to be intellectually absorbed in a task, paying close attention to what is being said, or being a "good sport" when being teased about something. Indeed, some of the qualities that the teachers thought it important to exemplify could hardly be called virtues at all, at least not in the usual sense. They were more like admissions of human weakness. Here is Ms. Morton, for example, talking about the importance of demonstrating to her students that teachers, too, can make mistakes:

Ms. M.: When you're a teacher, part of what you want kids to be able to do is to say to themselves that it's okay to make a mistake. . . . You have to constantly push into that unknown, and you make mistakes when you do that, and that is normal and kids need to know that, and kids need to know that grown-ups make mistakes. And that is okay, you don't have to feel guilty about it.

Another teacher, Mr. Jordan, expressed a similar notion, though one that focused on his students' shortcomings rather than his own. He said that he works hard at establishing a sense of trust in the classroom so that his students know that "it's okay to be confused, that the teacher is not trying to screw you up."

It was hardly a new insight to anyone in the group that teachers are constantly on stage and are presenting themselves as models even when they are not behaving in a heroic or manifestly virtuous manner. But a number of those present seemed not to have thought about this truth in any prolonged or systematic way. The process of doing so made some of them a bit more self-conscious than normal when they returned to their classrooms, or so they later testified. How long that effect lasted is a question we did not inquire into but it is part of a larger topic that we cannot ignore, which has to do with the long-term effects on both teachers and students of following the dual pieces of advice that run throughout this book — one calling for a systematic effort on the part of several different groups, from teachers in training to educational researchers, to view all that goes on within classrooms in expressive terms, the other calling on teachers in particular to become more conscious of their own potential as moral agents. We shall return to the all-important topic of long-term effects in due course. Before doing so, however, we must add one further insight to those that have already been depicted as emerging from discussions of the "we teach ourselves" idea. The label for this one came not from the teachers themselves but from a book of literary criticism that one of us had recently read.

The insight itself had to do with the common idea of "putting up a front," of being forced by circumstance to behave in ways that belied one's innermost feelings or "true" self. What emerged, as the group talked about the need for teachers to model the kinds of attributes that we have just discussed, was the recognition that in doing that kind of modeling, teachers usually exhibited a better self than the one they actually possessed, or at least better than the one they customarily credited themselves as possessing. It was not just that teaching often required them to put up a front, but that it called upon them to put up a very special kind of front, a good front, as opposed to a bad one (like that of the person who acts tough) or one that was simply false (like that of an actor in a play). That good front could also be called false, of course, and sometimes it is shown to be, as when a teacher reaches his limits of tolerance for certain kinds of student behavior and proceeds to lose his temper momentarily. But its basically desirable character is what distinguishes it from other forms of this particular brand of deception.

Here is where the phrase from the volume of literary criticism came in handy. In his book, *The Company We Keep,* Wayne Booth describes a similar phenomenon among writers. He points out that the "implied author" of a text (i.e., the person that the inquisitive reader might imagine the author to be in real life) is quite frequently, if not always, a better person than the real author turns out to be. Booth speaks of this flattering portrayal of the self as revealing a kind of "hypocrisy-upward"[13] on the author's part and it was that phrase, turned around to form "upward hypocrisy," making it a bit more grammatical, that the group immediately adopted when it was suggested to them one evening as a convenient term for what they had been talking about. Upward hypocrisy, they readily agreed, was an apt description of the posture that teachers frequently have to take — in other words, the posture of having to act better than they inwardly feel themselves to be. It was about then that they also began to see that upward hypocrisy may have payoffs for teachers above and beyond its benefits as a pedagogical strategy. Perhaps, they reasoned, if they succeeded in putting up a good front for a sufficient length of time (a few years or a full decade, let's say), it would no longer be a front at all but an integral part of their personality or character. In this way, therefore, teaching and other forms of activity such as parenting that call forth such upward hypocrisy might be seen as a means of self-improvement, a way of actually *becoming* a better person. Seen in this light, the group's favored expression, "We teach ourselves," began to take on a new meaning. It now referred not only to the fact that teachers constantly offer themselves as lessons to their students but, additionally, that by so doing, especially when the effort is a conscious one of trying to put up a good front, they are also inadvertently teaching themselves to be better persons.

The insight into human nature that says that virtuous conduct helps to create the virtuous person goes back to the Greeks and possibly beyond, as we all know. Aristotle, for one, made much of it in the *Nicomachean Ethics*. Yet that age-old proposition and others like it take on a degree of freshness when they are seen to have relevance to our current situation. That kind of insight occurred often in our discussions with the teachers. One of them commented wryly one evening, "We have just reinvented the wheel," in recognition of the group having just stumbled upon yet another ancient truth. But his remark was not intended to be unkind. It was simply his way of acknowledging what by then had become commonplace: yet another rediscovery of the type that often happens when a group of teachers begin to share experiences.

From the idea that upward hypocrisy may have beneficial consequences for teachers as well as students it was a short step to the allied notion that by constantly correcting the faults of others, teachers were also indirectly correcting themselves. As one of the teachers put it, "I see in each of my children one of my own faults; when I correct them, I am teaching myself." There is, however, in that remark a tacit recognition of a different kind of hypocrisy than the one we have been discussing. For if teachers really are guilty of the same faults they see in their students, we begin to wonder about their right to stand in judgment of others. "Physician, heal thyself!" is the adage that most readily comes to mind as fitting such a circumstance. However, what the teacher who made that statement probably meant by it (and what subsequent statements by her confirmed) was that in her students' errors or misbehavior she recognized certain tendencies that were latent in her own character or personality as well and that by correcting the students' behavior she was indirectly strengthening her personal resolve to hold those tendencies in check. Be that as it may, her point about the potential benefits to oneself of being a judge of others was a natural extension of the ideas that were brought to light and set in motion by whoever introduced the phrase "We teach ourselves."

The Bottom Line

It is time at long last to say a word (but hardly more than that) about the kinds of questions that often nag at readers who want more than a book like this can offer. Their questions cover an assortment of worries, many of them having to do with what some would call outcomes, others dependent variables, and still others something like the payoff or perhaps the bottom line. The line of questioning that expresses their unease might go something like this: What good will it do to adopt the point of view that has been advocated in these pages? Will it make students more moral? Will it make teachers happier? Will it make them become better teachers? More content with their lot? Indeed, does it make any difference at all in the long run whether teachers or teachers-to-be are led to think about the moral dimensions of their work? The most impatient of those questioners, reaching the end of his rope, might hurl out this one: What is the evidence that all of this talk about the moral life of schools and the moral dimensions of teaching amounts to more than a hill of beans when placed beside the real problems facing today's schools?

We have already addressed that line of questioning in several places and in several ways throughout this book, though hardly to the satisfaction of the genuine skeptic, we would guess. We have made abundant use of observational material, hoping to show, through many concrete examples, just how deeply embedded moral matters are within the fabric of classroom affairs. We have offered testimony from teachers, some of it attesting to the benefits of their becoming sensitized to the moral dimensions of their work and other portions describing the changes that take place within individual outlooks as the result of a continuing and freewheeling discussion of moral matters in the company of colleagues. We have spelled out in considerable detail our own reactions, both immediate and delayed, to what we witnessed in the classrooms we visited. The gradual changes in our own perceptions as observers and commentators were offered as further evidence of what happens as we persist in probing beneath the surface of ordinary classroom events.

We could easily have included much more of each kind of evidence and, if we had thought volume alone would be convincing, we certainly would have done so. We doubt, however, that simply adding more to what has already been said would do much to quell the skeptic's doubts. For what such an individual is calling for in his or her state of uneasiness is a different kind of evidence entirely, what some would call "hard" evidence, as opposed to the "soft" evidence we have offered. The skeptic, as envisioned by us, wants to see numbers and "facts" and wants to look at things like test scores of students that reveal genuine gains in moral understanding or proper "conduct" as a result of their teachers having participated in the Moral Life Project. At the very least, our skeptic wants to hear from those students themselves to be certain that what the observers saw, the students saw also. He or she also wants evidence of the changes the teachers say happened to them as a result of their participation in the project. But rather than more testimony, the skeptic wants quantitative data collected by trained

observers — frequency counts of how often the teachers did this
or that, before and after their experience in the project. None
of those things are found in this book.

   We cannot help the skeptic, much as we might like to try.
Moreover, we doubt that anyone else can, either. For much of
the evidence he or she is calling for is not only of a kind that
we don't have; it is not to be had by anyone, at least not in the
form the skeptic wants it. We know of no paper-and-pencil tests,
for example, that will gauge either the short-term or long-term
benefits of spending a year or so under the tutelage of an understanding and sensitive teacher. Nor do we know of any tests
that will measure the cost of having spent the same amount of
time in the presence of that sensitive teacher's opposite number,
who may be no further away than across the hall. Not only are
there no such tests that we know of; we seriously doubt the possibility of there ever being any. And, quite frankly, we do not
find that prospect troubling. For it seems to us, first of all, that
the question of whether there *are* effects associated with being
in the company of teachers who are either good or poor in moral
terms is not one that we need test scores to answer. We already
know the answer. We discover it on our own, within months
of our entering kindergarten. Moreover, it is a lesson repeatedly enforced throughout our school careers. This is not to say
that there remains nothing more to learn about how students
are affected by their school experience, but we may safely assume there are such effects without having to establish their existence every time around.

   Second, there is a sense in which it almost doesn't matter
whether treating students in a kind and understanding manner
or its opposite has any lasting effects whatsoever (although we
know it does), because the ultimate reason for behaving sensi-
tively toward students, or anyone else, for that matter, is not
an instrumental one at all, at least not principally so. Rather,
its rationale rests on moral grounds. It is a moral duty. Teachers,
in other words, live under an obligation to be as considerate
and understanding as possible in dealing with their students,
not because such treatment works pedagogically or has positive outcomes, which we may safely assume it does, but simply

because students *deserve* to be treated that way. It is their right as humans. That being the case, teachers also have a corresponding obligation, it seems to us, to learn as much as possible about their own potency as moral agents and about the moral potency of the schools and classrooms in which they work. It has been the latter obligation that formerly the Moral Life Project and now this book have sought to address.

So to the broad set of questions calling for hard evidence of student outcomes and asking whether it makes any difference at all for teachers to behave morally, we must turn a deaf ear, not because the questions themselves are unimportant — far from it! — but simply because we already know their answers sufficiently well to proceed. We also know that not all of those answers are empirical, that some depend upon the kind of life we choose to lead and the kind of treatment we believe others deserve. These points may themselves fall under the category of forgotten knowledge that we mentioned earlier — that is, truths that seem increasingly to have been lost sight of these days and stand in need of being revivified. All of which brings us to the changes testified to by the teachers who participated in the Moral Life Project. What shall we make of their testimony? Do we dare rest content with it as evidence of the benefits that can accrue to those who faithfully follow our advice?

One reason we are willing to do so is that we ourselves underwent similar changes during the course of the project. We, too, grew more sensitive to the moral dimensions of school life as we went along. We came to understand the importance of trying to put words to those vague presentiments and intuitions that goad the consciousness of all classroom observers who attend to what is going on within their own psyches as they gaze upon the scene before them. We experienced the reaffirmation of prior convictions that comes with sharing those convictions with others and hearing them reciprocally reaffirmed. And we came to appreciate the moral potency of the commonplace, of ordinary doings and happenings whose significance we had previously overlooked. In short, the teachers' testimony matched our own experience almost point for point. Were they just telling us what we wanted to hear? That possibility strikes us as being so remote and so contradictory to everything else that we came to know about those teachers that we feel no urge to put it to the test and would not do so, even if we knew how.

Finally, what shall we say to the charge that there are far more important educational issues facing our nation's schools today than the ones we address in this book? Our reply depends on what the person who would make such a charge might mean by the word *important*. Are there more pressing questions, issues of greater immediate urgency? Doubtless there are in certain quarters. Finding the money to maintain essential educational services in some communities or ridding the schools of drugs and violence in others would be good examples. Are there questions of higher priority in the public's mind and possibly also in the minds of many educators? We concede that they exist as well. Figuring out how to improve the educational opportunities of inner-city youth would surely be one of them. The prevention of dropouts within that same population of students would be another. Readers can probably imagine still others that would vie for the highest priority of public attention.

However, when it comes to questions whose answers affect *all* students, regardless of age or locality, we can think of none more important than those we have examined in these pages. What kinds of moral influence do our schools exert? How can teachers in training, as well as those already launched on teaching careers, become more attuned to the moral significance of their own actions and of the classroom environments they help to create? What can they learn from each other about such matters? How can they revitalize what they already know, making it once again a part of their professional outlook and thereby enriching the intellectual and emotional resources they bring to bear on their work? These questions, each of which we have sought to address in this book, remain to be answered in a more complete and satisfying way by all who teach and by all who aspire to help them.

POSTSCRIPT

Where Might One
Go from Here?

*O*ur central purpose in writing this book has been to encourage
all who care about education to become more attuned to the
moral significance of schools as physical settings and as cruci-
bles of human action. To the extent that we have been successful, our readers should by this point be prepared (and possibly
even eager!) to enact within their own schools and classrooms,
or within those made available to them by others, the ways of
looking and reflecting that we have tried to demonstrate. Many
will also want to explore further one or more of the key ideas
that we have treated at length in the course of our discussions.
Others may wish to do the same with topics that we have only
touched upon or ones that we were forced to overlook entirely
because of insufficient time and space.

For those wanting to extend their understanding through
further reading, we offer the following compilation of references,
roughly organized by topic. The four categories we employ and
the readings we include under each of them are not meant to
be comprehensive. Instead, they are more like those familiar
boxes of Whitman's Samplers that serve so reliably as gifts to
friends and relatives whose specific tastes leave us guessing. Each
list offers an array of delights from which to choose, though
hardly more than a morsel of any one variety. Readers wanting to pursue any subtopic in depth are left to do so on their
own. We would hope, however, that some of the items included

in the general references in each section would be of help to them, as would the bibliographies contained in many of the individual volumes.

As an aid to readers who might be completely unfamiliar with particular texts, we have supplied brief annotations following each entry or each set of entries by the same author. These comments, we must caution, are hardly more than whispered asides, intended only to give the reader a very crude idea of what the book is about, with sometimes a word or two about why we have included it, especially when this is not evident from the title alone. Above all, these scanty remarks are not to be read either as definitive summaries or as carefully considered judgments of the texts to which they refer.

To keep each list fairly short and to avoid items that many readers might find hard to locate, we have omitted references to articles in professional journals. In the general references section of each list we do name a few of the periodicals whose contents commonly pertain to that particular topic or set of topics. Readers interested in the very latest that is being said about a specific topic or idea should consult recent issues of those publications.

Expression and Expressive Qualities

Throughout this book, and especially in its final sections, we have given considerable attention to the way that various aspects of schooling — from how teachers behave to the way corridors are decorated — give expression to moral qualities. Considered in its fullness, that topic is both broad and deep. It touches upon philosophy, literary theory, psychology, and more. Each of the texts we list calls attention to the pervasiveness of the expressive within ordinary experience. Each has something to say about learning to perceive and to interpret those expressive qualities.

Abrams, M. H. (1953). *The mirror and the lamp: Romantic theory and the critical tradition.* New York: Norton.

Abrams, M. H. (1971). *Natural supernaturalism: Tradition and revolution in romantic literature.* New York: Norton.

Abrams, M. H. (1984). *The correspondent breeze: Essays on English romanticism.* New York: Norton.

Abrams analyzes the work of the English Romantics, who themselves have much to say about the expressive significance of ordinary objects and events.

Barfield, O. (1971). *What Coleridge thought.* Middletown, CT: Wesleyan University Press.

Barfield, O. (1977). *The rediscovery of meaning and other essays.* Middletown, CT: Wesleyan University Press.

Barfield defends the Romantics and their perspective on the symbolic meanings to be found in nature and in human life.

Booth, W. (1988). *The company we keep.* Berkeley: University of California Press.

Argues that what we read affects the kind of person we become.

Calvino, I. (1988). *Six memos for the next millennium.* Cambridge, MA: Harvard University Press.

Brief lectures on literary values, which are related to the values of everyday life.

Cavell, S. (1988). *In quest of the ordinary.* Chicago: University of Chicago Press.

Cavell, S. (1989). *This new yet unapproachable America: Lectures after Emerson after Wittgenstein.* Albuquerque, NM: Living Batch Press.

Cavell, S. (1990). *Conditions handsome and unhandsome: The constitution of Emersonian perfectionism.* Chicago: University of Chicago Press.

Cavell analyzes the roots of philosophical skepticism through readings of Emerson, Thoreau, and Wittgenstein, among others.

Csikszentmihalyi, M., & Robinson, R. E. (1990). *The art of seeing: An interpretation of the aesthetic encounter.* Malibu, CA: J. Paul Getty Museum and the Getty Center for Education in the Arts.

Interviews with museum curators, who speak of what it means to perceive meaning in an object of art.

Danto, A. C. (1981). *The transfiguration of the commonplace.* Cambridge, MA: Harvard University Press.

Distinguishes between art and nonart, using both real and imaginary instances.

Dewey, J. (1980). *Art as experience.* New York: Perigee Books. (Original work published 1934.)
Analyzes the connections between art, philosophy, and everyday experience. Many have called it Dewey's crowning achievement.

Eco, U. (1989). *The open work.* Cambridge, MA: Harvard University Press.
Treats the "openness" of art and the interactive process between reader and text.

Eisner, E. W. (1991). *The enlightened eye.* New York: Macmillan. Speaks on behalf of the importance of individual perception and critical reflection in qualitative research.

Goodman, N. (1972). *Problems and projects.* New York: Bobbs-Merrill.

Goodman, N. (1976). *Languages of art.* Indianapolis, IN: Hackett.

Goodman, N. (1978). *Ways of worldmaking.* Indianapolis, IN: Hackett.
Goodman's explication of expression ties the concept to both art and ordinary experience. *Languages* contains his fullest treatment of the subject but the two other volumes, which contain short essays, provide a useful introduction to the longer work.

General References

The works of all the English Romantic poets repay close study by all who are interested in the topic of expression, for they contain numerous examples of the expressive qualities to be found in everyday objects. Wordsworth's *Preface to the Lyrical Ballads* (numerous editions) and Coleridge's *Biographia Literaria* (numerous editions) explicate the theory behind the Romantic position. Many of Emerson's *Essays* (numerous editions), such as "Self-Reliance," "Circles," and "Experience," contain commentary on the expressive quality of ordinary experience. Contemporary journals that often include articles on the subject include *The Journal of Aesthetics and Art, Critical Inquiry, The Journal of Aesthetic Education, Studies in Art Education, Salmagundi, Raritan, Art in America,* and *Artforum.*

Perspectives on the Moral

In Western thought, discussions of moral education go back at least as far as the Greeks. Both Plato and Aristotle, for example, inquire at length into what it means to be moral and how one becomes a moral person. Those same questions continue to occupy today's moral philosophers, who approach them from diverse and often conflicting points of view. They also are of concern to developmental psychologists and to others interested in establishing programs and practices for the nurturance of moral qualities in persons of all ages but especially the young. We list below an assortment of references, reflecting both the historical continuity and the contemporary diversity of this enduring set of interests.

Blum, L. A. (1980). *Friendship, altruism and morality*. London: Routledge & Kegan Paul.
Emphasizes the moral importance of perception and emotional response in our relationship with others.

Bottery, M. (1990). *The morality of the school*. London: Casell.
Argues that morality is at the heart of schooling and provides practical suggestions about how to enhance the moral well-being of students.

Carr, D. (1991). *Educating the virtues*. London: Routledge & Kegan Paul.
A careful defense of moral education centered on the development of personal virtue and character.

Chazan, B. I. (1985). *Contemporary approaches to moral education*. New York: Teachers College Press.
Surveys the major conceptions of how moral education should proceed.

Damon, W. (1988). *The moral child*. New York: Free Press.
Reveals how adults as well as peers contribute to the emergence of moral sensibility in children.

Dewey, J. (1960). *Theory of the moral life*. Troy, MO: Holt, Rinehart & Winston. (Original work published 1932.)

Dewey, J. (1966). *Democracy and education*. New York: Free Press. (Original work published 1916.)

Dewey contends that moral considerations potentially infuse all of human conduct. We find his outlook to be compatible with the point of view taken in this book.

Durkheim, E. (1961). *Moral education: A study in the theory and application of the sociology of education* (E. K. Wilson & H. Schnurer, Trans.). New York: Free Press. (Original work published 1925.)
Lectures on duty, discipline, and authority and on their role in secular morality and moral education.

Eldridge, R. (1989). *On moral personhood: Philosophy, literature, criticism, and self-understanding*. Chicago: University of Chicago Press.
Argues that through the interpretation of narratives we come to appreciate the value of morals and the virtue of acting in accordance with them.

Foot, P. (1978). *Virtues and vices*. Berkeley: University of California Press.
Argues that virtues and vices are more important ethical notions than are the currently lauded ones of rights, duties, and justice.

Gilligan, C. (1982). *In a different voice*. Cambridge, MA: Harvard University Press.

Gilligan, C., Ward, J. V., & Taylor, J. M. (Eds.). (1988). *Mapping the moral domain*. Cambridge, MA: Harvard University Press.
Gilligan has inspired a rethinking of moral questions from a feminist perspective. She argues that women often enact a different moral sensibility than men.

Goodlad, J. I., Soder, R., & Sirotnik, K. A. (Eds.). (1990). *The moral dimensions of teaching*. San Francisco: Jossey-Bass.
Contains essays on the moral purposes of schooling and the ethical and moral significance of looking upon teaching as a profession.

Kagan, J., & Lamb, S. (Eds.). (1987). *The emergence of morality in young children*. Chicago: University of Chicago Press.
A diverse presentation of psychological research and theory dealing with the nature of moral development in children.

Kohlberg, L. (1981). *Essays on moral development: The philosophy of moral development* (Vol. 1). New York: HarperCollins.

Kohlberg, L. (1984). *Essays on moral development: The psychology of moral development* (Vol. 2). New York: HarperCollins.
Kohlberg viewed moral development as occurring in six stages. His view was very influential during the seventies and eighties and remains so today in many quarters, although it has been strongly challenged of late by Gilligan (see above) and others.

Larmore, C. E. (1987). *Patterns of moral complexity*. Cambridge, England: Cambridge University Press.
A critique of several major theories of morality that the author believes threaten to mask the actual moral complexity of human life.

Lickona, T. (1991). *Educating for character*. New York: Bantam Books.
A call for formal moral education in the schools by a forceful advocate of such programs.

MacIntyre, A. (1966). *A short history of ethics*. New York: Collier Books.

MacIntyre, A. (1984). *After virtue* (2nd ed.). Notre Dame, IN: University of Notre Dame Press.
MacIntyre offers an overview of moral philosophy from the Homeric Age to the twentieth century. His own work criticizes modern theories and practices and calls for a return to an earlier conception of morality.

Mitchell, B. (1980). *Morality: Religious and secular*. Oxford, England: Clarendon Press.
Discusses the place of the conscience in moral action and the relationship between listening to one's conscience and religious thinking and feeling.

Modgil, S., & Modgil, C. (Eds.). (1986). *Lawrence Kohlberg: Consensus and controversy*. Bristol, PA: Falmer.
Essays on Kohlberg's view of moral development.

Murdoch, I. (1985). *The sovereignty of good* (1970). London: Ark Paperbacks.

Murdoch, I. (1993). *Metaphysics as a guide to morals*. New York: Viking Penguin.
Murdoch offers a conception of morality that is at once literary and philosophical. Within it she grants a central role to religious thought and practice.

Noddings, N. (1984). *Caring: A feminine approach to ethics and moral education*. Berkeley: University of California Press.

Noddings, N. (1992). *The challenge to care in schools*. New York: Teachers College Press.

Noddings sketches a moral philosophy in which the "caring relation" is the central good. She argues that the main aim of schools should be to educate people to care about others, themselves, and the world of things.

Norton, D. L. (1991). *Democracy and moral development*. Berkeley: University of California Press.

Argues that moral action and moral education must be grounded in personal virtue rather than in external rules or codes of conduct.

Nucci, L. P. (Ed.). (1989). *Moral development and character education: A dialogue*. Berkeley, CA: McCutchan.

Contains a lively debate on conceptions of moral development and moral education.

Nussbaum, M. C. (1986). *The fragility of goodness*. Cambridge, England: Cambridge University Press.

Nussbaum, M. C. (1990). *Love's knowledge: Essays on philosophy and literature*. New York: Oxford University Press.

Nussbaum highlights the many difficulties and conflicts that stand in the way of leading a moral life. She makes extensive use of literature in doing so and goes on to argue that the latter is indispensable in furthering one's moral education.

Pincoffs, E. (1986). *Quandaries and virtues: Against reductivism in ethics*. Lawrence: University of Kansas Press.

Defends an ethic of virtue, as contrasted with one of duty. Highlights the complexity of moral conduct and the tensions it creates.

Power, F. C., Higgins, A., & Kohlberg, L. (1989). *Lawrence Kohlberg's approach to moral education*. New York: Columbia University Press.

Defends the idea of making the school itself the center of moral and democratic education.

Purpel, D. E. (1989). *The moral and spiritual crisis in education: A curriculum for justice and compassion in education*. Granby, MA: Bergin & Garvey.

Argues for a radical revision of educational purpose and procedure.

Shklar, J. N. (1984). *Ordinary vices*. Cambridge, MA: Harvard University Press.

Examines "ordinary" vices through readings of Dickens, Austen, Montesquieu, Faulkner, and others.

Sichel, B. A. (1988). *Moral education*. Philadelphia: Temple University Press.

Argues that character education must be at the heart of any conception of moral education.

Stout, J. W. (1988). *Ethics after Babel*. Boston: Beacon Press.

Criticizes MacIntyre (see above) among others and advocates the empirical study of the moral practices of the diverse communities in the United States.

Strike, K. A., & Soltis, J. F. (1992). *The ethics of teaching*. New York: Teachers College Press.

Presents case studies of ethical problems in teaching and suggests ways of thinking about how to resolve them.

Taylor, C. (1989). *Sources of the self*. Cambridge, MA: Harvard University Press.

Considers what it means to be a human being in today's world. Defends modern subjectivity against those who see it as moral decline.

Williams, B. (1981). *Moral luck*. Cambridge, England: Cambridge University Press.

Williams, B. (1985). *Ethics and the limits of philosophy*. Cambridge, MA: Harvard University Press.

Williams offers a sustained critique of contemporary moral philosophy. He urges a return to a set of ethical standards derived from a commitment to individual reflection.

General References

The writings of Plato and Aristotle remain rich sources of ideas for further reflection and discussion centering on issues of morality, as do most canonic religious texts, centrally, of course, the Bible, the Koran, and the Torah. Among Greek texts see especially Plato's *Republic, Protagoras, Meno,* and *Gorgias* (numerous editions of each) and Aristotle's *Ethics, Poetics,* and *Politics* (numerous editions of each). Contemporary journals that often feature articles on morality that might be of interest to educators include *Ethics, The Philosophical Forum, Common Knowledge, The Journal of Moral Education,* and *Educational Theory,* among others.

Schools and Schooling

This section contains references that pertain to all that transpires in today's schools. Many of the individual items describe ethnographic studies whose investigators spent large amounts of time observing in classrooms and talking to teachers and students. Others offer a more sociological perspective on the workings of schools.

Bennett, K. P., & LeCompte, M. D. (1990). *How schools work.* White Plains, NY: Longman.
 Analyzes schooling from a sociological perspective.
Cusick, P. A. (1973). *Inside high school.* Troy, MO: Holt, Rinehart & Winston.
Cusick, P. A. (1983). *The egalitarian ideal and the American high school.* White Plains, NY: Longman.
 Cusick explores the social dynamics of high schools, revealing the many real and potential conflicts between educational ideals and educational practice.
Everhart, R. B. (1988). *Practical ideology and symbolic community: An ethnography of schools of choice.* Bristol, PA: Falmer.
 Examines the assumptions behind the language of educational discourse and shows how they often conflict with actual practice.
Goodlad, J. I. (1984). *A place called school.* New York: McGraw-Hill.
 A broad investigation of current educational practices. Goodlad finds them resistant to change and failing to incorporate the recommendations of progressivists.
Grant, G. (1988). *The world we created at Hamilton High.* Cambridge, MA: Harvard University Press.
 Combines a close look at the recent history of a single high

school with a description of how a group of its present students went about trying to change the school's ethos.

Jackson, P. W. (1968). *Life in classrooms.* Troy, MO: Holt, Rinehart & Winston.

Takes a close look at what goes on inside elementary school classrooms.

Labaree, D. F. (1988). *The making of an American high school.* New Haven, CT: Yale University Press.

Traces across generations the shifting commitments, beliefs, and experiences of a single school's successive communities.

Lacey, C. (1970). *Hightown grammar: The school as a social system.* Manchester, England: Manchester University Press.

An inside look at life within a British grammar school.

Lightfoot, S. L. (1983). *The good high school: Portraits of character and culture.* New York: Basic Books.

Contains impressionistic descriptions of several American high schools said to be exemplary.

Lighthall, F. F., & Allan, S. D. (1989). *Local realities, local adaptations: Problems, process, and person in a school's governance.* Bristol, PA: Falmer.

Describes in detail one school's attempts to improve its governance procedures.

McNeil, L. M. (1986). *Contradictions of control.* New York: Routledge & Kegan Paul.

Illustrates how attempts to increase control in the governing of a school can sometimes backfire, leading teachers and students to subvert their real reasons for being there.

Metz, M. H. (1978). *Classrooms and corridors: The crisis of authority in desegregated schools.* Berkeley: University of California Press.

Metz, M. H. (1986). *Different by design: The context and character of three magnet schools.* New York: Routledge & Kegan Paul.

Metz examines how the informal cultures of schools vary from one institution to another and interact with formal organizational structure.

Oakes, J., & Lipton, M. (1990). *Making the best of schools: A handbook for parents, teachers, and policy-makers.* New Haven, CT: Yale University Press.

Develops a procedure for analyzing how well a school might be accomplishing its mission.

Peshkin, A. (1991). *The color of strangers, the color of friends: The play of ethnicity in school and community.* Chicago: University of Chicago Press.
Reveals how students in a multiethnic school convert that multiethnicity into a resource for forming personal identity and belief.

Powell, A. G., Farrar, E., & Cohen, D. K. (1985). *The shopping mall high school.* Boston: Houghton Mifflin.
Treats the academic compromises brought about by the high school's attempt to provide a curriculum that is satisfying to everyone.

Rutter, M., Maughan, B., Mortimore, P., & Ouston, J. (1979). *Fifteen thousand hours: Secondary schools and their effects on children.* Cambridge, MA: Harvard University Press.
Reports on the differences in ethos among several secondary schools in Britain. Traces a large measure of those differences to administrative practices.

Swidler, A. (1979). *Organization without authority: Dilemmas of social control in free schools.* Cambridge, MA: Harvard University Press.
Looks at the role of authority in schooling by studying schools that attempt to get along without it.

Willis, P. (1977). *Learning to labor.* New York: Columbia University Press.
Studies the last two years in school of a group of boys destined for low-skilled, low-paying jobs.

General References

Persons seeking to explore the vast literature on schools and schooling would be well advised to make use of general guides, such as *The Encyclopedia of Educational Research,* which has now gone through five editions, or *Education Index,* which is updated quarterly and provides a listing of articles that have recently appeared within any one of a large number of educational journals. Recently published handbooks that cover broad domains of educational research and inquiry, such as *The Handbook of Research on Curriculum* (Macmillan, 1992) or *The Handbook of Research on Teacher Education* (Macmillan, 1990), are often good places to begin one's search, as are volumes in *The Annual Review of Educational Research* and yearbooks of The National Society for the Study of Education. Journals worth consulting include *The American Journal of Education, Teachers College Record, Harvard Educational Review, Phi Delta Kappan, Curriculum Inquiry, The Journal of Curriculum Studies,* and *Educational Leadership.*

Teachers and Teaching Practices

This list contains references of two basic kinds, though the overlap between them is often quite great. One treats teaching phenomenologically, which is to say that it looks at teaching from an insider's point of view; the other treats it more objectively — that is, as seen from the outside. The former features accounts by teachers about their own experiences and ways of working but it also includes studies that make use of interviews, journals, and other forms of direct reports from practitioners. The latter features observations or tape recordings of teachers in action but it also includes case studies and historical analyses based on a medley of data-gathering techniques.

Allender, J. S. (1991). *Imagery in teaching and learning: An autobiography of research in four world views.* New York: Praeger.
Investigates the place of imagery in how persons learn.
Anderson, L. W., & Burns, R. B. (1989). *Research in classrooms.* Oxford: Pergamon Press.
Analyzes criteria for conducting and judging research on teachers, teaching, and classrooms. Includes exemplars of various approaches.
Booth, W. (1988). *The vocation of a teacher.* Chicago: University of Chicago Press.
Reflective essays on college teaching by a professor of English who loves to teach.
Brookfield, S. D. (1990). *The skillful teacher: On technique, trust, and responsiveness in the classroom.* San Francisco: Jossey-Bass.

An analysis of what it takes to be a skillful teacher, written especially for teachers of adults.

Bullough, R. V. (1989). *First-year teacher: A case study.* New York: Teachers College Press.
Examines the vicissitudes of a first-year teacher's experience in learning the ropes.

Cazden, C. B. (1988). *Classroom discourse: The language of teaching and learning.* Portsmouth, NH: Heinemann Educational Books.
Shows how classroom discourse varies in response to both institutional and cultural restraints.

Coles, R. (1989). *The call of stories: Teaching and the moral imagination.* Boston: Houghton Mifflin.
Makes a case for the importance of stories in learning how to lead a moral life.

Connelly, F. M., & Clandinin, D. J. (1988). *Teachers as curriculum planners: Narratives of experience.* New York: Teachers College Press.
Includes extensive testimony from teachers on how they go about deciding what to teach and how to teach it.

Cuban, L. (1984). *How teachers taught: Constancy and change in American classrooms, 1890–1980.* White Plains, NY: Longman.
Documents the remarkable stability of teaching practices over time and asks why they are so difficult to change.

Delamont, S. (1976). *Interaction in the classroom.* London: Methuen.
A sociological study of how and why students interact as they do in classrooms.

Elbaz, F. (1983). *Teacher thinking: A study of practical knowledge.* London: Croom Helm.
Looks at the constituents of teachers' personal knowledge, including cognitive, evaluative, and emotional forms of knowing.

Grossman, P. L. (1990). *The making of a teacher.* New York: Teachers College Press.
Compares teachers with and without formal training. Illuminates the value of a good teacher education program.

Haroutunian-Gordon, S. (1991). *Turning the soul: Teaching through conversation in the high school.* Chicago: University of Chicago Press.

Reports on the use of discussions of "great books" in high school English classes.

Hawthorne, R. K. (1992). *Curriculum in the making: Teacher choice and the classroom experience.* New York: Teachers College Press. Documents the highly personalized ways in which teachers select and implement what to teach.

Jackson, P. W. (1986). *The practice of teaching.* New York: Teachers College Press.

Jackson, P. W. (1992). *Untaught lessons.* New York: Teachers College Press. Jackson examines teaching from a variety of viewpoints, seeking to elucidate aspects of its practice that have been largely ignored.

Johnson, S. M. (1990). *Teachers at work.* New York: Basic Books. Calls attention to the relationship between the organizational features of schools and the aims and methods of instruction.

Lortie, D. C. (1975). *Schoolteacher.* Chicago: University of Chicago Press. An interview study of teachers as seen from a sociological perspective.

McDonald, J. P. (1992). *Teaching: Making sense of an uncertain craft.* New York: Teachers College Press. Defends teaching as a moral craft whose uncertainties help to illuminate its strengths.

Mehan, H. (1979). *Learning lessons: Social organization in the classroom.* Cambridge, MA: Harvard University Press. Studies language and social interaction within an elementary classroom.

Oser, F. K., Dick, A., & Patry, J. (Eds.). (1992). *Effective and responsible teaching: The new synthesis.* San Francisco: Jossey-Bass. Places research on effective teaching within a moral context. Offers varied perspectives on the nature of "good" teaching.

Page, R. N. (1991). *Lower-track classrooms: A curricular and cultural perspective.* New York: Teachers College Press. An ethnographic study of lower-track classrooms and what happens within them.

Paley, V. G. (1981). *Wally's stories: Conversations in the kindergarten.* Cambridge, MA: Harvard University Press.

Paley, V. G. (1986). *Molly is three: Growing up in school.* Chicago: University of Chicago Press.

Paley, V. G. (1988). *Bad guys don't have birthdays: Fantasy play at four.* Chicago: University of Chicago Press.
Paley reports on her own experience as a kindergarten teacher, making extensive use of conversations with individual children.

Perrone, V. (1991). *A letter to teachers: Reflections on schooling and the art of teaching.* San Francisco: Jossey-Bass.
Argues for the importance of having teachers focus on individual students.

Rose, M. (1989). *Lives on the boundary.* New York: Free Press.
An account of one teacher's attempts to help students overcome obstacles to learning.

Smith, L. M., & Geoffrey, W. (1968). *The complexities of an urban classroom.* Troy, MO: Holt, Rinehart & Winston.
Reports on a collaborative study involving a researcher and a classroom teacher.

Stake, R.. Bresler, L., & Mabry, L. (1991). *Custom and cherishing.* Urbana, IL: Council for Research in Music Education.
Describes how art is taught (or fails to be taught) in ten elementary schools.

Tom, A. R. (1984). *Teaching as a moral craft.* White Plains, NY: Longman.
Views teaching as a practical enterprise whose performance is value-laden.

van Manen, M. (1991). *The tact of teaching.* Albany: State University of New York Press.
Calls for the enactment of a thoughtful and receptive attitude toward all students.

Waxman, H. C., & Walberg, H. J. (Eds.). (1991). *Effective teaching: Current research.* Berkeley, CA: McCutchan.
Reviews the research on effective teaching, making use of new statistical techniques for massing independent studies.

General References

Almost all of the titles that appear in the general references at the end of the "Schools and Schooling" section could as well reappear here. Readers of this list who may not yet have examined those prior suggestions are advised to do so. To the handbooks named in the previous section we would add *The Handbook of Research on Teaching,* third edition (Macmillan, 1986), which covers a broad range of topics. The two earlier editions of that handbook are also worth examining and continue to be of more than historical interest. Readers wanting to travel a more literary route in their exploration of teachers and teaching might be drawn to any of a large number of novels whose central character is a teacher (e.g., Muriel Spark's *The Prime of Miss Jean Brodie*) or in which teaching figures prominently (e.g., the beginning of Dickens's *Hard Times*). The number of such works is far too great to even begin to list them here. Journals that focus principally on teachers and teaching include *The Journal of Teacher Education, The Elementary School Journal, The High School Journal,* and *Theory into Practice,* as well as numerous others that concentrate on the teaching of a particular subject, such as *The English Journal, The History Teacher,* and *The Physical Educator.*

❧ Notes ❧

1. John Bartlett, *Familiar Quotations,* 15th ed. (Boston: Little, Brown, 1980), 128.

2. Ralph Waldo Emerson, "Self-Reliance," *Essays & Lectures* (New York: Library of America, 1983), 166.

3. Umberto Eco, *The Open Work* (Cambridge, Mass.: Harvard University Press, 1989).

4. R. G. Collingwood, *The Idea of History* (New York: Oxford University Press, 1956), 42.

5. Emerson, "Self-Reliance," *Essays,* 166.

6. John Dewey, *How We Think* (Lexington, Mass.: Heath, 1933), 33.

7. John Dewey, *Democracy and Education* (New York: Free Press, 1916), 18.

8. Emerson, "Experience," *Essays,* 471.

9. Ibid., 170 179.

10. Ibid., 479.

11. Robert Hughes, *The Shock of the New* (New York: Knopf, 1991), 325.

12. Quoted in J. D. McClatchy, "Wildness asking for ceremony," *American Poetry Review,* 21 (March/April 1992), 18.

13. Wayne C. Booth, *The Company We Keep* (Berkeley: University of California Press, 1988), 254.

⮑ Index ⮐

The Authors

Philip W. Jackson is the David Lee Shillinglaw Distinguished Service Professor of Education and Psychology and a member of the Committee on Ideas and Methods at the University of Chicago.

Robert E. Boostrom is assistant professor of education in the Department of Teacher Education at the University of Southern Indiana.

David T. Hansen is an associate professor of curriculum and instruction in the College of Education, University of Illinois, Chicago.

∾ Acknowledgments ∾

The research project that serves as the basis for this book was generously supported by the Spencer Foundation, whose late president, Lawrence A. Cremin, also contributed his personal encouragement and warm endorsement. We thank the foundation for its support and we greatly treasure the memory of President Cremin's enthusiasm for our project. We trust that he would have approved this outcome of his faith in our endeavor.

Much of our writing and conferring was carried on within the Benton Center for Curriculum and Instruction, which is part of the Department of Education at the University of Chicago. We are grateful for the use of those facilities and are especially indebted to Diane Bowers, the administrative assistant of the center, who served us in more ways than we can name. From managing our budget to trafficking telephone calls and formatting manuscripts, she was always on hand when needed and more than willing to help.

Special gratitude is due the teachers and administrators who, by giving us access to their schools and classrooms, provided us with something to say. Though we are prevented by prior agreement from identifying any of them by name (the names that do appear are pseudonyms), we here acknowledge their indispensability in making this book possible. To the teachers in particular we offer our very deepest thanks. Beginning mostly as strangers, they all soon became our friends. We dedicate this book to them.

We are additionally grateful for the counsel of our editor, Lesley Iura, and for the critical advice of two anonymous reviewers. Our manuscript has been greatly improved as a result of their suggestions. We accept full responsibility for its remaining imperfections.

323